Communicating the New

METHODS TO SHAPE AND ACCELERATE INNOVATION

Kim Erwin

Cover designer: Anne Michele Abbott

Published by John Wiley & Sons, Inc., Hoboken, New Jersey.
Published simultaneously in Canada.

For general information about our other products and services, please contact our Customer Care Department within the United States at (800) 762-2974, outside the United States at (317) 572-3993 or fax (317) 572-4002.

Wiley publishes in a variety of print and electronic formats and by print-on-demand. Some material included with standard print versions of this book may not be included in e-books or in print-on-demand. If this book refers to media such as a CD or DVD that is not included in the version you purchased, you may download this material at http://booksupport.wiley.com. For more information about Wiley products, visit www.wiley.com.

Library of Congress Cataloging-in-Publication Data

Erwin, Kim, 1965-
    Communicating the new : how to make the complex, unfamiliar or still-fuzzy understandable to others / Kim Erwin.
      pages cm
    Includes index.
    ISBN 978-1-118-39417-5 (pbk.); 978-1-118-41761-4 (ebk); 978-1-118-42198-7 (ebk)
    1. Communication in marketing. 2. New products. 3. Business communication. 4. Communication in organizations. 5. Communication in management. I. Title.
    HF5415.123.E79 2014
    658.4'5--dc23
                                            2013002845

10   9   8   7   6   5   4   3   2   1

Communicating the New

TABLE OF CONTENTS

Introduction: The Mission and the Mess — 1

Challenges of communicating The New   3
What's in our way? Three communication myths   4
Reconceiving the role of communication   7
Five ways communication methods accelerate innovation   11

1 Finding the Conceptual Center — 16

Models and frameworks: Thinking with our eyes   19
How to make models work   28
Build-to-think prototypes: Thinking with our hands   42
Lists and open-ended writing: Thinking with words   50
The Takeaway: Five big ideas when seeking the conceptual center   62

2 Framing the Work — 64

Metaphors   69
Mantras and catchphrases   84
Contrast   92
Stories   98
Artifacts and images   108
How (and why) to use multiple frames to greater effect   112
The Takeaway: Five big ideas when framing the work   114

3 Targeting Your Constituents — 118

The communication plan   126
Mental model and orthodoxy analysis   129
Quad A diagnostic   135
The "Organization as Culture" framework   137
Segmenting and targeting constituents   141
The Takeaway: Four big ideas when targeting constituents   144

4 Introduce New Thinking   146

Exploratory experiences   155

Immersion experiences   160

Interaction experiences   165

Application experiences   172

Extension experiences   176

The Takeaway: Five big ideas when introducing new thinking   180

5 Expand the Conversation   184

Communication systems: Give them something rich and relevant   188

Performative presentations: Give them something to talk about   198

Demonstration artifacts: Give them something to show and share   208

The Takeaway: Five big ideas when expanding the conversation   228

Conclusion   230

Five big shifts in thinking (and doing)   231

Advancing the methods base   234

Under the hood: Theories, writers and references   236

Index   253

WHY THIS BOOK? WHY NOW?

What if you are working on a problem no one knows they have?
—Editor of this book to the author of this book

If you are holding this book in your hands, you may already be persuaded that communication is critically important to success when pursuing new products, services, businesses, or systems. Powerful ideas—the lifeblood of any modern economy—will be embraced, ignored, attacked, or rejected according to how well they are understood or represented.

You may also be holding this book because you believe something fundamental has changed, something that is making communication of The New more difficult, and standard communication techniques less effective. I have experienced this too, and I believe that a number of factors have come together to create a new context for communication:

We are working on problems of increasing complexity. This complexity is hard to manage, structure, and explain—and yet it is essential to establishing the relevance of The New. We cannot ignore the complexity nor reduce it to an elevator pitch without trivializing our work.

The creation of The New involves more people. The creative types—the scientists, designers, agency people, etc. have always had a hand in The New. Now, in an economy where speed of execution matters, we also need the "developers" —the engineers, marketers, and IT specialists. Most critically, The New must be understood and embraced by the "doers" —the sales staff, managers, and stakeholders of all kinds across the organization. This is no longer a problem of producing the best idea; it's a challenge of engaging, leveraging, and aligning the human systems inside organizations.

We presume communication is occurring when in fact it is not. In most organizations, we believe that delivering information—in presentations, in reports—is communicating to others. At a time when *co-creation* is becoming the norm, our communication techniques appear stuck in a *transmission* model. Our conventional arsenal of delivery-based methods is no longer up to the task.

Communicating the New steps into this new reality with a simple approach and toolkit for all creators of The New. It collects and describes methods for employing communication, in an integral way, throughout the creation of new products, services, messages, or experiences. It introduces concepts and methods to help manage complexity, accelerate synthesis, bring clarity, and exchange important knowledge with the people who need to act on it. It is written for everyone who is involved in creating The New—from the account planner in advertising, to the manager of an internal innovation center, to the entrepreneur with a big idea. The aim of the book is functional: to provide a practical framework and tools that individuals and teams can use to help tame and frame the inherent complexity of creating The New. And maybe, just maybe, it will make the hard work of creating The New just a little bit easier.

In this book, you will meet individuals at the forefront of creating The New. Some are early pioneers; others are new arrivals. Some practice as consultants; others work directly within organizations. All share a new attitude toward communication. They use communication to clarify rather than persuade, deploying it not only at the end, but *throughout* the process—to produce meaning and clarity, to advance ideas into concept, and to engage other people in advancing those ideas into the organizations and markets. This book draws from their experiences and organizes their contributions into a collection of methods for use by anyone who needs to communicate The New.

ACKNOWLEDGMENTS

Where to start? This has been more barn-raising than book writing.

I must first thank my husband, Tom Mulhern, my muse and my love. He is one of the most gifted communicators of The New that I know—and I'm not alone in that assessment. We met and fell in love on the job, and the thinking in this book is very much a product of our journey together. His support has been unflagging and his contributions incalculable.

To our boys, Joey and Dakota, for their patience, thoughtful encouragement, and restrained eye-rolling during this process.

To Hugh Musick, for his inexhaustible support for this project and his steady encouragement of me personally. Hugh's a talent in his own right. But he's also been instrumental to the promotion of ideas and others at the Institute of Design. Hugh's conviction around what matters is invaluable to all of us at ID, and to this book in particular.

I'd like to thank my editor, Margaret Cummins, for believing in a topic she wasn't sure anyone else would recognize and for putting money on a relatively unknown author. I believe that makes you a creator of The New, Margaret!

To Andy Parham—a central figure in this book—who takes risks every day, including sharing his inspiring story with an author he's never met. I hope others find his journey as remarkable as I do.

To all the practitioners who shared with me their wisdom and experiences, despite the many compelling reasons to say nothing at all. In an industry mired in nondisclosure agreements, your courage in volunteering even one story, one example, is central to our collective ability to transform an invisible practice into a visible discipline that every creator of The New can use.

To my colleagues Tomoko Ichikawa and Ruth Schmidt, for contributing their intelligence, time, and effort in thinking through the role of communication in the creative process. They are both talented communicators in their own right.

To ID students Twisha Brandenburg, Cristina Cook, and Philipp Böhm for their design and photographic help with the book. And to Farid Talhame and Douglas "Jeff" Hsu for modeling for us in the stifling August sun.

To all the talented students who have journeyed through the IIT Institute of Design and my classes. I thank you for your hard work, shown on these pages, and for your contributions to class projects that helped develop and illustrate the concepts promoted here.

MEET THE CONTRIBUTORS

If this book makes a contribution to how we think about the role of communication in creating The New, it does so with considerable cooperation and inspiration from three groups of pioneers: the practitioners who have been pushing the frontiers for years and who communicate The New every day for a living; the insiders who live the problem of The New from inside their organizations and who have been early adopters of the new communication; and the academics, whose generous conversations have provided useful theoretical frameworks. I have been privileged to listen to, watch, or work alongside these people, and it is their contributions that form the foundation of this book. In my effort to start a robust dialogue around the role of communication, I have been the ear, and they have been the voice.

Practitioners
early pioneers and
consultants

Hugh Dubberly
Principal and Founder,
Dubberly Design

Peter Laundy
Senior Innovation
Specialist, Doblin

Rick E. Robinson
Vice President,
SapientNitro

Michael Bierut
Partner, Pentagram

Kathleen Brandenburg
Principal & Co-Founder,
IA Collaborative

John Cain
Vice President,
SapientNitro

Photo by Chad Magiera

Martha Cotton
Partner, Gravity Tank

Shelley Evenson
Executive Director of
Evolution, Fjord

Megan Fath
Design Director,
Conifer Research

Photo by Bob Stefko Photography

Ben Jacobson
Partner and Founder,
Conifer Research

Photo by Bob Stefko Photography

© 2002 Daniel D. Chichester

Larry Keeley
President & Co-Founder,
Doblin

Tom Mulhern
Principal, Gensler

Dev Patnaik
CEO, Jump Associates

Steve Portigal
Principal and Founder,
Portigal Consulting

Heather Reavey
Managing Principal,
Continuum

Chris Rockwell
President, Lextant

Brianna Sylver
President and Founder,
Sylver Consulting

Michael Winnick
CEO, dScout
Partner, Gravity Tank

Photograph: Charles Best

Michael Wolff
Designer and Creative
Advisor, Michael Wolff &
Company

Gisela Gier
on her experience with
Skype's Experience
Research Group

Matt Leacock
on his experience as a
designer at Netscape
and Sococo, a startup

Tom MacTavish
on his experiences as
Director of research labs
at Motorola and NCR

Judd Morgenstern
on his experience as
an entrepreneur at
General Assembly

Danielle Nierenberg
on her time as Director
of *Nourishing the Planet*,
WorldWatch Institute

Andy Parham
CEO, Bick Group

Photo © Todd Owyoung

Melody Roberts
Director at McDonald's
Experience Design
Innovation Group

Tony Salvador
Senior Principle
Engineer, Experience
Insight Labs, Intel

(not pictured)
Steve Leeke on his
experience as a director at
Motorola New Enterprises

Academics
researchers and experts

Dr. John Cacioppo
Professor of Social Neuroscience,
University of Chicago

Dr. Mark Evans
Senior Lecturer, Industrial Design, Loughborough Design School

Dr. Gail Fairhurst
Professor of Communication,
Ohio State University

Dr. Charles Forceville
Professor of Cognitive Linguistics,
University of Amsterdam

Professor Anijo Mathew
Interaction and Communication,
IIT Institute of Design

Marty Thaler
Visiting Professor,
Product Design,
IIT Institute of Design

Photo by Junyoung Yang

The Mission
and the Mess

Eighty-two-year-old Jim Bick was dying of cancer when he called up Andy Parham and asked him to come lead his business as CEO. Jim owned a number of companies in newspaper and radio. But he also owned a company called Bick Group that designed and built data centers for large enterprises. Bick was a client from Andy's days as a management consultant, but Andy couldn't imagine why Bick was calling on him to run his almost 50-year-old company. Moreover, Andy didn't know anything about Bick's business. Bick responded, "I'm not concerned about what you don't know. I'm hiring you for what I think you can do."

It turned out that Bick's business was in real trouble. Beginning as a local punch-card machine sales business in 1964, the company had evolved to become experts in the design, construction, and operation of data centers and had customers across the world. Data centers were core to an IT model that reigned for over 25 years, but massive changes in the IT world meant that the era of that model was coming to an end. By 2007, revenues were down 85 percent from 2001. The aging and ailing Bick knew the business was going to have to change once more, but this time he wouldn't be there to lead it. According to Andy, "Jim knew that we were about to have another big change in IT. I didn't know that at the time, but he knew it and he knew that the company was going to have to pivot again, and that pivot is cloud computing."

At the time of Bick's visit, Andy was a partner at VSA Partners, a leading communication design and branding firm. Andy was an experienced strategist who had built and led some pretty big client accounts at VSA. But he had never been a CEO before.

Andy took the job, and under his guidance the Bick Group shifted its business. It acquired Blue Mountain Labs, a company with high visibility in the new cloud computing industry. Blue Mountain Labs was a small but mighty competency that, if nurtured correctly, could bridge Bick Group to the future. The acquisition allowed Andy to craft something new and relevant: It allowed him to go to clients and say that Bick Group could place them in the cloud.

But Andy's shift in strategy generated a tsunami of challenges, internally and externally:

I've got a hundred employees that have been there forever. They know how to design, build and operate data centers. They know about power and cooling, and they know how to consult around power and cooling. And I'm telling them that I think that our customers are going to buy less and less of that because of this new disruptive technology, and we've got to change. And now they're worried about their future. I've got another segment of employees who need to get a lot more sophisticated about the story that they tell because they're going to be selling a lot higher up the organizational stack. They've been calling on data center managers and IT directors. They now need to call on CEOs and CFOs and make a business proposition, not a technology proposition.

So now, I have multiple communication challenges. One of them is the cloud has hit the peak of the hype cycle and people are sick of it, and yet right now it's just getting real. Another is that business executives don't know what we're talking about when we talk about a cloud-based future, so we've got to find a way to help them see it. A third is the people inside of my own company don't know what the hell we're doing, and they're scared about it because they don't know what their future holds.

Andy is a man on a mission I'll call creating The New. It might equally be called "reinventing your business" or "innovation" or "designing the next great thing." But those terms are specialized, and Andy's story is more universal. Andy's mission is to create something new, relevant, and desirable. And his challenge is to do so for a complex and competitive market, shaped by dynamic and unpredictable forces, and without clarity or precedent to draw from. We might call this "the mess." Does his story feel familiar? It should. Everyone who is called to create The New—and there are more of us every day—faces a mission of vital importance and a mess of increasing size. The mission to create The New is now recognized by businesses and governments across the globe as vital to economic survival. As a result, this mission has stature, it gets respect and attention, it's increasingly understood (at least at a structural level), and it gets resources in the form of funding and research.

The mess, on the other hand, is different story. There is little glory and a lot less guidance in the mess. The mess that accompanies The New is harder to define and describe—it is sometimes called a business problem or an industry condition, but such descriptions are too narrow. The mess also includes emerging customer behaviors, long-wave cultural changes, advances in science, and increasing transparency in everything we do. Typically, a mess is deemed a problem. But when creating The New, the mess is essential.

Andy's mission (and his mess) is big and bold and a little intimidating, but it isn't unique. Andy's industry may be different from yours, and his budget may have more zeros, but his predicament is common enough. Andy is new to the job and to the level of responsibility and accountability. He's got a vision and a plan, but his organization can't see it yet. He's got a viable proposition for clients, with a promising trajectory, but it points to very different and as-yet unproven future. And he's connecting his proposition to a new information economy that is still emerging and so is hard to describe to others.

What makes Andy a little bit different—and ahead of other leaders—is that he saw his business problems as also being communication problems. So what he did next was equally uncommon: He hired a writer and a designer.

This is an old-school firm—they do things the way they do things. Even in our new company, the technology guys were used to putting together hundred-page PowerPoints with all these graphs and all this stuff. Nobody knew what they were saying. So I put them in a room with my designer and my writer, and I told them, "You will not deliver one thing to the client without it going through the filter of these two guys." They looked at me as if I had six heads, [and] told me they've always done it this way. They said, "OK, Andy, you're going to make it pretty." And I said, "I'm not talking about making it pretty. I'm talking about a level of polish and professionalism that inspires confidence and makes us look bigger than we are. And I'm talking about a level of communication clarity, that doesn't come through in this, which makes us look smarter and more trustworthy to lead through a complex challenge." I made these technology guys sit in the room and explain it enough times in enough ways for my two guys to understand it and be able to write it down themselves. And when it's written down, it is **completely** *different from the way that my technology guys were communicating it. Now I have them embedded on all the teams and everybody knows that there is no deliverable that goes out unless it goes through them. Period.*

Andy is on to something big—creating The New and communicating The New are inseparable endeavors. His belief that communication is not about making things pretty but is a strategic tool to manage complexity, to make the unfamiliar more comprehensible, to build alignment and to inspire confidence—in short, to manage the mess—suggests he's a little bit ahead on an important learning curve, a curve that most organizations have yet to even recognize.

CHALLENGES OF COMMUNICATING THE NEW

One of the biggest challenges in creating The New is to make it understandable to others and, not incidentally, to oneself. The challenge of clarifying new discoveries or concepts to organizational stakeholders—many of whom were not part of the development phase—is a notorious gap in the internal adoption and implementation of new ideas.

As Andy's story suggests, communicating The New is not one problem but a class of problems. I'd like to call out three in particular, each a part of the challenge, but each meaningfully different in nature and, therefore, in solution.

The complex

I distinguish the "complex new" from other forms of The New by its multidimensional nature. Public policy issues are a good example because they address a multiplicity of constituents, resources, circumstances, and existing laws in creating a new solution. The "complex new" is tough to explain to others because it involves a large number of factors that are connected and interrelated, and together they combine to describe the context for action. Andy's cloud computing proposition is fundamentally complex to his clients, less because of the technology involved than because of the broader transformations the cloud is enabling: big data, personal information economies, and mobile apps that transform the power relationship between consumers and producers.

The unfamiliar

The truly new is a tough proposition in its own right. How to explain something that is out of the range of conventional reference, or for which there are few precursors? Massive technology infrastructure projects—electrification, television, and the Internet—all defied popular imagination at the time. The core challenge of the "unfamiliar new" is helping others see new concepts with fresh eyes and from the perspective of the future, not in the context of the past and through the lens of what they already know.

The still-fuzzy

Ideas remain in motion for much longer than we'd like to admit, and the challenge of describing something unfinished or unstable is the case of the "fuzzy new." The inherent instability around emerging ideas is perhaps no surprise—just ask any startup that has experienced the path through multiple business models and products. But the surrounding forces necessary to shape these ideas are also areas in constant flux—consumer trends, emerging markets, scientific advances. The truly new has to anticipate what's next and what might matter in the future, and that means building on areas of life that are inherently in motion. In these cases, The New is a fuzzy image on an even fuzzier background.

Anyone testing out the logic of these definitions will quickly conclude that most new propositions are some combination of two or all of these. Andy's challenge, in fact, is all three—complex, unfamiliar, and still emerging. If we conceive of communicating The New as many problems, each involving many people—new team members, implementers, decision makers, etc.—and occurring throughout the course of a project, we can no longer consider it a trivial challenge to tackle at the end of a project. To succeed, we need to factor into our development processes the reality that communicating The New is an ongoing work stream, not an afterthought—and one that requires its own mindset, unique skill set, and specific tools.

WHAT'S IN OUR WAY? THREE COMMUNICATION MYTHS

Why don't more executives act like Andy and prioritize communication in their development processes? Why don't they hire writers and designers to work with their teams? Some do. But their conceptions of when, where, and how to engage communication are typically informed by conventional wisdom that doesn't account for creating The New. In fact, such conventional wisdom is badly out of date. For the sake of simplicity, I've boiled it down to three ideas that are rarely questioned, always present, *and no longer work*.

Communication myth 1: Simplification is the answer

One of the biggest challenges in creating The New is making it understandable to others. We are given a lot of advice about how to do this: the elevator pitch (get it down to two minutes), the Hollywood pitch ("X meets Y," to put it in familiar terms), the journalist's five Ws (compress key facts into a single positioning statement). But any entrepreneur who has had to use them will tell you that *reductionist approaches trivialize rich, nuanced ideas*. They strip ideas of what makes them special. And once you pull the wings off a butterfly, to paraphrase designer Massimo Vignelli, all you have is a bug.

Judd Morgenstern, an entrepreneur in New York's startup incubator, General Assembly, lives in a world where simplification is mandatory:

Every VC guy or investor says they want a new, innovative idea, but they ask you to describe this new, innovative idea in terms of something that already exists. A common pitch format is the X meets Y for Z format: describing your company in terms of a combination of other companies. So you're something like WebMD meets like ZocDoc for new mothers. At best, you come out describing your company as a kind of hybrid mash-up of two existing companies. And at worst the investors say, "yeah, we've already heard this one hundred times" or, "somebody already does that." And you're thinking, "Of course somebody already does that, I just told you two companies that are kind of like it because you asked me to."

The X meets Y formula is what I'd call a guaranteed near-miss: It can get people in the conceptual ballpark, but will ultimately fail because it focuses people on what's similar, instead of what's different and noteworthy.

Information guru Richard Saul Wurman says the worst way to manage complexity is throw out all the hard parts. Complex, potent ideas, such as the iPod/iTunes platform, simply don't reduce well. So if we can figure out how to convey a rich powerful idea, without trivializing its underlying nature or, as innovation consultant Larry Keeley puts it, "stripping it down to a caricature," we will have done something pretty powerful.

Communication myth 2: Packaging and selling are the objective

In most organizations, communication is conceived of as the grand finale, something that comes at the end of the project to promote the ideas and make them attractive to decision makers. This presumes that you have an idea, and that your idea is fully formed, but simply not packaged yet. In this context, communication provides the packaging and focuses on persuasion: gaining influence over "the audience," securing their compliance, and eliciting the desired behavior. Packaging and persuasion as the end state is the conception that the mass culture has always been aware of, and for which it has looked to creative people such as designers and advertisers. It is the driver behind communication-for-business books designed to "transform audiences," "drive action," "connect, persuade, and triumph," and "help ideas survive" (*Resonate* by Nancy Duarte, *Presentation Design for Impact* by Andrew Abela, *Tell to Win* by Peter Guber, and *Made to Stick* by the Heath brothers, respectively).

Packaging and selling don't work well in the context of creating The New because they don't address the pressing need to treat all legitimate stakeholders as participants. When you look at people as targets to be sold to, or as hurdles to get past, you can't focus on building important relationships, and so can't spark the organizational change and commitment required to implement The New.

Creators of The New need the active participation and enthusiasm of the people who are going to be problem solving those ideas months from now. As Lextant CEO Chris Rockwell notes, "Ownership is a big part of what we're trying to create here. If we throw the insights over the wall, if they haven't had a chance to hear it firsthand or be immersed in it throughout the process, then there's less ownership for it and there's less advocacy for it. If our clients don't own it and advocate it within their walls, those insights will whither and die, and old ways of thinking and behaving can re-emerge."

Communication myth 3: Delivering and transferring are the means

Here we come to the real root of the problem: Communication is trapped in a transfer model. In most organizations, communication means *delivering* findings and *presenting* ideas. It is about transferring knowledge to stakeholders at the end of a project, as concepts seek funding or move to implementation. This model puts communication after the development of The New, rather than making it an integral part of creating The New. The transfer model is the ultimate misfire because it frames communication as an event, rather than a process.

"The problem with conventional presentations is that they are a complete 'lean back' experience. It's all about being an audience member," says Dev Patnaik, CEO of Jump Associates. "Mats Lederhausen, who was at McDonald's for years, gave me a quote that I use over and over: 'It is far easier to act yourself into a new way of thinking than it is to think your way into a new way of acting.' If you really want to get executives to buy into your project, you need to get them to co-create the information. Creating sessions in which executives make something and then come to their own conclusions (hopefully conclusions you agree with), is essential."

This trifecta of communication myths—simplify, package, and transfer—may have been well suited to a different set of conditions. Maybe. But they generate blind spots and unproductive behaviors when you need to communicate something new. "Persuasion" requires proof. It causes us to lead with process and facts instead of stories and knowledge. The lack of immediate relevance to participants feels like a waste of their time. The transfer imperative compels us to be exhaustive, swelling presentations to 150 slides, when probably no more than 5 are relevant to any particular individual in the room. The simplification formulas lead to imprecise language and undue abstraction, both of which cause new ideas to sound indistinct and make them easy to misinterpret and dismiss.

Plenty of ideas go unfunded because they don't deserve investment. But the floors of corporations everywhere are also littered with promising concepts that failed because the communication began too late, stakeholders were not personally invested, and those ideas were described using communication tools of the past, optimized for discrete products launched at discrete times and for a few powerful audience members. These are different times, and we need a different mindset and more effective toolset to communicate The New.

RECONCEIVING THE ROLE OF COMMUNICATION

How we ultimately communicate our ideas—both to clients and to end users—is 90 percent of the job.

— Michael Winnick, Partner, Gravity Tank

How might we define the new context in order to understand the new role for communication? In my interviews with practitioners who make their living creating The New—innovation consultants, entrepreneurs, design planners, and research directors—they report an interesting shift in conditions. Project leaders now engage with an expanding number of stakeholders, more of whom are asking for near-constant participation in order to absorb general methodology and stay close to the project. Team members are now often on multiple projects, rotating in and out as their expertise is required. And as the imperative to innovate grows, organizations are now placing multiple bets, funding many projects and innovation teams simultaneously, creating internal competition for attention and resources.

For a practitioner, these shifts put a new premium on communication *throughout* the process—not only at scheduled moments or presentations. Project leaders must now connect to more people, most of whom have limited context, but who need to be included at multiple moments in the creation process. They also must ensure that the larger working team is invested in/committed to the work early and in meaningful ways. Last, if they want the project to succeed, they need to be mindful of the organization as a whole, not just the immediate working team. In this context, communication has become collaborative, pervasive, and central to the success of the project. In the situations and conditions described by practitioners, we are seeing new and critical missions for communication.

Communication mission 1: Create all-in, not buy-in
Gravity Tank's Michael Winnick observes that "a lot of people talk about senior executive *buy-in*, but I think in big companies you need senior executive *all-in*. It's the difference between an executive that tacitly approves something versus one that's driving it. Amazon's Jeff Bezos is all in—he's the guy scrutinizing the products,

working the product designers. He's very engaged in everything. In hierarchical organizations, *all-in* is a pre-condition for serious innovation, serious change." Michael's point is that we are aiming low when we shoot for acceptance, because acceptance is a weak commitment that can be withdrawn quickly and easily. Intel's Tony Salvador has said, "Innovation is violence," meaning that by its nature innovation is tough and disruptive to everyday people in organizations. If he's right, then we need more than buy-in; we need leaders to fully join our idea—to be involved in integrating it—not merely to accept it. If the idea is big enough and bold enough to disrupt the standard order of things, then "buy in" is no longer enough. It has to be all-in.

Communication mission 2: Build a common basis of judgment

Cross-disciplinary, collaborative work requires that teams have a shared conceptual model from which to proceed effectively. The lack of an effective shared model can derail a project early. This is a painful possibility in every creative effort that seasoned practitioners work hard to address. Consider this common scenario from Shelley Evenson, referencing her time as chief experience strategist at Scient:

In the past, we'd have a kickoff meeting, we'd formalize, we'd write down all sorts of things on flip charts. We had different people speaking different languages: business strategists, developers, designers, etc. Three weeks later we'd come back together and, while everyone had done stuff, one team thought the other team was going to do X and the other team did Y, and so on. There was no common ground. So we started creating what we called Territory Maps at the kickoff—visual representations of the project that include constituents and big themes. The territory map created that common ground and common language from the beginning. It's really critical to be able to leave a meeting saying that no matter what perspective we have, we agree on this thing.

For more on Shelley's Territory Maps, see the "Thinking with Our Eyes" section in the next chapter.

Many practitioners, such as Steve Portigal of Portigal Consulting, rely on *shared experiences* to create that common ground: "Even if we don't yet have conclusive models from, say, the research phase, we create shared experiences to generate shared vocabulary and shared interpretations. A shared conceptual model comes from a shared experience. It's essential now, and our clients demand it . . . no one should be surprised at what you are revealing in that final meeting." Design strategist and IA Collaborative co-founder Kathleen Brandenburg has also opted for shared experience in her company's development model because she's seen the transformative effect: "If you experience it yourself, you're in it, you know what's happening is real. That's why we bring our clients into the research phase. We will never go into the field again without our clients. That's not happening."

For an idea to maintain its coherence as it moves through an organization, its owners need to understand where it comes from, why it is what it is, and why it is not something else. When the time comes to brand, package, engineer, or sell The New, specialists in those areas require a deep connection to the conceptual model to do their job. Otherwise, they have little choice but to rely on conventional category practices and what they already know. This means that a potentially groundbreaking laundry concept will be packaged to look and sound like the category—complete with a sunburst and vague language about outdoor fresh scent—unless those downstream specialists share in some part of the creation experience. The only way to prevent a fallback to the familiar is to involve these potential collaborators early on, and to create powerful, shared experiences to forge a common basis of judgment going forward.

Communication mission 3: Build belief and conviction

"You can be smart and you can know a lot and you can tell a great story. But at the end of the day, somebody's got to have the courage—not just the authority, but the courage—to say 'yes' and put a bunch of money on the line." These are the words of Steve Leeke, a former director of Motorola New Enterprises, talking about the difficulty of getting a risk-averse organization to invest in an unproven future. "The guys who run these companies in billion dollar slices have to be the ones to give a damn, and it has to matter to them. You can't force that. You can't just sit down and explain it to them. It has to be genuine. [Former Motorola CEO] Chris Galvin once asked me over lunch, what experiences do I have to take these business heads through, for them to understand this? And I didn't get it at the time. I didn't really appreciate how profound a statement that was."

Michael Winnick does appreciate and respect this idea, and he calls it *building belief*: "In innovation-oriented work, it's not so much about proving or disproving. It is about getting people to believe things. And belief is different than proof. Belief is about taking leaps or developing a sense of intuition about what's next or asking, 'Why should I do something bold when there are an enormous number of really valid reasons not to do anything at all?'"

Facts alone can't mobilize an organization. There needs to be belief. Belief is the foundation for conviction, and conviction is what it takes to commit to a future that may look half as profitable as the present. As Conifer Research's Ben Jacobson says, "Yes, there's got to be a mission out there, there has to be a calling—but where does that come from? It doesn't come from an MBA asking if that idea can provide a $100 million worth of incremental revenue. If your company thinks that that's credible and realistic and wants to filter every possible idea through that, I think you've got a long way to go. Personally, I think it's hard to know a $100 million idea when you see one."

Winnick continues, "If you believe that belief comes from experiences, from doing things—from actually bothering to do the fieldwork as opposed to hearing someone tell you about it, or from playing with a prototype as opposed to having someone do that for you and report back on it—that's very difficult, because senior executives don't typically do that stuff." No, they don't. And while no one I spoke with had a ready answer, they agree on this: Belief and conviction are mission critical for big, ambitious ideas to succeed, and direct experiences are a powerful means to achieve that.

Communication mission 4: Move ideas through the organization

Whether you are part of an external consultancy or an internal innovation center, getting concepts to successfully move through the organization is often the biggest challenge. Kathleen Brandenburg puts it this way:

You can do the best work in the world—the best strategy, the smartest plan, the best design—and it can absolutely fail to progress into implementation if the people you're working with aren't able to communicate that work internally. So it's imperative to give them tools they can use not only to communicate the work but also to inspire others in their organization to champion it as well. Being a true collaborator means saying, "I'm not just doing the assignment, I'm going to help you carry it all the way through."

Heather Reavey at Continuum thinks carefully about how to draw others to work in the early stages:

In the strategy group I lead, our number one mission is to move things through the organization because we know that's the hard part. Ideally, an idea should move through the organization virally, and not require someone to pick it up and move it every day. So how can you transform a big idea or insight into a poster that's so appealing that people hang them up, and others start to ask about it? What other interesting artifacts might attract attention? At Continuum, this used to be something that came up after the ideas were formed. But now we start thinking about creating that connection right from the beginning of the project.

Heather and Kathleen are both saying that it's not enough to create a single communication experience delivered by you and your team. You need to give others tools *they* can use to communicate, to advance the organization's understanding.

Communication mission 5: Preempt the power of no

There are many opportunities to say no to The New. Anyone along the decision chain, from concept to rollout, can pull the plug or dig in his or her heels: too costly, too disruptive, too complicated, too, well, different. As Michael Winnick points out, in almost any organization it is both easier and safer to say no than it is to say yes. "This is why multi-stakeholder sessions early on are so critical," says Gravity Tank partner Martha Cotton, "and those sessions need to build empathy (with end-users), immersion (in both the reality and the potential of the situation) and engagement with the project and the team so that they understand and believe that something needs to occur."

Her point is also that oftentimes the issue isn't the idea at all—it's the lack of relationships with and among important stakeholders. Internal innovation centers are particularly susceptible to organizational rejection. As Heather Reavey notes:

A lot of our clients have started up innovation teams everywhere. In many cases these teams set themselves up to fail because they are different, often because they don't have the same accountabilities or metrics for their own work, and so they create antibodies throughout the whole organization. They can become this isolated group of people who are supposed to come up with ideas, but the rest of the organization is not behind them. We spend a lot of time with those teams trying to get them to forge relationships, so that once they have the idea, that larger working team will actually do something with it.

Complexity? Novelty? Fuzziness? Relationships? Experiences? Belief? Conviction? Engagement? Is this still communication we're talking about?

Larry Keeley suspects that maybe it isn't, at least not conventionally so. "Maybe calling this communication trivializes it. So let's call it *moments that matter* in a progression from 'we're ignorant about a problem but we know it's important and we sense that it's different or acute' to 'wow, here's this incredibly amazing new platform capability that nobody in a focus group ever asked for, nobody ever understood or anticipated, but suddenly we can't live without.'"

Let's define the New Communication as a team's journey through "moments that matter." And let's state that this definition is a *necessary* response to changing conditions: Today we all operate in a highly collaborative business world, with rising stakes and increasing complexity. There is constant demand for innovation and development processes that must operate in the realm of speculation in order to anticipate what might be emerging in the near future. In this world, conventional communication techniques such as the 200-page PowerPoint and grand finale presentations no longer work. They don't prepare the organization to execute. Persuasion loses its power over time or when new data is introduced. The transfer model has always been suspect, but because creating The New requires collaboration, it may be particularly ineffective now. What we need a new mindset and a toolset to help us keep pace.

FIVE WAYS COMMUNICATION METHODS ACCELERATE INNNOVATION

Many creators of The New are paying attention to the growing body of methods and frameworks for managing innovation. Methods are essential to any planning process because they help manage complexity, ensure effective output, and, hopefully, help teams achieve something significant in a more disciplined and reliable way.

But among innovation management methods, what is missing is an equally considered and robust playbook for explaining that work—to ourselves, to our teammates, and to others—and for engaging others in its development. In this book, I present a general model that project leaders, entrepreneurs, or anyone involved in the creation of The New can use throughout a project. It's not a formula; tailor your choice of methods to fit the organizational style and the stakeholder tolerance for engagement. Nor is it magic; it won't help the poorly conceived become viable. But what it can do is provide guidance and a checklist to advance the process of creating The New. This model organizes methods and tactics culled from many disciplines—design, social science, education, linguistics, creativity, and journalism—to help individuals and teams find just the right communication practices for the challenges they face.

5 ways communication methods accelerate innovation

Content		+ Users

1 Finding the center	**2** Framing the work	**3** Targeting your constituents
Sharpen your thinking, Know what you know	*Define the new space, Develop a story device*	*Fit knowledge to key participants*
Models + frameworks	Metaphor	The communication plan
Build-to-think prototypes	Stories	Mental model + orthodoxy assessment
Lists + open-ended writing	Mantras + catchphrases	Quad A diagnostic
	Contrast	Organization as Culture framework
	Artifacts + images	

Because The New involves a series of messes, helping teams know what they know takes time. This is particularly challenging for projects with tight time frames. Often we *mostly* know what we think is important, yet in practical terms we are still wandering around the conceptual space trying to identify its center point. At this point, individuals and teams need help reaching two critical objectives: achieving clarity around the problem or the proposition, and building that all-important alignment in the larger working team. Tools and methods that address this situation are considered in Chapter 1, "Finding the Conceptual Center."

Teams also need help framing their thinking about The New in ways they and others can understand and remember. The objective is to do so in a way that creates a fresh mindset, so that the new proposition has focus, meaning, texture, and accessibility. Linguistic tools are simple to experiment with and don't require special skills to execute. Language is a potent tool that experts have studied for decades to better understand its power. This is a great place for creators of The New to learn more about that power. Tools that help teams consider how to use language more consciously and to greater effect in their endeavors are explored in Chapter 2, "Framing the Work."

+ Engagement

4 Introduce new thinking	5 Expanding the conversation
Create emotional + intellectual experiences	*Reach new constituents* *Help ideas "go viral"*
Exploration	Communication systems
Immersion	Performative presentations
Interaction	
Application	Demonstration artifacts
Extension	

In business schools it has become standard practice to train students in stakeholder interviews. Few other professions focus on how to size up the human beings who need to be invested in the project; even the MBA programs tend to favor functional assessments (What do people do and buy?) over holistic assessments (Who are they, and how do they live?). If one critical communication mission is to build belief and all-in, creators of The New have to cultivate deep curiosity and acute empathy for the people who will be engaged in that New over the long haul. Yes, this is extra work. But professionals in my executive education sessions who invest the extra couple of hours almost always come away with a renewed clarity and a better grasp of the political dynamics they will face. Tools and frameworks—borrowed from the social sciences—that help teams understand and engage others in The New are explored in Chapter 3, "Targeting Your Constituents."

Educational theory tells us that experience is a powerful teacher that creates both intellectual and emotional engagement with content. Experiences are a vital platform with which to engage stakeholders of all levels. For purposes of introducing The New, experiences must break with corporate convention and borrow from the best precedents in theater and education. A model for creating unconventional but effective engagement—what I call the "design for experiences"—is at the core of Chapter 4, "Introduce New Thinking."

It's never too early to get insights into circulation, to build organizational empathy with end users, or to begin priming an organization for a change. The objective, as Heather Reavey characterizes it, is to help projects "go viral" inside the organization by creating a platform for stories and conversation. We need to draw attention to an initiative before synthesis is finished, laying early groundwork for what comes later. This requires a bit of design, maybe a bit of theater, to dramatize the work. These tools for getting the word out and creating widespread support for The New are the subject of Chapter 5, "Expand the Conversation."

Even though the chapters are arranged in a linear sequence, any tool in the toolkit might be useful at nearly any stage of your development process. In the work of creating The New, you will find yourself facing challenges such as finding the conceptual center or introducing new thinking to stakeholders at multiple points. The book is designed to help you find the inspiration and practical advice to better communicate, and create, your New as you encounter these challenges.

1
Finding the conceptual center

MODELS AND FRAMEWORKS

BUILD-TO-THINK PROTOTYPES

LISTS AND OPEN-ENDED WRITING

Externalize thinking.

Achieve clarity around what's known, what's desired, and what's proposed.

Build alignment and shared meaning among team members.

We have a condition, when creating The New, of needing to process the mess of inputs we have gathered. We have quantitative data, qualitative data, industry reports, trend reports, rumors, stories, our own experiences. We've read it all. We may have lived it through direct experience with users and their lives. Now we must make sense of the soup. And we must make meaning from it. How do we decide which of all the things we have lived, read, and seen really matter most to the challenge at hand?

HOW TO "KNOW WHAT YOU KNOW"

Neuroscientists tell us 95 percent of brain activity is unconscious. For the sake of argument, let's say most of that activity is not worth conscious thought—digestion, walking, and cell division likely work better without our input. But while our brain's ability to operate and store information unconsciously makes us efficient, it may also be a problem: What if we need some of that 95 percent? What if some of what we have sublimated is important to the challenge at hand? An important first step in creating The New is finding a way to surface and organize the massive number of inputs our brains have so efficiently and automatically stored. We need to make it all top of mind again.

This is where communicating The New starts: surfacing what is known and then finding and articulating the conceptual center of the work. No effective communication can take place if we don't know what we are trying to say. No effective progress can take place if a team does not have a shared conceptual model of what's important. Articulating what we mean, whether on our own or as part of team, is a critical stage in communicating The New.

The challenge of "unspeakable data"

In creating The New, we face an early-stage condition of *unspeakable data*—the data of our senses, thoughts, and emotions. This is author Peter Turchi's phrase for capturing the fiction writer's condition in his book *Maps of the Imagination: The Writer as Cartographer.* In the context of creating The New, "unspeakable data" refers to all the rich details and information we have ingested as we framed our challenge, conducted research, and began to explore directions. Much of that experience now lives in a subconscious state that some might understand as intuition. We know our bodies take in information through our five senses at a speed and depth that we are largely unaware of, but that we are richly wired to interpret and apply with little conscious thought. This may explain why so many designers and innovators rely on field research methods to better understand the reality of their customers: Research teams go into customers' homes and workplaces and cars and coffee shops so that they may observe with their eyes and with their hands, noses, and ears the everyday context and activities of the people they are creating for. In these cases, our bodies are our field instruments as much as our field notebooks. This data becomes "unspeakable" because it is often deeply embedded in our sense memory, and it may or may not ever make it to the pages of our field notebooks. We know it, but we may not *know we know it*.

How to surface unspeakable data? Or unspoken knowing? What are effective processes for working through the mess and finding that conceptual center? In this section, we look to the fields of design, engineering, education, and journalism to identify methods for early-stage synthesis. And we go back to basics to include those often ignored ways of knowing that are part and parcel of our conceptual system. On the basis of my research, I cluster these methods into three basic categories:

- MODELS AND FRAMEWORKS
- BUILD-TO-THINK PROTOTYPES
- LISTS AND OPEN-ENDED WRITING

The ROI and PFP (Pain for Progress) of these approaches

Although helping individuals and teams align on what they know is a critical milestone, it's actually not that hard to do. Years of professional practice and teaching tell me this: For all the confusion and mess, people in the early stages of projects know more than they give themselves credit for. We are, after all, sense-making machines driven toward answers. But self-doubt, piles of facts, and a fair bit of ambiguity can impair a team's vision and clarity in ways that are uncomfortable and time-consuming. Too often, getting to conceptual clarity is where the team collides with the uncompromising requirements imposed by the project's Gantt chart.

If thirty minutes of open-ended writing (one of my favorite accelerants) or two hours of rough prototyping could save a team days of unfocused meetings and group gropes, would that merit stepping out of the Gantt chart? In the pages that follow, I propose no method or approach that I have not used myself. These require no specialized knowledge, equipment, or software. They work on the train ride in, or at the lunch table. They work for individuals and for teams.

What they require is a willingness to ask an open-ended question, "What do we know?" and to proceed from there as if the answer is within reach. Because it is.

MODELS AND FRAMEWORKS:
Thinking with our eyes

All models are wrong, but some are useful.

—George P. Box, statistician and author of *Empirical Model-Building and Response Surfaces*

WHAT CAN MODELS DO FOR US?

Models or frameworks are abstract, diagrammatic representations of information or observations. Models represent a particular view of reality, and so can be partial and subject to change, and may even represent incorrect interpretations. What makes models useful is their ability to abstract and simplify complex content.

Models are particularly useful in the early stages of creating The New, when a team may find itself awash in data and in search of meaning. Models are effective at this stage because they remove distracting detail and anecdotal content to reveal an underlying structure or pattern in the information. Models install boundaries on the system of ideas, telling us where the conceptual space begins and ends. All this de-cluttering and distillation fosters clarity. It builds consensus (or at least supports conversations that can lead to consensus) and opens up questions about what could exist in the future. This may explain why so many practitioners who favor models say that the process of making models may be more useful than the model itself: Model creation requires reflection, editing, negotiation, and storytelling. These are all excellent activities for individuals or teams in search of synthesis and convergence.

Because they are visual expressions of thought, models do something that text cannot: To borrow a phrase from quantitative visualization guru Stephen Few, models allow us to *"think with our eyes."* Our eye/brain hardware has optimized over thousands of years to process the visual world for patterns and meaning, and we can do so in a fraction of the time it takes to read and translate that meaning from text. This intelligence is not only faster, it's higher bandwidth: We can process much more visual data simultaneously than we can textual data, which demands a linear process. Thinking with our eyes provides a different channel into a conceptual space: one that is highly complementary to verbal methods, such as writing or talking, but uniquely able to compress a sprawling problem into a compact space and to support conceptual play with its parts and pieces. Using a model, a team can see the whole conceptual space at once, and then dive into a specific portion of the space without losing sight of the whole.

Let's look at three examples of how models can help teams find the conceptual center:

- MODELS FOR MANAGING COMPLEXITY
- MODELS FOR BUILDING A SHARED BASIS OF JUDGMENT
- MODELS FOR CREATING ALIGNMENT

MODELS FOR MANAGING COMPLEXITY

How does Internet search work, anyway?

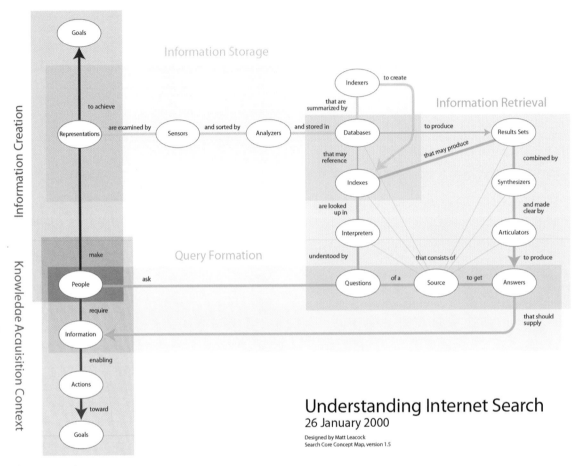

Understanding Internet Search
26 January 2000

Designed by Matt Leacock
Search Core Concept Map, version 1.5

© Matt Leacock

In 1999, it was still the Dark Ages of Internet search. Industry leader Netscape had just acquired a small startup with an expertise in search.

Netscape was still in the process of folding this new capability into its search services when the VP of products approached design lead Hugh Dubberly, and asked him to manage a redesign of the search interface. Hugh assigned promising young designer Matt Leacock to the team, a

group composed of "fairly aggressive, opinionated engineers," in Matt's words. The first meeting didn't go well. "He'd been basically almost kicked out," says Hugh, "they didn't know why he was there."

To state the obvious, Internet search was an amorphous and complex topic to someone outside the field. Hugh handed Matt a vintage copy of Gowin and Novak's *Learning How to*

Learn, which outlines in detail how to create concept maps as a tool for managing unfamiliar, complex subjects. Matt followed the protocol: He interviewed the engineers, project leader, and an external subject expert or two. He drafted his model, which Hugh reviewed and liked, and went into the next meeting to present it.

"He comes back after the meeting, and he's kind of all hangdog," as Hugh tells it. "I asked him what happened, as I thought the map was fine and that everyone had bought into it. He said, 'Yeah, you wouldn't believe it, though, a fight broke out.' Matt's map had brought to the surface the fact that the mental models among various engineers for what was happening were not consistent." As Matt recalls, "There was a lot of contention around how to differentiate the search engine and where to drive user interaction with the product—the search page or the directory." Through the model, the team had discovered something very important—they were working to code a system they didn't agree on.

And so Matt was able to go on and be a productive member of the team and earn their respect. "He went from being an outsider who didn't really know anything in this process to being a person in the room who had the best view of the whole thing. He wasn't a deeper subject expert in any particular part of the domain, but nobody else had the whole domain," observes Hugh.

Matt suspects the process of creating the model was more critical to his success than the artifact. "The model was a tool for individual understanding and to get everyone on the team on the same page with same language. But my interviewing the team showed interest in them. It built credibility, and created a history of agreement when there was no history of trust. It also helped them understand what I did."

For Hugh, concept mapping at various levels of abstraction has become a regular tool in the development of software and services. Matt took the lesson, too. He has continued to make maps in his professional progression through Netscape, Yahoo, and then startup Sococo. He likes them for their ability to communicate how a complex system operates, but he cautions: "At the end of a day, a model is just the description of the system, and what you really need is a reason to be making the system at all."

MODELS FOR BUILDING A SHARED BASIS OF JUDGMENT
How to reinvent the college textbook?

For its textbook publisher client, Conifer Research went back to school to observe in person how and when college students use textbooks to prepare for papers and exams. Using ethnographic field methods, Conifer tracked and compiled data on study behaviors, time management, and any study tools used by students. What they discovered contained some challenging news for the client about the role and value of textbooks: Textbooks are abandoned at test time, and some students don't use the textbook at all.

When the news is hard to hear, building organizational belief can be particularly difficult. Like many established industries, textbook publishers have long-standing assumptions and conventions about what their product should be. This client would need a big dose of belief and a shared basis of judgment in order to mount a robust and coherent response to the findings about their core business.

It was the user experience model that opened up those assumptions and conventions for discussion. Conifer's Megan Fath has built a reputation for her deftly executed user experience models. In the textbook case, her time-based model visualized two key discoveries: First, at test time, students abandon the textbook; second, not all students even use the textbook. Some students began preparation earlier, utilizing the textbook, while others skipped the textbook altogether in favor of abbreviated and mobile materials.

This difficult news was not "delivered" to the client; it emerged from collaborative efforts with the client. Fath and the client evolved the experience model together, exchanging

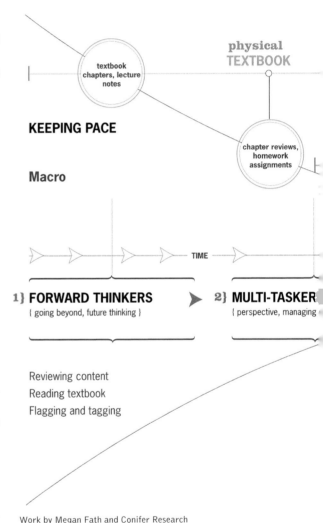

Work by Megan Fath and Conifer Research

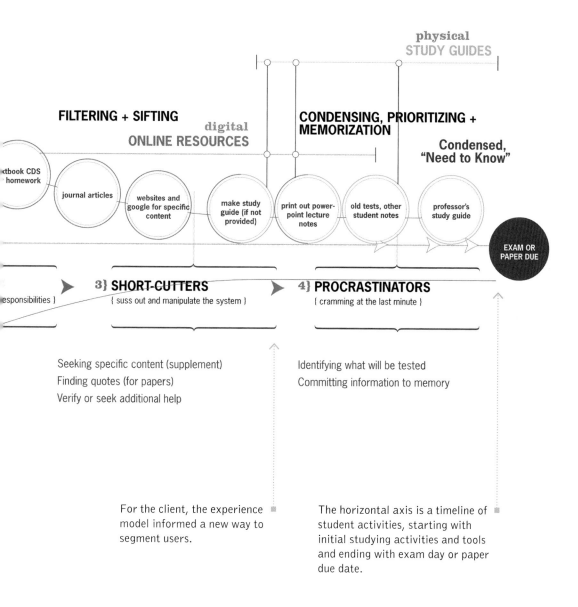

physical
STUDY GUIDES

FILTERING + SIFTING
digital
ONLINE RESOURCES

CONDENSING, PRIORITIZING +
MEMORIZATION

Condensed,
"Need to Know"

textbook CDS
homework

journal articles

websites and
google for specific
content

make study
guide (if not
provided)

print out power-
point lecture
notes

old tests, other
student notes

professor's
study guide

EXAM OR
PAPER DUE

responsibilities }

3} SHORT-CUTTERS
{ suss out and manipulate the system }

4} PROCRASTINATORS
{ cramming at the last minute }

Seeking specific content (supplement)
Finding quotes (for papers)
Verify or seek additional help

Identifying what will be tested
Committing information to memory

For the client, the experience
model informed a new way to
segment users.

The horizontal axis is a timeline of
student activities, starting with
initial studying activities and tools
and ending with exam day or paper
due date.

stories around data and building a shared understanding of what the team was learning. Megan underscores that "co-creating models with our clients is essential. It not only builds shared understanding, it ensures that the visualization will be utilized as a communication tool after our collaboration ends."

The final version of the model was printed out in large format and ultimately became the platform for multiple team events and development efforts. As Megan tells it, "We used this final visualization in the client workshop to anchor ideation and navigate discussions of key insights. The ideation verified that we were effective in communicating the need to reframe the textbook and to reexamine several of their established textbook conventions. To extend the value of the learning, the client printed out several more copies of the poster to use in team collaborations moving forward." The model became a unifying force across different teams and product development efforts. It ensured that new concepts, whether developed by different teams or over time, would spring from a shared conceptual root.

The model became the shared basis for multiple ideation sessions across stakeholder groups.

New concepts with stakeholders all began with a first page that said, "We listened."

MODELS FOR CREATING ALIGNMENT

Which factors matter most in patient care for seniors?

Work done in collaboration with the Mayo Clinic Center for Innovation, with Melissa Cliver, Dave Passavant, and Christina Payne Earle for Designing + Leading a Business, a graduate course at Carnegie Mellon University, with Professors Boni, Evenson, and Weingart

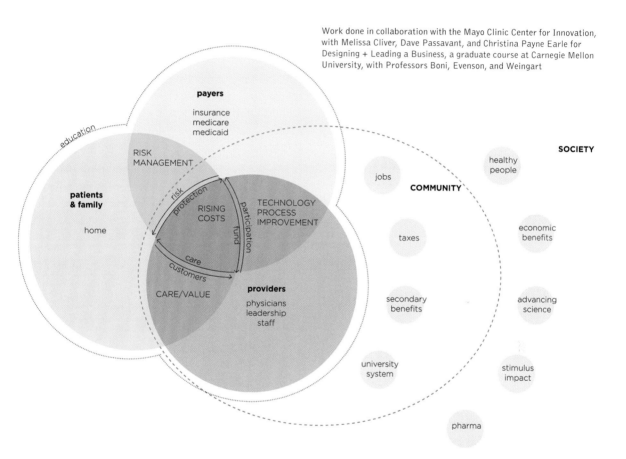

Since the mid-1990s, designer and strategist Shelley Evenson has been championing collaborative creation processes. She and her late husband and frequent collaborator, John Rheinfrank, were ahead of their time in this; conventional practices presumed closed creative processes that delivered finished work at the end, with little input from clients. Shelley's professional trajectory, however—from Fitch to Doblin, Scient, Continuum, Microsoft, and

Graduate students of Carnegie Melon University kicked off a project with the Mayo Clinic's Center for Innovation by jointly creating a Territory Map to define the scope, theme, and relevant constituents to be considered. The objective of the project was to design a disruptive business model that would decrease costs and improve efficiency and quality of care.

- Draw out existing preconceptions and knowledge

- Create a shared language

- Visualize the problem statement

- Help bound later research activities

- Create a shared vision of the project by team members

Facebook—provided her with strong evidence that collaborative construction is key to creating The New. "Organizations are doing a better job of breaking down silos, but the silos are still there. Working across different committees and different domains, and understanding how everyone can be successful in those efforts, is still the crux."

A notable trouble spot in interdisciplinary, collaborative work is the kickoff meeting, where project scope is defined and expectations are set. To succeed, everyone needs a shared "north star" to guide their actions and unify their efforts. But team members from different domains have their own culture and ways of thinking, and often speak in their own language, with differences in meaning that are not always apparent until later. Dialogue around project scope also typically includes high-level, abstract terms such as "innovation" or "research" or "transformative" that, at a practical level (and often at the end of a project), turn out to have a spectrum of interpretations. As a result, project funders, team members, and important stakeholders are often out of alignment from day one.

Shelley, in collaboration with Hugh Dubberly, has developed a tool called a Territory Map as a first step to create early-stage alignment. Territory Maps visually capture the territory the team thinks it is tackling together. Territory Maps are collaborative efforts built by project participants in a work session. The maps factor in all the constituents who will likely be impacted, and can even propose a rough stab at the future vision that is shared by team members.

As Shelley tells it, "I knew there was something to it when we were working on a project for a client of Scient, an Internet consultancy, in the early 2000s. At the kickoff meeting, we had the designers, coders, and client-side team, including the CEO of the client organization, go through the process of creating a Territory Map. Later in the project, the CEO was reviewing things and asked, 'Is that in our map? If it's not in our map, I really want to understand why we are going to increase that. We agreed on the set of attributes that mattered.' So the map also became a way to have a conversation about what was in and out of scope, which is always really difficult as projects go forward."

"What's key," notes Shelley, "is that the map is co-constructed with relevant stakeholders and senior-level executives. Because it's collaboratively created, it builds cohesion and shared vision. Of course, the things you put in the map can change over the duration of the process, but creating a map gets everyone to a common starting point and a common story, and gives them a shared language for talking about it. And because project definition is built from the ground up by the people involved, there's no need to convert others in the room to a way of thinking or to impose a point of view on others. *Territory maps work because they are negotiated, not imposed.*"

HOW TO MAKE MODELS WORK
How might we use the mighty model to find the conceptual center of our work?

Models are excellent tools at this stage if we keep in mind two important principles:

Models are not about being right

"There's this perception or belief that a single framework emerges from the work—that there is a *right* answer, a *right* model. And there isn't." These are the words of SapientNitro's John Cain, but he speaks for many experienced practitioners when he stresses that models are a means to an end: "There are a lot of possible models for any given project. When I take students through the six or eight constructs we created for a case, and I ask which one's *the* framework, I get a bunch of blank stares. And this is the problem: We can learn a lot of stuff [from consumers] about cleaning or getting a cold, but there is no 'truth for all time' framework that is going to emerge from this research process. There are just ways of constructing different ideas to serve some sort of purpose in the project."

In other words, models at this stage are *provisional.* They are a means to multiple end states. As a thinking tool, the value of models comes through variation and the multiple stories they allow us to tell of the same problem space. This brings us to the second principle. . .

More models are better than one

Models express a way of thinking about a problem, but often the most relevant way to express a problem isn't obvious at the outset. Creating a series of models in response to questions—What if we model it by time? What if we look at structural relationships?—generates a productive progression in thinking that can

help teams triangulate around what's relevant. Social scientists use the expression "interrogating the data"—asking questions of the data to discover meaning and pattern. Through creating multiple models, teams can interrogate their own knowledge and prototype their thinking. The advice, then, is not to make a model, but to make *many* models: Vary the questions, vary the visual forms, and see what surfaces.

THE USE SCENARIO FOR MODELS

Managing, not eliminating, complexity

Creators of The New embrace complexity because they know the answer to "what's next" lies in it. Businesspeople recoil from complexity because it's hard to manage and creates inefficiencies in their processes. Their answer to managing complexity is to manage it down, to get rid of as much of it as possible. This, however, is not an option for creative teams, who must cultivate a messy, multidimensional problem space to produce novel, timely, and relevant output. As a result, in the early stages of creating The New, complexity, ambiguity, and confusion are pretty much the norm.

Models and mapping are particularly well-suited to managing early-stage complexity. For example, says Kathleen Brandenburg, "at IA Collaborative we use frameworks both for top-down and bottom-up understanding of complex information. Frameworks provide a sense of confidence—especially with topics as large and complex as redesigning airline travel, or uncovering needs in an emerging market, or how technology might best be utilized in healthcare. For example, taking time to list and see that the activities and interactions of users are, in fact, *finite* can provide a great sense of clarity and direction for a project." Whether it's a user experience model or a concept map or a mind map, models provide an alternative to reductionist thinking that would have us manage valuable complexity by getting rid of it.

Creating critical conceptual alignment to hold the mission together

When The New is in the "still fuzzy" stage, building a shared vision of the concept with collaborators is hard because the thing itself is still emerging. For entrepreneurs such as Judd Morgenstern, working with the still-emerging is the natural state for startups. This has predictable problems: "We recently did a user experience evaluation with a startup product, and the user was really confused on whether or not you could do a certain action, like follow a person. As we started talking about that, it turned out the two co-founders strongly disagreed on whether or not a user could follow a person, and whether or not the user should be allowed to follow a person. Well, I'm not surprised that the user experience is totally confusing because the two founders don't even agree on how it should work."

In reality, ideas always do and must change. They are affected by data, by interaction, even by the act of communication. Until the ideas are fixed, alignment of stakeholders needs to come from someplace deeper, from a larger conceptual framework that stays stable even as the ideas themselves evolve. Models are useful here, too, because they can map out important conceptual territory that holds the mission together.

Building a shared basis of judgment to stay true to the work

Models can anchor for people a way of thinking about the problem. This provides a common platform for development and decision making, for collaborators who may need to work in different locations or on different parts of the problem simultaneously. A model that has been collaboratively built is understood by all participants, and so can provide cohesion and integrity to work developed across groups. The fact that models are compact and visual is also an asset: It is easier to carry and reference a model than it is to work with a slide deck in which key information is distributed over many pages.

HOW TO GET STARTED

Some models emerge naturally from data; others require coaxing. On the following pages, I borrow questions and structures from the field of information design to inform a simple process for extracting models from data.

Information designers know that different visualizations of the same data can direct your attention in meaningfully different ways. Data organized sequentially yields a different picture than that same data will yield when organized by importance or by theme. What information designers also know is that discovering the most useful forms for any given data set requires experimentation and iteration. The process of creating variations itself is often revealing, because it requires you to touch all the data multiple times.

HOW TO MAKE MODELS WORK
Structuring the Mess

What kind of questions help drive discovery? The number of possible questions is open-ended. But here are five that will advance your thinking:

1. Does time or sequence matter?

2. Are some aspects more important than others?

3. What is the relative impact of any part to the whole?

4. Is there an underlying system at work?

5. Is there a central concept anchoring the topic?

On the following pages, we'll see how to use these questions to drive visual variations and reveal different perspectives on the data.

Most "messes" start with a pile of information or insights. As an example, let's look at a relatively simple and accessible pile of information—an in-home study of how children brush their teeth. Using individual pieces of information, we can build a lengthy list of insights. But to advance our understanding more deeply, we can model this information in multiple ways, using different questions to drive visual variations.

Waaaa! It must be toothbrush time. Getting kids to get started is half the battle. ▪

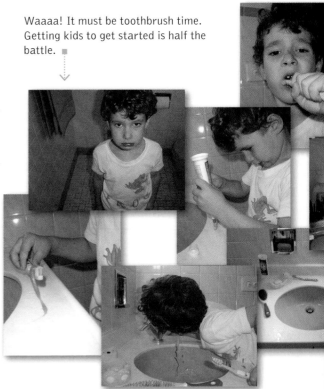

▪ The "fountain slurp" is a common rinse tactic.

■ Some kids have two brushes: one for them, one for the parent.

■ Brushing with brother makes her feel like a "big girl."

■ Motorized brushes add fun, complexity.

■ Older kids get more freedom.

■ Whose job is it really? Parent involvement is high with young kids.

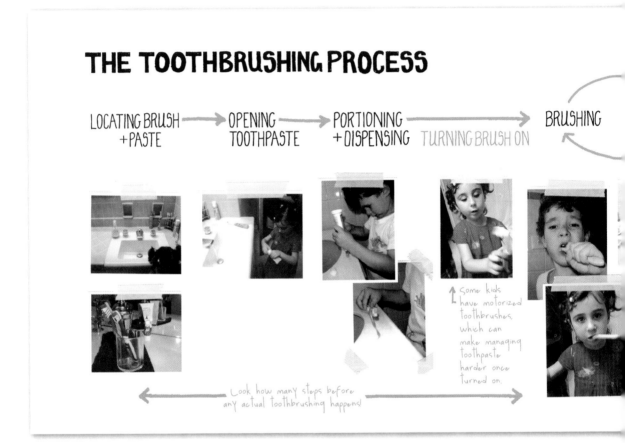

THE TOOTHBRUSHING PROCESS

LOCATING BRUSH + PASTE → OPENING TOOTHPASTE → PORTIONING + DISPENSING   TURNING BRUSH ON → BRUSHING

Some kids have motorized toothbrushes, which can make managing toothpaste harder once turned on.

Look how many steps before any actual toothbrushing happens!

Most of us intuitively start with time-based or process-oriented models. This makes sense; we are creatures bound in time and space, and so these are natural organizing principles to apply when trying to sort out information. When I give these toothbrush images to teams to sort, nine out of ten times the organizing structure is sequence. It needn't be—in the case of kids brushing their teeth, it would be just as productive to sort the images by object usage or spatial issues—but most teams go for a linear process breakdown. Time-based sequences feel natural, familiar, and so are a great place to start.

Sequence models are useful because they direct our eyes to:

- Stages and handoffs: The visual form can draw attention to gaps in the process that are not well understood or supported.

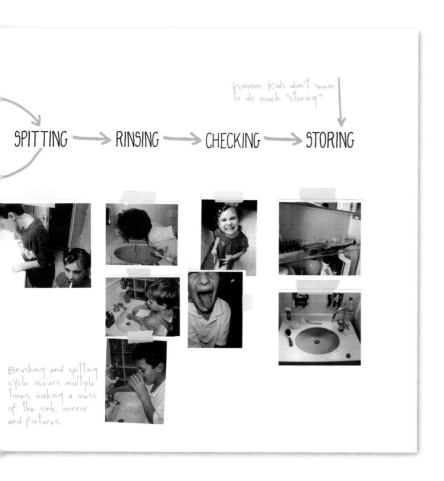

SPITTING → RINSING → CHECKING → STORING

hmmm. Kids don't seem to do much "storing"

Brushing and spitting cycle occurs multiple times, making a mess of the sink, mirror and fixtures.

- Progression: Sometimes the number of elements in a sequence tells its own story about the complexity of the subject. If a customer experience has 14 stages, that's courting trouble!

- Variations: Charting a sequence can surface important variations in flow, helping teams understand differences between the ideal process and the actual experience.

- Boundaries: Deciding where a subject starts and ends, for instance, can help teams commit to what is in or out of project scope.

HOW TO MAKE MODELS WORK

2: Are some aspects more important than others?

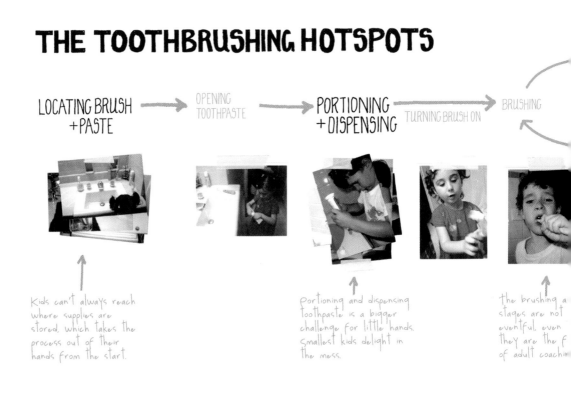

THE TOOTHBRUSHING HOTSPOTS

LOCATING BRUSH + PASTE → OPENING TOOTHPASTE → PORTIONING + DISPENSING → TURNING BRUSH ON → BRUSHING

Kids can't always reach where supplies are stored, which takes the process out of their hands from the start.

Portioning and dispensing toothpaste is a bigger challenge for little hands. Smallest kids delight in the mess.

The brushing a stages are not eventful even they are the f of adult coachin

Sequence and time-based models are useful because they offer a complete view and establish firm boundaries of a process. But sometimes this flat visual form obscures the fact that some aspects matter more than others—they happen in quantity or with intensity. We can call attention to factors that have particular relevance by adding size or color to parts of a model, giving them prominence on the page so that our eyes find them quickly.

Priority models that call out what's important or intense are useful because they direct our eyes to:

- Quantitative factors: These draw attention to high-frequency events or high-cost issues.

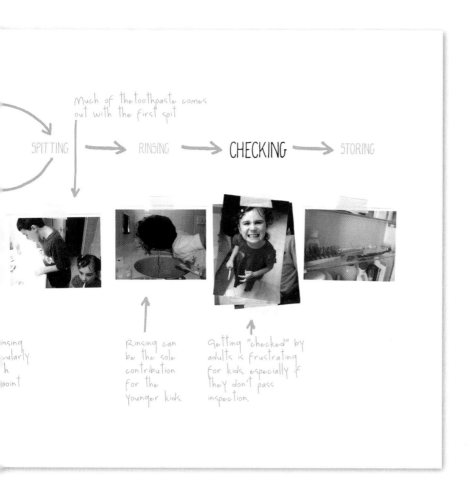

Much of the toothpaste comes out with the first spit

SPITTING → RINSING → **CHECKING** → STORING

...nsing ...ularly ...h ...oint

Rinsing can be the sole contribution for the younger kids.

Getting "checked" by adults is frustrating for kids, especially if they don't pass inspection.

- Emotional factors: These layer observed human responses, such as frustration or delight, onto otherwise functionally-driven models.

- Opportunities: These draw attention to elements that appear particularly problematic, out of step, or ready for reinvention.

HOW TO MAKE MODELS WORK
3: What is the relative impact of any part to the whole?

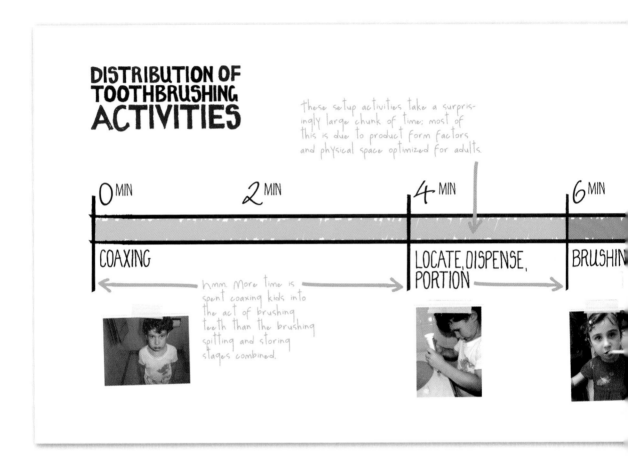

DISTRIBUTION OF TOOTHBRUSHING ACTIVITIES

these setup activities take a surprisingly large chunk of time; most of this is due to product form factors and physical space optimized for adults.

0 MIN   2 MIN   4 MIN   6 MIN

COAXING   LOCATE, DISPENSE, PORTION   BRUSHIN

hmm. More time is spent coaxing kids into the act of brushing teeth than the brushing spitting and storing stages combined.

Breaking large topics into smaller parts and pieces is essential to careful analysis, clear thinking, and to ensuring coverage of a topic. But sometimes we need to put those discrete parts back together to remind ourselves of their relationship to the larger topic. Pie charts and segmented bar charts are both visual forms that attempt to clarify how much a given part contributes to the whole. Often times these representations add more value when

created after conventional tagging and sorting of data is done, as they force us to step out of the details and reassess the topic from a holistic perspective again.

Impact models that highlight the relationship between parts and whole can help us:

• Correct our assumptions: Preconceived ideas about what's important can fall away when we

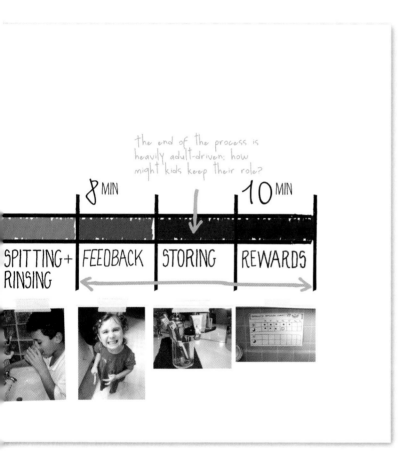

the end of the process is heavily adult-driven: how might kids keep their role?

8 MIN   10 MIN

SPITTING + RINSING | FEEDBACK | STORING | REWARDS

can see more accurately the role of a part in the larger context of the whole.

- Resist undue influence: It's easy to undervalue or overweight some factors, such as physical discomfort or emotional distress, until they are recontextualized in the larger picture, where their impact becomes more obvious.

4: Is there an underlying system at work?

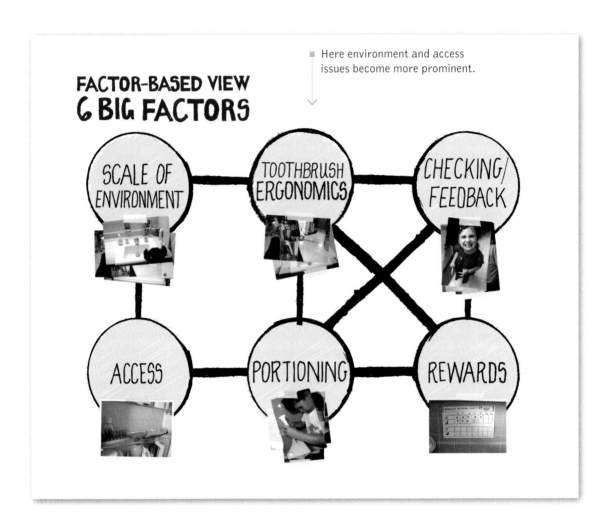

FACTOR-BASED VIEW
6 BIG FACTORS

■ Here environment and access issues become more prominent.

SCALE OF ENVIRONMENT

TOOTHBRUSH ERGONOMICS

CHECKING/ FEEDBACK

ACCESS

PORTIONING

REWARDS

Models that focus our attention on variables and clusters can blind us to larger, less evident forces that might be influencing the topic in question. This includes cultural, environmental, and other latent factors that we take for granted and therefore fail to see. In systems design, engineers engage in "factor analysis," which aims to identify any underlying structure that might organize a large number of variables, and then models the relationship between those factors.

Systems models are useful because they direct our thinking to:

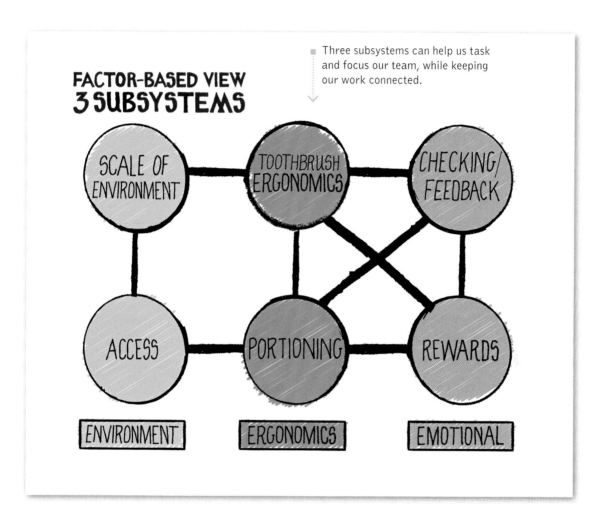

FACTOR-BASED VIEW
3 SUBSYSTEMS

Three subsystems can help us task and focus our team, while keeping our work connected.

SCALE OF ENVIRONMENT

TOOTHBRUSH ERGONOMICS

CHECKING/ FEEDBACK

ACCESS

PORTIONING

REWARDS

ENVIRONMENT

ERGONOMICS

EMOTIONAL

- Latent factors that are hard to see: A systems model is high-level and exhaustive, making it easier to spot logic gaps or spy important concept that are missing.

- A reduced number of elements: The visual form combines multiple factors into smaller groups.

The smaller set is easier to remember and creates focus.

- Factors that interrelate: Identifying relationships between elements highlights factors that influence each other, and therefore should be evaluated and possibly resolved together.

5: Is there a central concept anchoring the topic?

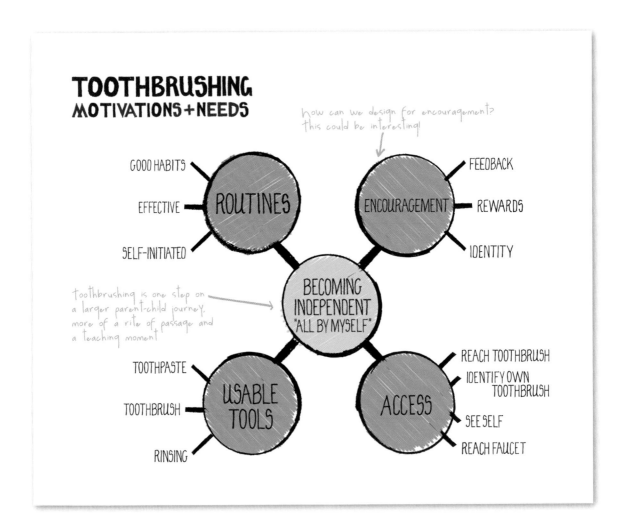

TOOTHBRUSHING MOTIVATIONS + NEEDS

how can we design for encouragement? this could be interesting!

GOOD HABITS — ROUTINES
EFFECTIVE —
SELF-INITIATED —

ENCOURAGEMENT — FEEDBACK
— REWARDS
— IDENTITY

BECOMING INDEPENDENT "ALL BY MYSELF"

toothbrushing is one step on a larger parent-child journey. more of a rite of passage and a teaching moment

TOOTHPASTE — USABLE TOOLS
TOOTHBRUSH —
RINSING —

ACCESS — REACH TOOTHBRUSH
— IDENTIFY OWN TOOTHBRUSH
— SEE SELF
— REACH FAUCET

Step back from the data and ask yourself: Is there a linchpin issue? Among all the important facts and observations, is there one key concept at the center of it all? Mind maps are one of the most common visual forms for organizing variables so as to identify dependencies and, most importantly, to surface meaning. Identifying the center node of a map is often a point of discovery, surfacing the unstated or tacit driver of the topic. To be effective, then, the center node needs to articulate clearly the "why" that explains the existence of all the other nodes in the network.

A mind map can be revealing when we use its form to drive:

- Order: To see the various elements grouped into a hierarchy brings order to the smaller details observed along the way.

- Synthesis: To edit is to decide—mind maps drive negotiation and editing for relevance.

- Priority: The center node is the conceptual center, which in turn influences how all other factors on the page are interpreted.

BUILD-TO-THINK PROTOTYPES:
Thinking with Our Hands

"You learn things from building," says Marty Thaler, "maybe especially when building before ideas are fully developed." Marty is a respected product designer who has worked for IDEO and whose work is displayed at the Art Institute of Chicago. Early stage prototyping, or building models of ideas that are underdeveloped and unfinished, is, in effect, thinking with your hands. Using your hands to build still-emerging ideas forces decisions, reflection, and synthesis. Marty calls it "build to think."

Most of us have been socialized to believe that making things, whether sketches or models, is for creative people (not us), people with talent and hand skills (again, not us) and who understand the mysteries of color and proportion and form. This is a discouraging, art-based paradigm in which the value of the work is perceived to be in the output and its aesthetic properties.

There is a more productive and encouraging paradigm for making artifacts that focuses on discovery, rather than outcome. Let's call it a learning-based paradigm, in which the value of building is in the process of experimenting and surfacing of meaning. "Build to think" is a low-cost, high-impact method for helping teams find the conceptual center of their work.

On the following pages we look at three ways prototypes can help us find the conceptual center:

- **PAPER PROTOTYPES TO ASK "WHAT IF?"**
- **"FRANKENPROTOTYPES" TO EXPLORE AND ALIGN**
- **MODULAR PROTOTYPES TO CONFIGURE AND CONVERSE**

BUILD-TO-THINK AS A PATH TO KNOWING

In their courses on early-stage prototyping at the Institute of Design, Marty Thaler and Anijo Mathew introduce an important distinction between fidelity and resolution. Fidelity refers to the level of similarity to the actual experience you would like to convey. Resolution is the level of detail needed to convey it. Prototypes can vary in both fidelity and resolution. And practitioners, say Marty and Anijo, need to choose the right level of both to achieve their goals at any given point in the process.

Most people are familiar with late-stage prototypes—detailed physical models that articulate a product, environment, or brand before it heads into production. They tend to be produced when concepts are well defined and need to be communicated to decision makers, funders, and implementers. Marty calls these "build to decide" prototypes.

The distinction between "build to think" and "build to decide" is important: Late-stage, "build to decide" prototypes require high-resolution execution, because the job is to fully convey the potential of the concept or business. They allow teams to test the concept for various forms of consumer "fit" (cognitive, physical, contextual). They allow the team to socialize ideas in a concrete way with important stakeholders. High-fidelity, beautifully executed prototypes are also a point of pride: They attract attention, build excitement, and advance careers.

In a "build to think" prototype, the target is low resolution and low fidelity—just enough experience to imagine the concept, without distracting detail and quality craftsmanship that signal a more developed idea. The role of a "build to think" prototype is not to be pretty or complete or accurate; it's to help the team learn, experiment, and develop unfinished ideas using tangible objects to imagine a future state.

"Build to think" prototypes are useful because they are never intended to be right. Their job is to inform the problem. Building to think helps teams externalize assumptions, biases, and gaps in the team's knowledge base. It surfaces weak, timid, and close-in thinking. Building to think can quickly flush these routine impulses from the team's system, opening up the conceptual space for more nuanced and interesting ideas. Building to think can rule out directions, too, illuminating stronger directions by having raised and made evident the weakness of other directions. At this stage, there should be no stake in final outcome, only the decision-making and resulting conversation that comes from having an artifact to review.

How to spend your building time wisely

When teams work in low resolution, stake-holders need to be prepared for the rough-hewn, provisional nature of the prototype. Once those expectations have been set, limit the amount of investment in the visual to hit this note: just enough refinement to make the proposition self-evident, not so much as to make it look finished. Heather Reavey calls it "credible but sketchy":

I'm a big advocate, especially in the messy phase, of making sure that things aren't too finished. It used to be I'd do a sketch of something, and then use Illustrator and add nice colors to make it art. At one point one of my clients, with whom we were collaborating heavily, said, 'Why are you doing that? Because where I come from the fact that you have all these sketches is like magic. We see the computer stuff all the time.' That made me realize that people are so much more open to things that don't look finished in this mess stage. And when you do make it look good, it can look too done. And then they start thinking about why it's wrong. Or maybe they start thinking about how they might actually have to implement it, and they get scared. So it's really important in the early stages to make sure things still look sketchy . . . credible but sketchy.

Build-to-think prototypes serve several important functions:

1. They allow teams to experiment with multiple "right" answers at little cost or commitment.

2. They accelerate learning, helping to surface opportunities and limitations early on.

3. They take the abstract and make it tangible and touchable, and therefore open to review by stakeholders both on the team and outside of it.

4. They change the conversation around the table and create that all-important alignment teams need to proceed in concert.

There is almost no downside to building to think. Even provisional prototypes can change the conversation in a room in important and surprising ways, cutting through the false concreteness of words to reveal ambition levels, tolerance for change, political no-no's, sweet spots, and other hard-to-identify factors that cause teams to slap their foreheads and groan three months later: "If we'd only known." You can know it: Build early and discover.

PAPER PROTOTYPES TO ASK "WHAT IF?"

How to impact global food loss?

Two hours. Three colored markers. One carefully cut piece of cardboard. With a simple set of resources, one Institute of Design planning team imagined what the world might be like if farmer-innovators in developing countries could collect and diffuse food-saving innovations to other farmers who need them.

Working with Danielle Nierenberg, director of the Worldwatch Institute's *Nourishing the Planet* project, the planning team was challenged to look

at global food loss issues in India and Western Africa to imagine how to diffuse crop-saving inventions among farmers within and across a region. In their research, the team had expected to discover a scarcity of solutions to post-harvest food loss problems. Instead, they learned there is no shortage of low-cost, easy-to-implement ideas. But these solutions were locked up in dense public policy reports, often inaccessible to on-the-ground organizations in contact with the farmers.

What if those innovations could be seen by everyone? What if anyone who had a good solution could share it? The team envisioned an online site that would aggregate the stories and solutions of on-the-ground farmers that are technically and culturally appropriate for their regions. When the team met with Dani, they walked her through a paper prototype of their concept, inserting hand-markered pages into a cardboard "screen" to demonstrate use scenarios. For Dani, it was an epiphany.

"I love that paper prototype. I had been thinking of an innovations database since the Nourishing the Planet project started in 2009, after we got funding from the Gates Foundation. I had this amorphous idea, but couldn't grasp exactly what I wanted. When I saw the prototype, it was like opening a gift up on Christmas morning. It crystallized what it should look like in a way that I couldn't conceptualize on my own."

The low-resolution paper approach added value: "I expected them to have some sort of computer program or a slide show. But this was a nice surprise because paper is *hands-on*: You can flip through the pages and then spread them out and then put them back together. That means of being able to handle it and look at it all laid out on the table is very different than looking at something on a computer screen. It wasn't just another thing I was viewing on my laptop. It was something I could feel and visualize in a very different way."

Even in rough form, the prototype opened up important conversations: "Looking at it, everything clicked for me in a different way. Now I can describe it to a funder, a farmer, a researcher. I can describe how it might work and what it might do and can say to stakeholders, 'Hopefully this is the advantage we will all get from it.' It gave me confidence when describing it and trying to get funding for it. I think I had doubts before about whether it would actually work or whether we could actually use it. But having it together in that cardboard bundle made me think, 'Of course we can do this, and we can do this easily.'"

Work done by Institute of Design master's degree students Helen Wills, Alisa Weinstein, and Russell Flench for Danielle Nierenberg and Worldwatch Institute; photographs by Russell Flench and Helen Wills.

Imagining a wireless device in 1989: The top half was an LCD screen (with spreadsheet—of course!) and windows for multitasking. The lower half imagined multiple input devices—trackball, function and character keys—with a microphone and speaker zone for telephony and multimedia. ∎

"FRANKENPROTOTYPES" TO EXPLORE AND ALIGN

How to envision a wireless world?

Build-to-think prototypes are useful because they surface important questions about objectives that the entire team needs to align around: Why build this at all? Is this a productive direction? What would it need to really work? But not every team has a band saw, lathe, or router in their office to prototype new products. How to prototype early-stage ideas in a resource-constrained setting?

Marty Thaler and Anijo Mathew advocate the "Frankenprototype" to quickly mock up 3-D ideas with found objects or easy-to-use parts. As the name implies, craft skills are not required or even of value in making Frankenprototypes—the objective is a low level of detail to support a low-fidelity but still clear experience. Frankenprototypes are a low-cost way to get to learning faster. And they work in ways that allow others to contribute and participate because the prototype is so obviously unfinished.

It was the autumn of 1989 when Tom MacTavish and his colleagues made their first Frankenprototype. He was director of engineering at NCR's Wireless Communications and Networking Division near Utrecht, The Netherlands. He needed some way to inspire engineers and product managers to envision and discuss a future in which wirelessly-connected devices would be common. "The block of wood prototype was created by our Director of Product Management, John Buswell, as a result of a late afternoon dialogue between us: What would wireless devices look like? What would they be used for? Where could we identify opportunities for our core competencies in radio frequency communications and chipset design? John and I wanted to inspire focused thinking by using tangible artifacts, rather than sketches on an overhead projector." The block of wood prototype was born that night.

It was an open question at the time as to how mobile, wireless devices should behave and what they would provide to users on the go. The prototype helped teams imagine mobile computing—no wires, no desks—and proposed features that might leverage application-specific, integrated circuits for dedicated processing to manage costs. For example, there is a small zone on the tablet for entering handwritten characters that could be recognized by the computer and instantly shown on the display. Touch screen technology was prohibitively expensive at the time, and the prototype's reduced size addressed this issue. Its ugliness was key to its success.

"We used the prototype as part of a daylong strategy discussion with senior executives from NCR Headquarters. Then we used it for local team discussions for the next few weeks. Then, we circulated the prototype among the sixty local employees, from desk to desk. Finally, we placed it in the lobby in a glass showcase with recently-produced products to suggest that it might be part of a continuum of successful products. After that, I hung it on the wall of my office, so that I could use it as an example of rapid prototyping and learning. Ultimately it ended up in my home as a treasured memento."

Work by Tom MacTavish and John Buswell for NCR; photo by Philipp Böhm / boehmphilipp.de

MODULAR PROTOTYPES TO CONFIGURE AND CONVERSE

How to think about customer-led store design?

Photo courtesy of Gravity Tank

Sometimes it's more effective to turn the prototyping over to stakeholders, to allow them to build insight into the problem and conviction around opportunities. Gravity Tank has been creating modular store prototyping kits for use with retail clients for years, after early experiments proved effective in getting clients to engage in focused conversations.

"People are much better 3D thinkers than 2D thinkers," says Michael Winnick, "so if you're trying to build a new store, people can argue about it forever, about something even as basic as where the accessories should go. So, we give them store dioramas and all the tools for deciding what's supposed to go in there. And we ask them to build a store. Using the dioramas, they work

with each decision, understand the trade-offs and think about the effects of that decision on the real estate, on the product placement, on accessory placement, on the service staff, on the checkout stations, on the customer flow through the store—all of that has to play out in a box that's not that big."

When stakeholders are engaged in prototyping, they develop a different relationship to the problem space and to what's possible. Michael explains, "By giving them stuff that's not formed, and letting them do the forming, you're putting them in a position to gain a deeper understanding of the problem and also to take more ownership of the solutions. It can be a little awkward at first to get people to try to do something like this. You force people to create first, as opposed to being stuck in framing or analytical problem solving, which is where their comfort zone is. But in my experience it's a relief to people to be able to work this way—it's a little bit naughty. There's a freedom to not getting so caught up in analyzing everything to death."

It's the conversations and early-stage alignment around the problem that are the real benefits: "When people walk into an exercise like that, each one has a rough but ill-formed vision in their head about what they might do with their store. Our job is probably not to get them to the one store everyone agrees on, but to get from fifteen ill-defined visions down to four more clearly articulated directions. In this sense, it's really prototyping to have a conversation—to make their conversation tangible. It's prototyping for consensus-making."

LISTS AND OPEN-ENDED WRITING:
Thinking with words

Perhaps the simplest way to "know what you know" is to just write it down. Writing is the shortest, fastest path to clarity and synthesis. It is uncomplicated and low-budget—no batteries required. And it's portable, so you can do it on the train, at lunch, or in bed. Writing is highly productive for even the most minimal time investment. In fact, all the techniques I propose here require an initial investment of only 10 minutes or less.

And yet writing is a trauma for some. When I suggest a writing task in executive education sessions, I can feel the energy leave the room. I see it in their faces: My participants are suddenly back in school, where writing was *graded* and *technical* and ultimately *depersonalized* and maybe a bit *humiliating*. Writing education has divorced many of us from a most natural mode of expression and self-learning.

Write to think, not to be right

I am proposing a different role for writing, one whereby writing is a process for thinking, not a means of producing finished work. Writing gets substantially easier and more productive in helping us find the conceptual center if we stipulate the following:

- The writing doesn't have to be right.

- The writing doesn't have to be complete.

- The writing doesn't have to be shared.

It's *your* writing. It helps organize your thinking, accelerates synthesis, and prepares you to be a productive team member. So think of writing less like mom's broccoli, and more like Popeye's spinach.

HOW DOES WRITING HELP US FIND THE CONCEPTUAL CENTER?

Writing creates room for reflection

Even in collaborative work, team members need dwell time to process what they've seen and heard. Heather Reavey believes quiet time is when things come together: "I don't believe that big ideas happen in rooms of eight people. I think that the kernels of those ideas happen when people are at their desks. In fact, when I manage these big collaborative teams, because the collaboration is so frequent, I make sure that people still have their dwell time. Even with clients onsite I'll say, 'Ok, we're going to take the next three hours and everyone's going to go to their quiet place and think and come back with something.'" Writing stirs up what's in the unconscious or subconscious mind, and allows it to come together in a new way.

Writing accelerates insight

It is my experience that teams always know more than they think they do. But that thinking is scattered across databases, sticky notes, human beings, and even geographies. Writing is a powerful synthesis tool: It pulls those pieces together and puts them in one place. When I ask people to write, they discover they "own" more of the relevant issues than they knew. And when I ask them to write in timed increments—no more than 10 minutes—they discover they can be surprisingly productive in short bursts. Writing in general is a sense-making tool; writing under constraints can kickstart nonlinear thinking, generating important transformations in perspective.

Writing is prototyping

Like sketching and building models, writing is a form of prototyping. It can bring about various outcomes depending on word choice, choice of lead, and story sequencing. We know this in practice: Executives and students alike complain that whoever touches the PowerPoint last ultimately controls the idea. Language choice is powerful. When we experiment with words, we change the idea.

Why is that? The answer lies in two theories about how words work in relation to thinking.

The "cloak" theory proposes that language simply expresses what we think. Language drapes over our thoughts, much as a cloak drapes over the body, conforming to its shape. In this conception, language takes on the shape of our thinking. Here language is passive and reflective—it merely makes our thinking visible to others.

The "mold" theory proposes a more dynamic relationship between language and thinking. In this theory, words give shape to our thinking, like pouring liquid into a mold. Language choice in this theory has great power, not just to express thoughts but to *cause* belief one way or another. When we follow the advice of pop psychologists who tell us to look in the mirror and repeat that we are worthy, we're using our language to prompt a way of thinking.

Both of these ways of looking at language can be of great use to us in communicating The New. We need language to express our ideas in ways that others can understand. But we can also vary that language to put ideas back into our own heads, to change our way of thinking. Writing is not just prototyping our expression of thought, it is prototyping our very thoughts themselves. Perhaps this more expansive conception of language and writing will be enough to help blast past the "writing to be right" orthodoxy that holds so many of us back from using writing as a means to think.

Let's look at some examples of how to use writing to think:

- USE SIMPLE LISTS TO ELICIT INSIGHTS
- USE STRUCTURED LISTS TO INTEGRATE INSIGHTS
- USE WRITING TO PROTOTYPE

USE SIMPLE LISTS TO ELICIT INSIGHTS

See what you know

Philipp Böhm / boehmphilipp.de

In a fact list, write everything you know about your challenge. At the bottom, list anything you don't know but wish you did.

For a hunch list, write everything you think might matter or be important (you can add qualifiers or rank items in terms of credibility later)

For the spark list, write anything that stands out, seems interesting, or just cool (it will soon become evident if these have a role to play, so reach into those "adjacent" spaces for quirky trends, technologies or startup stories that get you thinking)

It's easy to underestimate the power of the lowly list. The list is an excellent tool for externalizing what's known about a project in the early stages. One practitioner (who would prefer not to be known as the "list guy") told me he keeps open multiple lists about his projects: things he knows, things he doesn't know but should, things he thinks could be relevant to the case, things he thinks are cool but unclear in terms of relevance. He puts his lists out where he can see them, keeping the project visible and his thinking top of mind. He appraises his lists, killing and adding elements as his thinking changes. His lists are personal; he doesn't bring them to team meetings. But they prepare him for team meetings—they help him know what he knows.

Lists are useful because they allow parallel tracks of information to emerge. It's a good mental discipline to keep separate what's verifiable from what's interpreted, to keep the observed and the surmised in separate columns. Useful lists to keep include:

Fact lists call out the solid ground—what's known and can be validated. This can include anything from market facts to business conditions to direct observations of customers.

Hunch lists surface intuition and add new variables into the mix. Hunches can be the seeds of transformation, but are often fuzzy and indistinct in the early stages. They need a bit of air and time to grow. It's important to separate hunches from facts, however, since hunches are subjective and can be wrong; they should be tracked separately but in parallel with objective information.

Concerns lists track anything that weighs on you, or that needs to be revisited or resolved before project end. These can include barriers, misgivings, or even inconvenient realities, such as competitor efforts, organizational issues, or implementation challenges. These may morph into "to do" or "next step" lists later in the work.

Spark lists are for the enthusiast in you. They keep you in touch with delight factors that creators of The New know add magic and depth to concepts: What if a jewelry designer designed the phone? What if we added an accelerometer to the shopping cart? How can we leverage educated stay-at-home moms in the business model?

In my teaching experience, list making produces considerable clarity for very low time investment. When I ask executives and students to engage in 15 minutes of list making, I routinely hear *I knew more than I thought I did.* They seem surprised, but I'm not. The first step toward clarity is getting everything out and in one place. Lists are excellent channels for externalizing.

USE STRUCTURED LISTS TO INTEGRATE THINKING
Build and evolve your mental models

If simple lists are about isolating relevant, interesting, or troublesome factors, structured lists are about assigning order and priority to those elements so as to create a more complete picture of the conceptual space. In the process of structuring lists, we focus on relationships and hierarchy between list elements, creating and naming the resulting clusters.

There are many approaches to structuring lists. Some people find it intuitive to create "mind maps," in which list elements can be spatially arranged to make relationships. Some prefer the hands-on, large-format approach of using sticky notes on a wall or index cards tacked into corkboard. And some prefer more computational—but less visual—list-processing tools, such as Excel. Each of these approaches has advantages and drawbacks. All of them, however, get the job done, considering that the job is to further structure the mess and find the conceptual center.

Mind maps fit smaller endeavors and individual processes

Many people find that mind maps are a great place to start in externalizing and ordering their thoughts. Mind maps do what all visualizations do: compress a large, sprawling problem into a compact space so that it may be seen all at once, and visually differentiate types of information so that our eyes can scan and isolate distinct groups as needed. Mind maps hit a wall, however, when the number of elements nears 50. It's hard for the eye to process that many instances, no matter how carefully organized or color-coded.

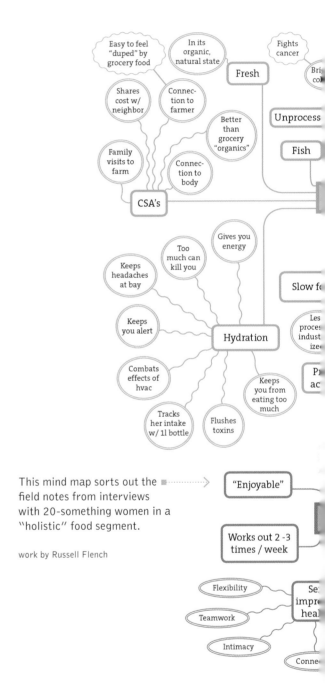

This mind map sorts out the field notes from interviews with 20-something women in a "holistic" food segment.

work by Russell Flench

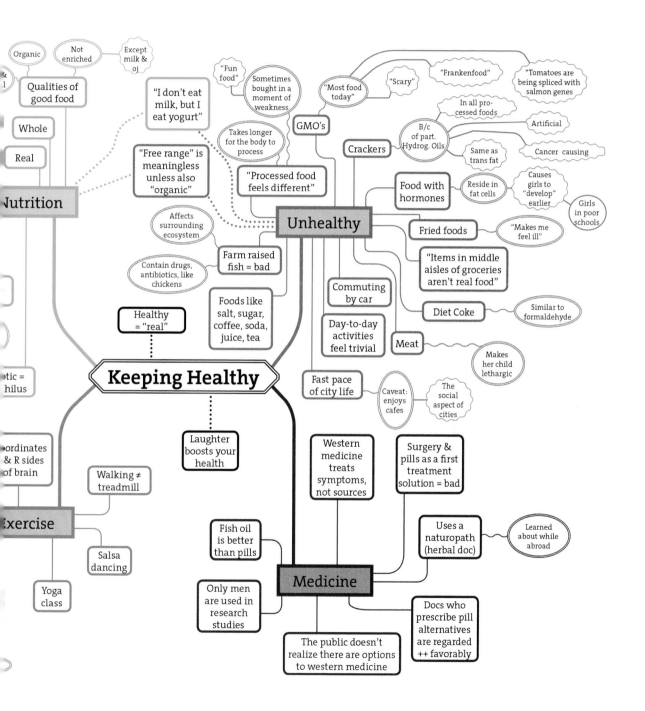

Organic

Not enriched

Except milk & oj

Qualities of good food

Whole

Real

Nutrition

"I don't eat milk, but I eat yogurt"

"Free range" is meaningless unless also "organic"

"Fun food"

Sometimes bought in a moment of weakness

Takes longer for the body to process

GMO's

"Most food today"

"Scary"

"Frankenfood"

"Tomatoes are being spliced with salmon genes"

In all processed foods

Artificial

B/c of part. Hydrog. Oils

Same as trans fat

Cancer causing

Crackers

Food with hormones

Reside in fat cells

Causes girls to "develop" earlier

Girls in poor schools

"Processed food feels different"

Affects surrounding ecosystem

Unhealthy

Fried foods

"Makes me feel ill"

"Items in middle aisles of groceries aren't real food"

Contain drugs, antibiotics, like chickens

Farm raised fish = bad

Commuting by car

Diet Coke

Similar to formaldehyde

Healthy = "real"

Foods like salt, sugar, coffee, soda, juice, tea

Day-to-day activities feel trivial

Meat

ptic = hilus

Keeping Healthy

Fast pace of city life

Caveat: enjoys cafes

The social aspect of cities

Makes her child lethargic

ordinates & R sides of brain

Laughter boosts your health

Western medicine treats symptoms, not sources

Surgery & pills as a first treatment solution = bad

Walking ≠ treadmill

Exercise

Salsa dancing

Fish oil is better than pills

Uses a naturopath (herbal doc)

Learned about while abroad

Yoga class

Medicine

Only men are used in research studies

Docs who prescribe pill alternatives are regarded ++ favorably

The public doesn't realize there are options to western medicine

Moving from the most concrete (facts or quotes) at the edges to the most abstracted synthesis in the center helps make logic explicit. ▪┈┈┈┈┈>

work by Helen Wills

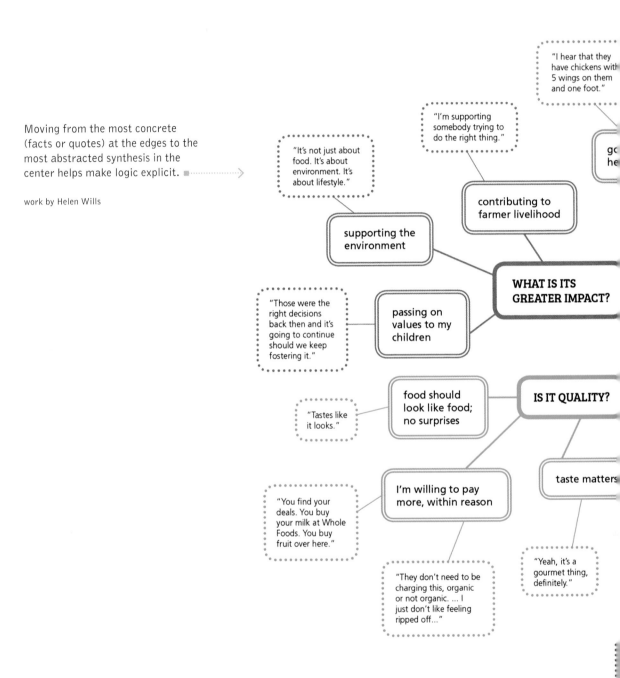

"I hear that they have chickens with 5 wings on them and one foot."

"I'm supporting somebody trying to do the right thing."

"It's not just about food. It's about environment. It's about lifestyle."

contributing to farmer livelihood

supporting the environment

go
he

WHAT IS ITS GREATER IMPACT?

"Those were the right decisions back then and it's going to continue should we keep fostering it."

passing on values to my children

food should look like food; no surprises

"Tastes like it looks."

IS IT QUALITY?

I'm willing to pay more, within reason

taste matters

"You find your deals. You buy your milk at Whole Foods. You buy fruit over here."

"They don't need to be charging this, organic or not organic. ... I just don't like feeling ripped off..."

"Yeah, it's a gourmet thing, definitely."

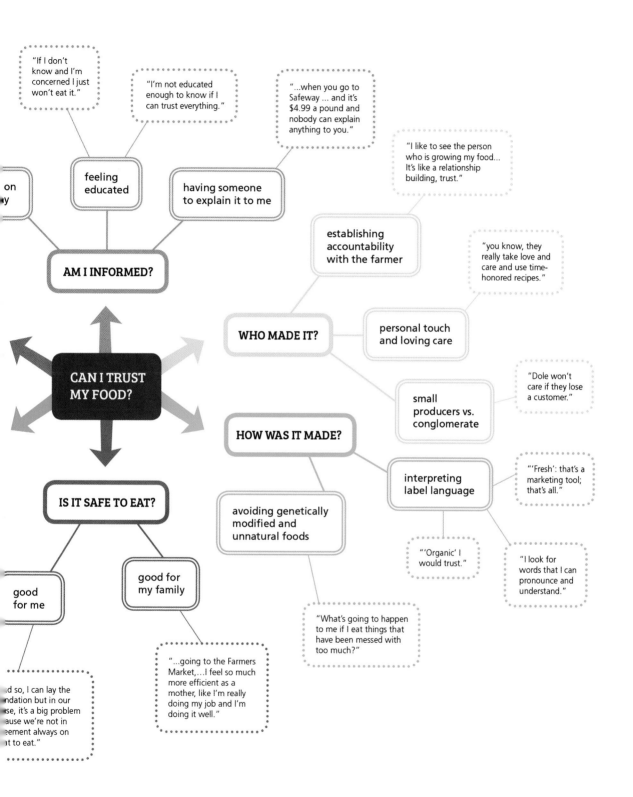

"If I don't know and I'm concerned I just won't eat it."

"I'm not educated enough to know if I can trust everything."

"...when you go to Safeway ... and it's $4.99 a pound and nobody can explain anything to you."

"I like to see the person who is growing my food... It's like a relationship building, trust."

feeling educated

having someone to explain it to me

establishing accountability with the farmer

"you know, they really take love and care and use time-honored recipes."

AM I INFORMED?

WHO MADE IT?

personal touch and loving care

CAN I TRUST MY FOOD?

small producers vs. conglomerate

"Dole won't care if they lose a customer."

HOW WAS IT MADE?

interpreting label language

"'Fresh': that's a marketing tool; that's all."

IS IT SAFE TO EAT?

avoiding genetically modified and unnatural foods

"'Organic' I would trust."

"I look for words that I can pronounce and understand."

good for me

good for my family

"What's going to happen to me if I eat things that have been messed with too much?"

...d so, I can lay the ...ndation but in our ...se, it's a big problem ...ause we're not in ...eement always on ...at to eat."

"...going to the Farmers Market,...I feel so much more efficient as a mother, like I'm really doing my job and I'm doing it well."

Sticky note and wall-based clustering fits midsized endeavors and team-based processes

Sticky notes are iconic tools for creating The New and have been enthusiastically embraced by innovation-tasked teams everywhere. Because their use is well documented in other methods books, I will not elaborate on this approach except to offer two contrary but considered opinions from practitioners I respect. Heather Reavey first: "I'd like to put my vote in for stopping the use of Post-its® in the thinking phase. For me it's about making connections between things, so I can put Post-its® next to each other, but I need to draw a line or visually show something more than just a cluster.

I also try to teach people to be really deliberate about how they describe things. Post-its®, because they're small, breed shorthand and word choices that are close but not precise. I'm for bringing big paper back—butcher paper or whiteboards or big spaces to write on so people don't feel constrained to the two inch by two inch surface." The language issue is alive in a different way for Ben Jacobson: "I would say failure mode equals a bunch of people having a discussion that yields Post-it® Notes with scribbles on them—even sorted, clustered Post-it® Notes. The truth is that what any one person meant when they scribbled two words on that Post-it® Note can mean something quite different to another person in the same room with them, let alone an audience that walks in an hour later to say, 'What did you guys do for three hours?'"

Sticky-note-based lists and wall-based clustering are terrific tactics for making teamwork visible and sharable. But, as Heather and Ben point out, they are tactics with limitations that directly impact how and what we think. These cautions are useful, and PowerPoint has attracted similar criticism as a format that has shaped and limited our thinking. All tools influence how we think, and so we need to be mindful of their impact when we use them.

■ This spreadsheet contains hundreds of diary entries by working moms, who logged how and when they used the Internet to manage their homes and families. Visually coding list elements with color, font, icons can help us quickly spot issues— here the tall yellow line of entries tagged "other" is too big and needs investigation.

Spreadsheets fit dense, complex data and work for individuals and small teams

The complexity involved in creating The New typically involves hundreds, often thousands, of information elements, demanding more robust processes and tools. Most practitioners I know use spreadsheets to manipulate lists for insight. The matrix structure of a spreadsheet is highly flexible, and supports the bottom-up process of evaluating data, assigning relationships, using additional columns to add insights and visual cues. Spreadsheets permit easy data entry—one idea per row. Rows can also hold identifying data, such as the interviewee names, cities, or dates that can be used to sort and structure the list further. A spreadsheet's sorting and filtering features provide for fast prototyping of clusters, making patterns in the data easy to spot. The ability to play with data and to shape and reshape lists to uncover potential meaning is a powerful path to discovery, and to the conceptual center.

USE WRITING TO PROTOTYPE
Nine ways to find the lead

In creating The New, teams are constantly in the process of articulating their story. For a number of reasons, not the least of which is credibility, it is important that teams have a shared narrative about the project, its trajectory, and its potential. Oftentimes, the only thing a team knows for sure is a problem statement, the original objective that kicked off the work. And this leads to the classic rookie mistake: the linear recitation of the project when called to account. You've probably sat through this, and you've probably done it. But it is a communication mistake, and it goes something like this:

We were tasked with answering the following questions [insert business questions here]. So we did research into the topic [perfunctory process recitation goes here] and performed some analysis [show inscrutable diagram or table]. Let us show you what we've learned.

This is a mistake because the most relevant and interesting part of the work comes ten minutes into the story, when the window of attention has closed. I was once told by a genuinely kind and personable client that he might book me for an hour but I really had five minutes to grab his attention before he'd start managing his e-mail. To spend those five minutes on process and other secondary issues is to waste an opportunity. Instead, I propose we lead with knowledge.

The agony of square one

Writers and journalists know that getting the story started is often the toughest part. This problem is bigger than just the blank page syndrome that everyone has faced at one point or another. The problem is the endless number of starting points, and the potential for any one starting point to make the story relevant. Or worse, to make the story *irrelevant*.

Prototyping the project narrative, in any stage of the work, can help teams find the conceptual center of their work. Shown here are nine generic but useful formulas to help prototype that narrative and find the real news faster. You may have seen these all before—they are not new, and by no means are they my inventions. But they work, especially when struggling to clarify the conceptual center, and so I've collected them all in one place.

1 THE FACT

Is there a stark statistic that anchors the issue? Here's an astonishing fact that a student team used to great effect: 60 percent of crops in starving countries never make it to market. Facts can also be of the odd-but-true variety to add intrigue, a bit of mystery. Facts of any kind have the added benefit of suggesting that the team has done its homework and is knowledgeable about the topic area.

2 THE QUESTION

Creating The New tends to begin with a relevant question—is there a variation that might capture the current state of the work? Questions can be rhetorical ("Do we really want a world where...?"), pragmatic ("How might we...?"), or futuristic ("What if we could... ?"). The added benefit of using a question as the lead is that it invites others into the problem space with you, which encourages a participative, constructive mindset.

3 THE QUOTE

Quotes can serve multiple purposes. Not only can they convey facts and relevant opinions, but referencing others is also a good way to signal expansive thinking. Quotes can be philosophical (invoking the sage), everyman or commonsensical (Forrest Gump was good at this), or ripped from the headlines (to tie the project to something particularly relevant).

4 THE STORY

Is there a human drama at the center of the action? In the fieldwork or from personal experience, is there a short iconic story that captures the human challenge? Stories can explain complex work in accessible terms, creating an emotional connection.

5 THE MARCH OF HISTORY

Is a sense of time or context important to the project? A brief but sweeping retrospective can help tie a project to the bigger picture and put the efforts into perspective. Drawing attention to cycles and evolutions attaches the work to cycles of change, to things in flux, or establishes it as being set on the precipice of an emerging and important change.

6 THE SITUATION

Oftentimes in creating The New, it is important to establish a context by summing up the current condition or the state of our knowledge. For example, "In eight years we have gone from industry leader to industry follower, from pioneer to laggard. We don't own a single capability in the hottest tech sectors. We are dangerously behind." This becomes the setting against which the project's importance and contributions become more relevant and timely. When starting with the current condition, the team is setting the stage for a transformation.

7 THE SCENARIO

"Picture this" is a tried and true way to heighten the vividness or potential of The New. In this approach, you might start softly with "Imagine yourself here..." and bridge to the work. Or lead more directly with "It's the future, and here's what's happening..." As is the case when leading with a question, sketching out a scenario invites participants into the future with you.

8 THE THESIS STATEMENT

The thesis or problem statement can be the simplest way into the premise of the work. In creating The New, this has the added advantage of being easy to evolve over time. Thesis statements don't have to be dry; they can be bold or shocking statements that position the work as maverick and edgy ("We are learning how to lie with visualizations."), or outrageous ("We are reinventing motherhood.").

9 CONVENTIONAL WISDOM (IS WRONG)

Is there an industry or organizational orthodoxy that the work is up against? If so, starting with "Most people think X, but we've discovered Y" creates a clean, focused conception of the work that has the added advantage of sounding like an important contribution.

THE TAKEAWAY
Five big ideas for finding the conceptual center

This section proposed a number of methods and tactics for advancing the thinking of individuals and teams. Which method is the best for you? That depends on your time frame, your collaborators, and the nature of your New. Communication is not a formula. Whatever method you choose, and however you tailor it to your circumstances, the general principles are the same:

1. Don't just think. Make.

The act of creating forces decision making that shapes our thinking. This is important: To create is to commit to a new reality, however provisionally, that we can assess. We can step back and squint and ask, "Is this what we know? Does it feel real, promising, important? Do we feel conviction around this?" Building belief starts here.

2. Don't make one. Make many.

Creative fields know that when a person or team builds a single instance of a concept, they become emotionally involved in that creation. The learning stops because they have too much invested. This is why creative fields thrive on rapid prototyping, creating many variations that allow teams to experiment with multiple entry points, multiple perspectives on the problem at hand. Because writing, building, and structuring models are all creative acts, expect to make several variations to better see which of the possible expressions of the future is best suited to your project.

3. Don't be "right." Be curious.

What if there isn't a right answer? Or what if there are multiple right answers? Our job is to find a future state that matters, that is significant and worth the life energy it takes to bring it into being. This requires a different mindset than being right: We need to cultivate curiosity, openness, and a willingness to experiment. "Right" and "best" are not the same thing, and the mindset to get to either is not the same, either.

4. Build in time to reflect.

Collaborative processes are important but are more productive if balanced out with individual dwell time. So build in time to reflect, and experiment with synthesis methods that presume a reflective mode, to better prepare collaborators to come together with new energy.

5. Create room to engage.

Building belief really does start here. So find a mix of methods to engage others and help them experience, if not build, the work. This includes making work visible (so stakeholders can see it), visual (so informal participants don't have to engage in the manual labor of reading), and sharable (so others can stay in touch and contribute).

2
Framing the work

METAPHORS

MANTRAS AND CATCHPHRASES

CONTRAST

STORIES

ARTIFACTS AND IMAGES

Define the new space in a way everyone can
understand and remember.

Give the concept shape, texture, and accessibility.

Provide clarity around what the proposition is not.

Anyone who pays attention to politics, perhaps especially
in election years, has experienced framing in action. Who could ignore Arnold
Schwarzenegger's call to his fellow Republicans to not be "economic girlie-men" in
the 2004 election? Or Bill Clinton's "It's the economy, stupid" catchphrase of 1992?
The framer's ability to use language in a compact, vivid, and memorable way—and
to direct our attention towards or away from important meaning—is what makes the
technique so effective.

Somewhere between objective description and outright persuasion is a set of
language-based techniques called framing. Framing is the intentional description and
positioning of an event or concept so as to control its interpretation. If this sounds
manipulative, it certainly can be, and this is why framing is most often studied in the
context of politics and public rhetoric.

In communicating The New, we aren't running for election, but we do need the
candidate's command of the message. In this stage, our mission is to *frame the work*,
so that it can live and thrive outside the friendly confines of the team in which it
initially took shape. Framing as a *process* is an important transition step—it closes
out the content synthesis stage, helping teams consolidate their insights and sum up
their work in a memorable way. This is important because it builds the alignment and
shared conceptual platform teams need to move forward. Framing as a *communication
method* is productive because it pushes teams to capture some underlying truth in the
work that resonates immediately and demands action—a first test of how to explain
the work to outsiders. Once a discovery has emerged during a creative process—
especially if it is a complex or unfamiliar concept—it is still tenuous, and yet it needs
to be circulated and worked with by others. People need to understand the discovery,
need to approve further effort and funding, need to make contributions to it that will
make it stronger.

Bridging the work to others, especially those who were not part of the early stages,
can be an involved process. To start, we need to create fresh eyes in order to break free
of ingrained mental models that limit how others see the problem. Next, we have to
open up a new space for thinking, so that others are primed and ready to hear about
a complex, unfamiliar or still-fuzzy New. Then we need to set our "new" apart from

other things that may be perceived to be similar. To do all this is no mere language challenge. It is a massive mental model and chain-of-logic challenge, with language as a key point of leverage.

Because language plays such a critical role at this stage, and because language is the heart of framing, I want to spend a little time orienting the discussion to the potential and limits of language as a creative tool.

FINDING THE LANGUAGE OF THE NEW

In his thoughtful essay "A Linguistic Model of Innovation," writer and artist Hugh Musick muses about the evolution of pidgins. "Pidgins" are the linguistic workarounds created by people who don't speak the same language but need to communicate with one another; historically, these have evolved along trade routes to support commerce. Hugh calls these language modifications *wordarounds*— "adaptations made in the context because the existing languages and corresponding mental models do not meet either party's needs." Pidgins are effective because they act as linguistic bridges, offering a simple, hybrid language both parties can understand and employ.

We may not require the pidgins of these early entrepreneurs, but in creating The New we share their need for wordarounds. Language can be a potent ally in the planner's quest for distinguishing The New. Whether we are tinkering at the word level or inventing new technical jargon, the strategic use of language can heighten, brighten, and define a new conceptual space. But if language has power, it is also fraught with difficulties.

Language often lags

Because we operate in a field that routinely tasks us with discovery, we often find ourselves at the edge of language. New ways of thinking often call for new language because the existing vocabulary may not accurately express that which is still in formation: emerging human behaviors, evolving mindsets, trajectories of cultures, and hybridizing product categories. Language is notoriously poor at capturing continuous processes—how to play a guitar or maintain a motorcycle. It may be even less suited to describing that which is not fully in existence yet.

Language is elastic

That language is elastic and evolving is not new. Consider the linguists' growing catalog of *retronyms*: words added to existing terms to distinguish them from newer expressions. Thus, "store" becomes the retronym "bricks-and-mortar store" to respond to the emergence of online retail. Similarly, "offline shopping" emerges to distinguish traditional shopping from online shopping. Language, far from being a stable set of bricks we can arrange and rearrange to give shape to our ideas, requires negotiation to work. In communicating The New, that negotiation is our job.

Language is a negotiation

Shared meaning arises from dialogue. It's negotiated and socially constructed, not looked up in a dictionary. As communicators of The New, we can use words, but we cannot simply deliver meaning. We must build it together.

Language always frames

"All language is framing," says author and academic Gail Fairhurst, "because framing is about creating meaning. To the degree that you are communicating, you are attempting to create meaning. It's just whether you see communication as the transfer of knowledge or the creation of meaning. If you are wedded to the transfer model, then you are not really focusing on the meaning potential of language." In creating The New, we are all building meaning together and using language, among other tools, to do so. So, why aren't we more often in agreement? Dr. Fairhurst's point is that some framing—the conscious kind—is more effective than other kinds. That's why working with defined framing structures is a good idea: Structured framing causes us to engage in *conscious* language manipulation. This not only makes us more aware of our own thinking, it makes us aware of the thinking and framing practiced by others.

HOW TO FRAME THE NEW

Because framing is set of techniques for the intentional construction of meaning, it is a particularly effective intervention when dealing with the complex, unfamiliar, or still fuzzy. In this chapter, we look to the work of academic experts in language, psychology, and organizations, and adapt that work to the context of creating The New. While I am inspired by the scholarship of George Lakoff, Mark Johnson, Andrew Ortony, and Charles Forceville, I am particularly indebted to the research of Gail Fairhurst, whose work on framing in the context of organizational leadership has proven to be especially relevant. Using her constructs, I offer five tactics for framing The New:

- METAPHORS
- MANTRAS AND CATCHPHRASES
- CONTRAST
- STORIES
- ARTIFACTS AND IMAGES

A word of caution about framing

Framing techniques are commonly used by marketers and advertisers, whose objectives are meaningfully different from ours. Advertisers typically seek to create associations, awareness, and recall, rather than to spark genuine understanding. And advertisers want us to buy what they're selling, not just engage with it as a concept.

Persuasion, rather than understanding, is the job of framing in their context, and its function is to stimulate desire that the consumer didn't know she had.

In communicating The New, desire is too ephemeral to bind stakeholders to the mission over the long haul. We need to create deep, substantive contact that resonates and persists with teams and stakeholders. The challenge to everyone using framing in this context, then, is the hard work of keeping the framing *functional* and *authentic*, rather than slick or superficial.

This requires conscious effort. As a culture, we have internalized deeply and without full awareness the methods of advertising: The "snap, crackle, pop" jingle or the "Just Do It" slogan is a form of expression to which we have been exposed from a young age. Too often, early-stage framing efforts mimic this approach. This is a problem, because just as surely as we have internalized this way of thinking, we have also evolved strong radar for this kind of manipulation and developed defenses against it. As a result, framing efforts that settle for slick are likely to backfire for two reasons: First, stakeholders will likely spot and challenge glib framing language because it provokes questions as to whether or not there is any substance to the work. This line of inquiry is damaging to the credibility of the project and its leaders. Second, advertising-like framing language is often itself thin on content, and so ultimately fails to capture the conceptual center of the work.

If a team working in constant contact with a discovery process can't keep aligned around its core output, how can investors, managers, or implementers? The mission for clarity starts at home, with the team. And a deliberate use of language and framing can help.

"The planet has a fever."

AP Images

"The planet has a fever." In 2007, Al Gore made front page news in every major newspaper in the U.S., and many across the globe, with this simple, powerful reframe of climate change. In a few short words, he cut through the complex science, the myriad of opinions, and the political finger pointing. And he set up an imperative: If the planet has a fever, what are we to infer about the problem? And what is the implied course of action?

As psychology Professor Andrew Ortony describes it, this is what metaphors do. They simplify complex ideas. They explain in compact and vivid terms. They transfer large chunks of understanding, often at a subconscious level, in just a few words. And they imply a course of action. Metaphors are powerful tools for framing unfamiliar and complex ideas, and Gore has proven a master of metaphor. He popularized the term "information superhighway," and in so doing managed to convince 99 of his fellow U.S. senators—none of whom, safe to say, had ever sent an e-mail, and most of whom had never heard the term—to invest billions of dollars in 1991 to build what we now call the Internet. Throughout his advocacy, he framed other technical components of the issue with metaphors such as "supercomputers are the steam locomotives of the information age," making the point even then that locomotives were not of much use until tracks were laid.

Metaphors work by explaining what we don't understand by comparison to something we do. All metaphors work this way, say Lakoff and Johnson in their influential book *Metaphors We Live By*, because they "allow us to experience or understand one subject in terms of another." Lakoff and Johnson then go on to assert something rather astonishing: This process of comparison is how we learn just about anything abstract. We learn unfamiliar concepts by comparing them to that which we already know. Metaphor, rather than a decorative (and therefore largely optional) expression of thought, is *how* we think: Our fundamental cognitive processes are metaphoric in nature.

That's a powerful insight. If this is how we learn, it suggests that metaphor is pivotal in creating and communicating The New because so much of what we do is about exploring and explaining the unfamiliar. In fact, try communicating The New *without* using a metaphor—it's exceedingly difficult, as my graduate students quickly come to learn. This may be why we see inventions cast in terms of the things they intend to replace: *the horseless carriage*, *liquid paper*, *mobile phones*. And it may also explain why so many examples in this section of the book, and in professional work in general, leverage metaphors even as they use contrast, stories, mantras, or artifacts. Metaphors (and their close cousin, the analogy) are the essential conceptual tool in making the unfamiliar familiar.

But the fact that metaphor excels at explaining the new and novel in ways that feel familiar—something J. J. Gordon, in his book on creativity, *Synectics*, called *making the strange familiar*—leaves unaddressed the second half of the challenge. Gordon has a term for this, too. He calls it *making the familiar strange*, and this construct addresses a standard piece of process in creating The New: forcing distance from preconceived notions of the problem so that we can examine it again with fresh eyes and an open mind. Metaphors, it turns out, are excellent tools for this circumstance, too.

Metaphors can help *reframe the familiar* in useful ways:

- METAPHORS CAN DRAMATIZE EMOTIONAL QUALITIES

- METAPHORS CAN RECAST EVERYDAY EXPERIENCES

- METAPHORS CAN SHIFT OUR CONCEPTUAL MODELS

Metaphors can help *frame the unfamiliar* in useful ways:

- METAPHORS CAN FRAME THE EXPERIENCE OF THE NEW

- METAPHORS CAN EXPLAIN HOW THE NEW WORKS

- METAPHORS CAN DESCRIBE PRODUCT FEATURES IN NEW WAYS

METAPHORS CAN DRAMATIZE
EMOTIONAL QUALITIES

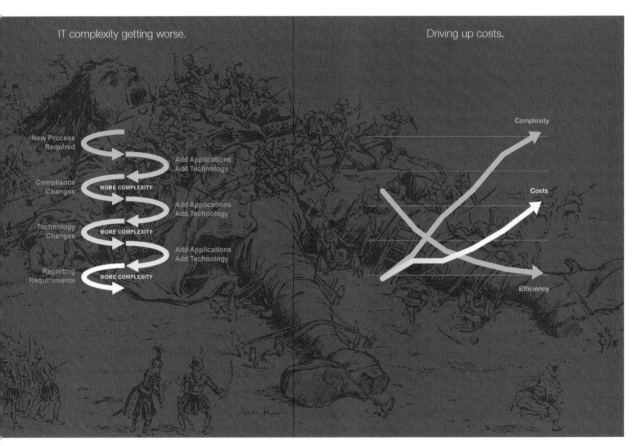

IT complexity getting worse.

Driving up costs.

New Process Required

Compliance Changes

MORE COMPLEXITY

Technology Changes

MORE COMPLEXITY

Reporting Requirements

MORE COMPLEXITY

Add Applications
Add Technology

Add Applications
Add Technology

Add Applications
Add Technology

Complexity

Costs

Efficiency

Work by Jim Fisher (writer), Paul Bussman (designer), and Andy Parham, Bick Group

Perhaps most executives feel trapped like Gulliver, here held hostage by the Lilliputians, no matter their industry. But in explaining cloud computing to health-care executives, Bick Group CEO Andy Parham had a more specific point in mind: Pricey, proprietary IT models were holding the industry down, trapping its data, and limiting leaders' ability to move. In Andy's words, "We showed them an image of Gulliver tied down by the Lilliputians. And we told them that this is essentially what they are because their data is trapped behind all these silos and all these integration points. They can't move to make the slightest change without so much effort. Getting 'unbound' has been our theme in describing the new, cloud-based model of IT services. And the executives always chuckle when I throw this image up there."

© Gabriel A. Biller, with Professor Kim Erwin advising

The air travel experience hasn't been the same since 9/11, and frustrated flyers have parodied airport security processes in numerous ways. The "touch my junk" t-shirts and a slew of slogans ("it's not a grope; it's a freedom pat") don't appear to be changing the collective mind of global airport security. But the metaphor of passenger as helpless sheep and the security agents as powerful wolves delivers the experience instantly.

METAPHORS CAN RECAST
EVERYDAY EXPERIENCES

Inbox (127)

My inbox is the first thing I check in the morning. I try to keep it organized but find that cleaning it out is a chore I have to set aside time for. I don't want anyone peeking over my shoulder into my inbox despite that everything in there has been publicly seen by at least one person. There are certain items in my inbox that I keep promising to get back to, but never do. Similarly, I'm afraid to purge anything from my inbox, so I end up moving it to a drawer or bin. Sometimes, I'd just like to close my inbox.

Work by Hanna Korel, with Professor Kim Erwin advising

Recasting the inbox as a closet highlights the clutter of inbox management, the challenge of keeping order and finding important items, and the sense of volume that threatens to spill over. This metaphor also invokes the anxiety, the shame and embarrassment, and other identity issues that are intertwined with how we keep house—or fail to manage our e-mail. The good news is that, like all metaphors, the inbox-as-closet is only a partial description: Inboxes don't actually run out of room, but they don't really have a door to close, either.

Far from a spa moment...

skin care
is a chore

Requires a regiment,
feels like a burden

Lots of product, little
difference = no loyalty

Time-consuming
and endless

Unfinished products pile
up and take over

Specialized products:
what works together?

Concept by Chelsea Holzworth, with Professor Kim Erwin advising

Advertisers would have women believe that skin care is a pampering act of self-care, complete with lux products that will transform our literal and figurative face to the world. Any qualitative researcher can tell you that the reality is quite different: Skin care is a tedious task with complicated regimens that are decidedly not glamorous to implement. Like cleaning products, skin care products claim task-specific benefits, requiring multiple products to get the job done. But these products don't always work well together and sometimes don't work at all, and so half-used products accumulate over time, cluttering closets and cabinets. This metaphor makes an apt comparison: Skin care is far from a coddling experience; it's a *chore*.

privacy

a door, not a wall

METAPHORS CAN SHIFT OUR CONCEPTUAL MODELS

What if we conceived of privacy more like a door and less like a wall? Lakoff and Johnson tell us that we often draw on our experiences of the physical world—buildings and containers, for example—to explain abstract concepts. We speak of being "in love" (a container) or "the cornerstone of our strategy" (architectural element).

Oftentimes these mental models go unnoticed and unexamined, and so they lock us into a way of conceiving what is possible. But to change the underlying metaphor, such as reconceiving privacy as a door that could be partially open or fully closed, as needed, is to change how we conceive of the topic, and to open us up to new ways of thinking.

Work by Dania Harris, with Professor Kim Erwin advising

For mobile workers, electrical power is a critical resource that keeps essential technologies up and running. Like thirsty animals, these users seek out sources of power, jostle for space next to the outlets, and have instincts about where to find power when out in the wild. Not all spaces were designed for energy-hungry appliances, however, and so users often cluster around makeshift power outlets such as extension cords and power strips. The need for power can empty out power-impoverished spaces, and create unexpected density in other areas. In today's spaces, power needs to flow to wherever the thirsty are, increasing and decreasing to fit their numbers and migration patterns.

Work by Leslie Nichole Hicks, with Professor Kim Erwin advising

METAPHORS CAN FRAME THE EXPERIENCE OF THE NEW

Brand work by Radiant Brands; image © Ask.com

Up until in the mid-1990s, when the Internet was called the World Wide Web, all spelled out, database search had been the domain of experts. These experts were trained in Boolean logic to better speak the language of databases, and they paid handsomely to access proprietary repositories of information. As we now know, the Internet changed that dynamic forever. But the question at the time was how to orient a world of new users, primed to think of search as the province of professionals, to believe that they, too, could navigate the growing information repository of the Internet. Ask Jeeves, now ask.com, was the first natural language search engine on the Web. It allowed users to get answer to questions posed in everyday language. To make the ease of use evident, its founders likened the use experience to having a personal valet who would do all the hard work and deliver the best possible answers. The valet was based on Jeeves, Bertie Wooster's fictional valet from the works of P. G. Wodehouse. As a metaphor, it framed a complex technical system as a competent but deferential companion.

Behavioral metaphors frame the underlying model of a new concept in light of something we already understand. These metaphors set expectations about how the new concept will act, and help define our role in using it. This is what two entrepreneurs needed to explain when pitching the dho-Dala (a washing machine designed for low-income populations in developing countries) to a large, India-based manufacturer. They needed to plausibly explain how an electricity-free washing machine could help users wash clothes. By framing the behavior of washing as being "as simple as swinging on a backyard swing," they also described the literal motion required to make the machine work. By tethering the core invention to the familiar image of a rocking swing, the team quickly built a mental image for investors. The team received initial-stage funding, and the concept has proceeded into development. ■ ············>

Work by Viraj Patwardhan and David Kodinsky, with Hemmant Jha advising

Washing clothes with dho-dala is as easy as swinging on a swing in a backyard.

dho-Dala consists of a frame and a cradle. The cradle sits within the frame to hold the bucket. The cradle is pivoted on either side to the frame, allowing it to move freely back and forth.

The bucket is designed to lie horizontally within the cradle and is rocked back and forth to create the necessary agitation to properly wash clothes.

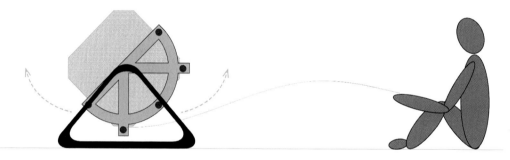

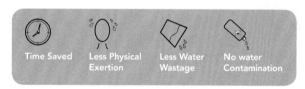

Time Saved   Less Physical Exertion   Less Water Wastage   No water Contamination

The manual washing machine is intended for use in the developing world, specifically targeting low-income populations. In many developing countries, individuals suffer from limited and unpredictable access to water and electricity.

The non-electric washing machine presents an opportunity to improve the washing process by reducing the amount of time, physical effort and exposure to harmful chemicals, significantly improving an individual's overall comfort and health.

dho-Dala
Changing the way India does laundry

METAPHORS CAN EXPLAIN HOW
THE NEW WORKS

food irradiation:
freshness preserved

Work by Lawrence Abrahamson, with Professor Kim Erwin advising

The fields of science and technology often bring us innovations that can't be seen or touched. And yet we need full comprehension in order to invest, advance, or adopt the proposition. As with Al Gore's simple declaration that "the planet has a fever" to explain global warming, visual metaphors can be equally powerful in framing The New. In the case of food irradiation, proponents have decades of study that show food irradiation is safe and effective as a tool for food safety and for extending the shelf life of produce. But is that the whole story? This wry visual metaphor counters by directing our attention another way: What do we mean by "fresh"?

When the meeting is over and you're out in the real world facing temptation everyday, you need to know you can call on your friends.

Weight Watchers

myRock for Weight Watchers
Get group support the moment you need it.

The WeightWatchers **myRock** fits easily into your pocket. When you're in a tough situation, give it a squeeze and a signal is sent out to your support group. As emails and text messages of encouragment are sent, **myRock** squeezes back to let you know you're not alone. You've got backup.

Work by Elizabeth Taggart, with Professor Kim Erwin advising

Where is that support group when you need it most? For this student project, the weight loss challenge of staying on track while in a social setting filled with tempting foods calls for a new device—the myRock. The myRock is a tiny signaling device that members can carry in their pockets. Squeeze it, and it puts out a distress call to the weight loss support group. When group members respond with texts or e-mails, myRock squeezes back to let the member know that others are there for them, responding and supporting.

From phone to camera
with a familiar flip.

Seamlessly transition from
phone to camera mode with a
physical flick of the wrist.

zp0

METAPHORS CAN DESCRIBE PRODUCT FEATURES IN NEW WAYS

Working with Motorola in 2009 to imagine future phone concepts for new user groups, the *zp0* concept phone targeted would-be rockers by riffing on the wrist-flip of the lighter. The wrist-flip was intended to be a familiar but novel interaction to help users switch modes, in this case from phone to camera.

Work by Joseph Shields, with Professor Marty Thaler advising, for Motorola Mobility Inc.

Sure, we all understand it now, but back at market launch, what simpler way to frame the iPhone/apps proposition than by comparing it to the multifunctional Swiss Army Knife?

Work by Suk Jun Lim, with Professor Kim Erwin advising

MANTRAS AND CATCHPHRASES

Too often when framing the complex, novel, or still emerging, we find ourselves challenged by vocabulary. Communicating The New benefits from words and expressions that are fresh and free of baggage—expressions that don't make The New sound like everything else. Most words suffice for expressing the present or the past: The expression "mobile worker," for example, emerged and evolved in response to a new behavioral pattern in our culture that needed attention. Our language caught up to that need. Words and expressions that point to the future, however, are often in short supply.

Mantras and catchphrases are useful workarounds for this circumstance. Mantras and catchphrases are alike in that they are both short, memorable expressions of a topic. Mantras tend to be directive—they are used to offer guidance and to direct action, much the way McDonald's mantra to "get better, not bigger" reminds the organization of the shift in strategy to grow through in-store sales versus new store openings. Catchphrases, by contrast, tend to be descriptive—they don't aim for advocacy so much as for compact clarity. As a result, catchphrases tend to be less self-evident because of their brevity: "Jumping the shark" is a non-obvious catchphrase for running out of ideas and stretching the limits of credibility. But if you've seen the episode of the TV show *Happy Days* in which Fonzie, on water skis, actually jumped over a shark, you understand the reference pretty well.

Linguists have a term for new words or specialized terms that express ideas in novel ways—they call them *stunt words*. Stunt words are new words created so as to stand out or attract attention. Comedian Steven Colbert's "truthiness" is one example: He coined the term to refer to a changing standard of truth, in which individuals claim that a belief is true, without regard for logic or facts, simply because of their "gut sense" or internal conviction. (Author Farhad Manjoo noted the trend, too, and expressed it as "living in a post-fact world.") Stunt words are an interesting workaround to holes in expressive language. Like "Spanglish" or "metrosexual," new words can serve as bridges, building from a current conception of the world toward what's changing and new.

In communicating The New, mantras and catchphrases can work this way, too. They can act as compact expressions that don't summarize The New—summarizing can strip work of important nuance and so ultimately undermine the work—so much as *point* to it. In this way, mantras and catchphrases act as proxies for larger sets of ideas and understandings. To invoke the mantra or a catchphrase, then, is to invoke everything it stands for.

In communicating The New, mantras and catchphrases can address multiple framing challenges:

- **MANTRAS CAN DISTILL A COMPLEX TOPIC**
- **CATCHPHRASES CAN ACT AS POINTERS TO COMPLICATED CONCEPTS**
- **MANTRAS CAN PROVIDE FOCUS, DIRECT ACTION**
- **MANTRAS CAN DEFINE A NORTH STAR**

MANTRAS CAN DISTILL A COMPLEX TOPIC

Eat food.
Not too much.
Mostly plants.

"Real" food is food as close to its original state as possible—not the processed foods found on grocery store shelves. This small expression points to an expansive set of ideas that form Pollan's book: What is food, really?

Limiting food consumption makes sense, but not to the economic interests of institutions that advocate for, manufacture, or sell food.

Plants have an enduring nutritional profile, whereas manufactured foods are reengineered to reflect the health fad of the moment (delete the oat bran; add omega-3s). Pollan channels this into a broader discussion: "Nutritionism," he notes, "is good for business" if not for the eater.

Sometimes details get in the way, and a reductive restatement can distill complex thinking to its essential elements. Author Michael Pollan famously did this when he summed up two decades of detailed food science and complex "healthy eating" research with this short mantra: "Eat food. Not too much. Mostly plants." Simple on the face of it, the mantra brushed aside what Pollan believed was a confused conception of food and unnecessarily complex advice around

eating. His mantra sought to displace a scientific preoccupation with nutrients, which he termed "nutritionism," with a simplified reframe that focused on food itself. His reframe was more than a summary of advice—it became a platform that allowed Pollan to start fresh. It provided him with new essentials: "real" food, from the earth not factories, and in moderation. And with these simple building blocks, Pollan advanced a new conception of eating.

Just-in-place learning

What if an object could narrate its story?

TIME CAPTURER

Time Capturer is an application designed to experience the past histories of places and objects. The application compiles and embeds information and pictures captured in a place that can be experienced by users at a later date and time. The concept promotes "just-in-place learning" by providing informal and experiential information.

When complexity doesn't reduce easily or well, a fresh catchphrase can act as a proxy for the fuller set of ideas. It can't summarize those ideas, but it can act as a compact reference to them.

The research of IIT Institute of Design Professor Anijo Mathew is a good example of this. He coined the catchphrase *Just-in-place learning* to refer to an area of his work that looks to distributed technologies and sensors as a means for informal learning enabled by places. The underpinnings of the work are complex. It challenges two conventions: first, that learning needs to take place in a set environment like a classroom, and second, that sensors and technologies embedded into an environment are best used for monitoring and passive data collection on that environment. Just-in-place learning proposes something quite different: What if place-based technologies could capture

Work by Aparna Unnikrishna, Nikhil Mathew, and Matthew Swift, with Professor Anijo Mathew advising.

the rich information and history of a given place and make that accessible just as an individual was standing in it? Professor Mathew sums it up this way: "It is when we stand in front of a bridge that we are most intrigued by it, and our heads are filled with questions. At this moment, the bridge becomes an incredibly rich learning environment where information is relevant and useful for that one student who stands in front of it—one that has yet to be tapped as a learning resource."

Imagine that bridge, he says, virtually layered with information about its design, construction, usage over time, and essays and research that reference it.

This is a transformative future that he proposes, one not well suited to an elevator pitch. The catchphrase, however, can start the critical conversations, and in dialogue the richness of the concept can begin to emerge.

AMSTERDAM

Tuesday 9:30 am rush hour traffic

City of pedals: The world's most bicycle-friendly city with over 249 miles of bike lanes and dedicated paths with separate bicycle traffic lights, and ubiquitous bike racks throughout.

"Tax the driver credit the biker"

Urging the City of Chicago
to emulate the transportation ecosystem of Amsterdam

We as environmental planners urge the city to encourage biking in the city by providing subsidies or tax credits to bicycle users. We also urge the city to explore the options of creating bike friendly "eco lanes." By making it safer and more convenient, dedicated bike lanes encourage people to get out of their cars and start peddling.

Work by Shilpa Rao. Amsterdam image © Aija Lehtonen, 2012, used under license from Shutterstock.com; bike lane image © Diego Cervo, 2012, used under license from Shutterstock.com

MANTRAS CAN PROVIDE FOCUS, DIRECT ACTION

Tax the driver; credit the biker

Creating The New often requires multiple, simultaneous courses of action to take a concept from the drawing board to the real world. Mantras can provide focus and direct action that organizes an effort and keeps teams progressing in concert.

For example, as a part of a Sustainable Mobility project, a design team studied cities around the world that invest in sustainable modes of transportation. The team addressed the results of its analysis to the mayor of Chicago, Richard Daley, and showcased the vibrant bicycle culture of Amsterdam as a model for improving

sustainable mobility in Chicago. Among other proposed actions, the report encouraged the city leadership to explore the options of creating bike-friendly "eco lanes" and providing subsidies or tax credits to bicycle users. "Tax the driver; credit the biker" evolved as the mantra for the proposed initiative, which called for multiple actions on the part of the city, including enhancing street infrastructure and formulating new local government policies, to turn Chicago into a City of Pedals—a secondary catchphrase to describe the new mobile urban landscape.

MANTRAS CAN DEFINE
A NORTH STAR

Free the data,
share the data,
apply the data

We take the turn
toward transformation.

And we provide
this roadmap
to guide us through
the transformation.

The signposts along
the road are clearly marked.
They read:

Free the Data

As Chief Technology Officer at the Department of Health and
Human Services, Todd Park has been given an impossible
assignment: to take a virtual ocean of public health data that
the US government continuously collects and transform it into
useful healthcare information. By Park's own admission, if he
were to rely strictly on his own insight and his own department's
quite limited resources, then he would likely make little headway.
Instead, he opened the data to the public; he invited health
experts and technological entrepreneurs to use this vast resource,
this truly big data storehouse to pioneer new applications,
to deliver new services and even to produce new game-like
products that entice others into useful exploration and l
earning related to community health outcomes.

Sometimes creating The New demands a dramatic shift in thinking or a long-term behavioral change that runs counter to current practices of the organization. These are leadership moments, for sure. But mantras and catchphrases can advance these changes by defining the vision, giving it coherence, and providing a memorable metric against which to judge plans of action.

Consider again Andy Parham's challenge to explain to executives the massive changes underway in how consumers expect to engage with their own data, such as electronic medical records. As Andy puts it, "I've got to somehow convince these health systems executives that the future is moving away from what everybody in the industry is doing, which is locking up their data with systems like Epic. I

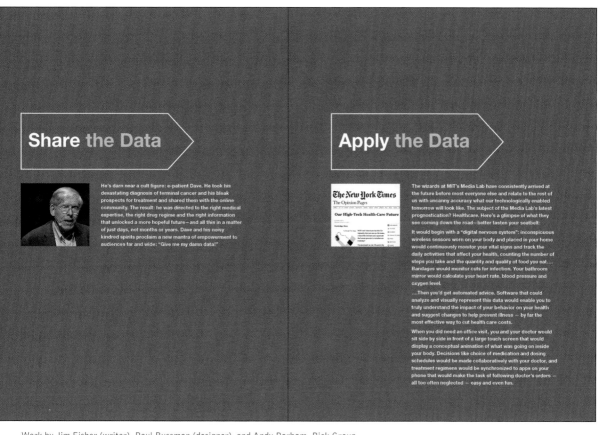

Share the Data

He's darn near a cult figure: e-patient Dave. He took his devastating diagnosis of terminal cancer and his bleak prospects for treatment and shared them with the online community. The result: he was directed to the right medical expertise, the right drug regime and the right information that unlocked a more hopeful future—and all this in a matter of just days, not months or years. Dave and his noisy kindred spirits proclaim a new mantra of empowerment to audiences far and wide: "Give me my damn data!"

Apply the Data

The wizards at MIT's Media Lab have consistently arrived at the future before most everyone else and relate to the rest of us with uncanny accuracy what our technologically enabled tomorrow will look like. The subject of the Media Lab's latest prognostication? Healthcare. Here's a glimpse of what they see coming down the road—better fasten your seatbelt:

It would begin with a "digital nervous system": inconspicuous wireless sensors worn on your body and placed in your home would continuously monitor your vital signs and track the daily activities that affect your health, counting the number of steps you take and the quantity and quality of food you eat.... Bandages would monitor cuts for infection. Your bathroom mirror would calculate your heart rate, blood pressure and oxygen level.

....Then you'd get automated advice. Software that could analyze and visually represent this data would enable you to truly understand the impact of your behavior on your health and suggest changes to help prevent illness — by far the most effective way to cut health care costs.

When you did need an office visit, you and your doctor would sit side by side in front of a large touch screen that would display a conceptual animation of what was going on inside your body. Decisions like choice of medication and dosing schedules would be made collaboratively with your doctor, and treatment regimens would be synchronized to apps on your phone that would make the task of following doctor's orders — all too often neglected — easy and even fun.

Work by Jim Fisher (writer), Paul Bussman (designer), and Andy Parham, Bick Group

don't want them to make a billion dollar bet on the industry standard. I want them to make a 250 million dollar bet on me. I want to help them get their data out of all their current applications, build a data model that they own, that they master, so that when new cloud apps arise they're going to be able to plug and play with them, and create a better experience for their patients and physicians."

To help executives see the changes coming and to mount a response, Andy and his design team paint a picture of a three-stage process: *free the data, share the data, apply the data*. "This is a really, really tough communications challenge, and we have to do it in lots of different ways. But executives and technical people understand this expression. They see it and it makes sense. It's a start."

CONTRAST

As Gail Fairhurst defines it, *contrast* defines a situation "by stating what it is not." This is what General Motors did when it famously declared, "This is not your father's Oldsmobile," using contrast to draw attention to its new car's departure from an outdated past. Similarly, when British Petroleum chose to promote the BP acronym as "Beyond Petroleum," it was attempting to direct public attention to a fuzzy future state that was potentially transformative and bigger in scope than BP's current business in oil. In both these cases, the use of contrast was for marketing and positioning. And in both these cases, BP and Oldsmobile attracted cynical responses for their open-ended use of contrast to promise nothing of real substance.

In the context of communicating The New, contrast is one of the most potent framing techniques because we have something of substance that needs defining. In our context, contrast is productive because it can frame the current discovery as distinct from what currently exists or has existed, and can do so in a clear, crisp way. This is especially useful when the "new" is not easily definable, or is still in motion, because if you can't say what it is yet, you can get started by saying what it's not. Contrast can also be used to create comparisons with things that currently exist, calling out similarities and differences that can be instructive in emphasizing the novelty of The New.

Some examples of how contrast can frame The New:

- **CONTRAST CAN FRAME AN OFFERING AS OUT OF STEP**

- **CONTRAST CAN REFRAME CONVENTIONAL THINKING**

- **CONTRAST CAN REFRAME PRODUCT FEATURES AND BEHAVIORS**

CONTRAST CAN FRAME AN
OFFERING THAT IS OUT OF STEP

Work by Doblin, a member of Monitor Group; photo © Roger-Viollet / The Image Works

It used to be that when you shopped for linens, you would spend some time conferring with the salesperson about what you desired. After a short consultation, they would display a range of linens on the table for your approval.

In today's retail environment, consumers get to feel the package, not the fabric, while personalized service and sales expertise are scarce. Doblin took a long look at the retail experience from the consumer's point of view and discover that:

it's not shopping—
it's *work.*

Sometimes customer expectations evolve and industries don't. Take the bed and bath category: Video cameras hung in stores showed customers repeatedly stooping, bending, and getting on their knees to extract the popular queen-sized sheets, inevitably stored near the floor. Shoppers walked around the store over and over to try to mix and match items to complete a bed. They scrutinized packaging full of technical language—a euro sham? 400 thread count?—which confused them and led to the search for a salesperson. And it was hard for shoppers to know what they were buying: They could feel the packaging, but not the fabric.

After investing 30 or 45 minutes, more than a few shoppers pushed their carts to the side and left without buying anything. This wasn't shopping in the conventional sense—this was *work*. And for any bed and bath manufacturer, with little control over retailing, packaging suddenly becomes very, very important.

Contrast is a simple, powerful way to convey a critical gap between the culturally dominant conception of an activity (shopping that is delightful, exciting) and an industry experience that is out of sync with that.

CONTRAST CAN REFRAME
CONVENTIONAL THINKING

Work by Amber Lindholm, with
Professor Kim Erwin advising

This isn't your typical 9 to 5.

She cleans houses by day and creates expressions of life and beauty by night. She eats, sleeps and breathes with her paintings in a one-room studio called home. She doesn't strive to be well known, but she needs to be able to share her voice. She focuses on today because tomorrow's path seems so unclear. **This is the life of an artist: a 24/7 job.**

Sometimes preconceptions stand in the way of change. Contrast can take on conventional wisdom or unexamined beliefs by calling them out. In explaining the life of an artist, the contrast starts with what the artist's life is not: It's not predictable, it's not bounded, and it's probably not like yours, gentle reader. For those who may be unfamiliar with the hardships of being an artist, particularly gallery owners, city agencies, or even arts patrons who have the resources to help

artists, this contrast conveys that artists have very different needs than most. While conventional work may end at 5:00 pm, artists work late into the night to survive and to fund their art. And if conventional 9-to-5 work occurs in a cubicle with a computer and stacks of paper, the artist's desk tells a different story with its analog tools and messy, rich textures. Contrasting conventional wisdom with reality is a powerful way to set the stage for change.

CONTRAST CAN REFRAME PRODUCT FEATURES AND BEHAVIORS

It's common for most manufacturers to focus on the things they can control: product performance, weight, packaging, and size. It's also common to ignore things they can't influence: context of use, evolving consumer behavior, and changes in workplace culture. This is a problem because too often it's the second set of factors that determines whether a product is considered by consumers at all. In communicating The New, contrast can be a powerful way to spotlight that an industry is focused on only half of the equation.

For the "notebook computer" industry, as it was called in the mid-nineties, manufacturers were obsessed with technical specs and building "better, faster, cheaper" laptops. Missing from the development processes was a focus on the human beings who were using them, and a deep understanding of what those human beings were attempting to do. In a study of mobile workers, it was clear that mobile computers were far from mobile. Battery life was short. The computers were delicate but cumbersome to carry. They had no protection from what might happen out in the wild—weather and accidental falls could kill a product. They required a long boot-up cycle to get going, and they needed a lot of maintenance to keep going. As notebook computers were building their base of technical features, they were lacking the physical and cognitive affordances that would make them truly mobile.

This simple use of contrast highlighted the differences between a truly mobile technology, a motorcycle, and a technology that was mobile in name only. This framing of the problem set the stage for a larger strategic conversation, one that called for a shift in practices from technology-centered engineering to user-centered engineering, to allow manufacturers to better understand the issues that mattered but that they could not control.

Work by Doblin, a member of Monitor Group; photo by Philipp Böhm / boehmphilipp.de

Here's a truly mobile worker scooting into the information age. Consider that the portable computer and motorcycle in this picture likely cost this guy about the same amount of cash. Which was a better buy?

Notebook computers have a high initial price compared to their desktop counterparts; even when well-made, they have a low resale value; they are difficult to confgure, operate and modify; they require nearly continuous maintenance and attention.

Motorcycles are moderately priced compared to automobiles; when well-made, they have a high resale value; they are relatively uncomplicated to operate as well as fun, and require moderate maintenance and attention. They also have strong cultural appeal. And, oh yeah, you can drive it right out of the showroom.

The mobility and connectivity business will bring computing systems to the same degre of appeal and utility enjoyed by common transportation systems.

STORIES

Much has already been written about types of stories that can be told—*leadership stories* that executives use to manage their organizations, *personal stories* designed to create identification with others, *anecdotal* or *folk stories* told to transmit lessons and insight to others, and the list goes on—so I'll not recount this vast body of literature here. The pertinent question for us in framing The New is probably less about what kind of story to tell, and more about when to tell a story at all.

In a bullet-point-driven world, stories and narratives have a particular edge in framing The New: They give us time to get familiar with ideas. And they give complex ideas room to breathe. Fairhurst refers to stories as "the much larger linguistic unit" for making meaning, as compared to other framing techniques, and perhaps size is why we respond so well to them. Stories can provide context, invite us into the narrative, and they build emotional connection to information that makes it easier to recall later. And research shows that human beings have tremendous facility for making sense of information through narrative—it engages our cognitive abilities for pattern recognition, analogous reasoning, and other sense-making processes.

A well-designed story can address particular challenges of framing The New in ways that other methods can't do as well: A story has the room to dimensionalize the current situation in nuanced and revealing ways. A story can sequence ideas so as to reveal complexity slowly over time. A story can nibble away at existing mental models that limit what others are able to see, and instead open up a new space for thinking. A story can set a proposal in the context of a longer wave of change, making that proposal logical and even necessary. And, most importantly, stories don't have to be about the present. In fact, stories from the future can be particularly powerful (as long as they are credible).

I'd like to call stories that address these needs *framing narratives,* and offer here a starter set that is particularly well suited to the need states we have in communicating The New:

- **THE ICONIC USER EXPERIENCE**
- **THE STORY OF A FUTURE WORLD**
- **THE RETROSPECTIVE: STORIES THAT SET CONTEXT**
- **THE ANALOGOUS STORY**

THE ICONIC USER EXPERIENCE

Today's perfect rental car customer?

A man who is physically fit. Can read and follow procedures. Steady income. Respects authority. Can carry own luggage. Can stand in line for long periods of time. Can go a long time without food, water, or bathroom break. Will face and persevere in any type of weather. Versed in map reading. Will take necessary actions to protect official property under his care. No kids – or none that he travels with. Speaks English fluently. Courteous and deferent – will return car with full tank of gas. Carries all necessary information and paperwork. Will not engage in any unlawful activities. Will proceed forward with little information, bolstered by faith in the system. Will enjoy renting, especially if it's an order.

Here is the opportunity: don't wait for customers to adapt to the system. Adapt to their needs first.

Work by Doblin, a member of Monitor Group; photo by Philipp Böhm / boehmphilipp.de

Stories from field research are standard fare in creating The New because they exemplify a problem that needs resolution. Iconic stories, or stories that typify the problem in ways that are particularly clear and representative of a larger pattern, can be hard to come by. But, done well, these stories can crystallize the challenge. And stories can help deliver bad news, sometimes by injecting a dose of humor.

Parodies can make for an effective iconic story when the message might be hard to hear but nonetheless needs to be said. For a high-volume car rental site that had not seen a redesign in years, this parody of the perfect car rental customer spoke volumes about what was being asked of current customers. The image of the military man, soldiering through his rental experience, was snapped by a field researcher on-site. It inspired the story of a difficult customer service environment and the observed customer workarounds, as renters tried to negotiate the rental site and process. As an iconic story, it was strong but humorous in presenting a point of view, and it created a compelling case for change.

Although our work is serious, it can still afford to be human, even whimsical. *Illustrated narratives* can add charm and introduce information indirectly—a useful technique when the story is tough news, and the audience for it is even tougher. This story about the light bulb "wall of hell" at hardware stores is certainly iconic. But your average manager might consider the problem relatively trivial and brush it off; after all, customers are still buying light bulbs. But perhaps that manager might relate more to the frustration of getting home and discovering that the bulb doesn't fit or lights the room in an unpleasant way, knowing that another trip to that store may produce the same outcome. That marginal customer experience is now a brand issue, and that's a more substantive problem.

A word about user stories: I would like to advocate that we avoid telling superficial user stories that recite a litany of irritations or outrages and are told under the guise of "building user empathy." You know the stories I'm talking about: "Jill is a busy mom, always on the go with her two kids, and here she is trying to get the minivan door open with her hands full of groceries. This makes Jill's life hard." This is overused, overt in its agenda to manipulate others, and ultimately it will fail if Jill's situation comes across as contrived. A stronger approach is to tell a story that builds around a single message: "Jill works harder because her minivan doesn't" is more focused, but "mobile users like Jill are ahead of the technologies designed to support them" may be more productive because it opens up a broader conversation about what needs to be in place for customers.

Work by Jamie Munger, with Professor Kim Erwin advising

WELCOME TO THE LIGHTBULB DATING GAME!!!!!

LET'S MEET OUR CONTESTANTS...

WHO'S THE LUCKY BULB?

THE END.

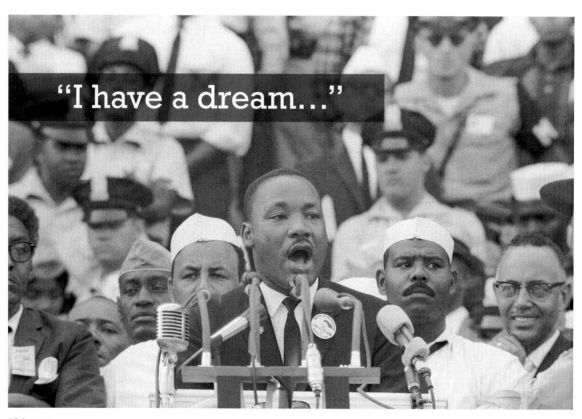

"I have a dream..."

AP Images

Stories can frame a picture of a future world that is both revealing in its vision and powerful in its call for change. Nothing speaks of this potential more than Martin Luther King's famous 1963 "I have a dream" speech on the steps of the Lincoln Memorial. Widely considered to be the most influential speech of the twentieth century, King's narrative imagined a world devoid of racial inequality, in which all men really were counted as equal and where his children would be "judged not on the color of their skin but on the content of their character." His vision addressed more than just a future state; it challenged everyone's comfort with living in a world where these things were not true.

Few of us have the rhetorical skills of Dr. King. But even everyday leaders of The New can use stories to frame The New from the future. Future stories invite others to imagine it with us, and they provide an early logic for considering change. This is especially useful when, as Dr. King knew, the path to change was likely to be painful and challenging to the status quo.

A word of caution, here, too: Future stories can fail when they stretch credibility or make improbable claims about how we are likely to live or how products are likely to behave in the future. Future stories are equally open to derision when they pose as visionary but in fact present linear extrapolations from the present. Technology "visions videos" are, paradoxically, prone to both these failure modes at once. Future stories are more successful when they make a case for change, as Dr. King did, but don't propose a fully finished solution. Unfinished stories, as famed storytelling guru Stephen Denning likes to point out, are more likely to enroll others in creating the future because they will have had a hand in defining it.

THE RETROSPECTIVE: STORIES THAT SET CONTEXT

For organizations that are mired in past practices or are particularly slow to change—let's call them industry laggards—the retrospective can remind them of a time when they were in synch with the culture, maybe even riding a cultural wave to success. And then the retrospective can highlight when that alignment fell apart. A longitudinal perspective can be of great use in both building pride in the past and illustrating that an offering is out of step and in need of reinvention.

1920's

Convenience stores got their start when Americans bought cars...

- Curbside service let car owners be seen
- Corner store became gas stations, and gas stations became stores offering ice, milk and other staples

1960's

When American work life changed, c-stores responded...

- Women in the workforce needed a simple way to grab grocery basics on the way home.
- Factory shift work drove late night, "7-11" hours
- Signature drinks offered something for kids

2

Today

When pay-at-the-pump kept customers outside, stores tried to draw traffic by adding inventory

- It's hard to shop when your car is at the pump.
- Counter is crammed, busy — signaling you should get in and out.
- Employees aren't accessible.
- Noisy environments don't invite browsing.
- Latte machines are timely but not distinctive offerings.

Today, while owners focus on inventory, customers are asking **"what's so convenient about convenience stores?"** *It's time for c-stores to find their cultural connection again.*

| 3

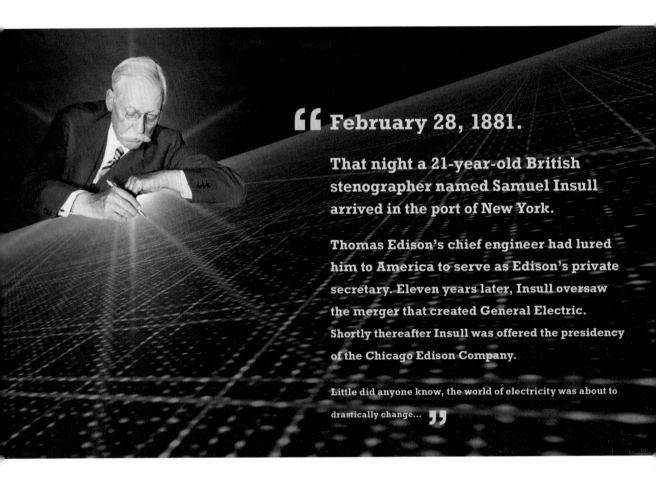

" February 28, 1881.

That night a 21-year-old British stenographer named Samuel Insull arrived in the port of New York.

Thomas Edison's chief engineer had lured him to America to serve as Edison's private secretary. Eleven years later, Insull oversaw the merger that created General Electric. Shortly thereafter Insull was offered the presidency of the Chicago Edison Company.

Little did anyone know, the world of electricity was about to drastically change... **"**

To help executives grasp the coming transformation led by cloud computing, Andy Parham talks about something they all understand—electricity—and then recounts the radical transformation of the production and distribution of power in the early twentieth century, brought on by the shift to AC power. Thomas Edison was committed to DC power, even in the face of growing evidence that AC, or alternating current, was a vastly more efficient way to deliver electricity to businesses and homes. AC power could also send power farther out through the lines. This meant that expensive power-generation facilities could be centralized, *and* distribution could increase. As Andy tells it:

In 1908, like 7 percent of companies and homes were using alternating current; by 1930, 90 percent were, and the world had fundamentally changed. So I draw those parallels to what's happening with utility computing, and I tell them that it's about math and utilization. I say here's the difference in utilization with cloud computing, because you have shared resources over your own computing where you run at about a 7 percent utilization rate. And I show them that the equivalent cost per core is $3000 for today's model and it's $300 in the future model. And so they get it. Cloud computing is bringing a massive shift in efficiency and cost-effectiveness over the current IT model, just like the shift from DC to AC power.

ARTIFACTS AND IMAGES

Most people have heard the adage that a picture is worth a thousand words. We know from experience that an image can visually deliver an effective, compact expression of complex phenomena in ways that words cannot. Artifacts are much the same. Artifacts can tell stories—of the people who used them, of their activities, of their values and social structure. This is why archeologists and cultural anthropologists seek out and study objects and spaces: As creations of the people who use them, artifacts communicate activity and meaning. Artifacts are clues.

For many, the intentional use of artifacts as a communication device is less intuitive, although in fact as human beings we "interpret" and assign meaning to artifacts constantly: The colleague who comes to a meeting sporting the disposable Starbucks coffee cup is interpreted quite differently from the one who carries his coffee in the handcrafted clay cup. Interpretations may vary, but the coffee cups have succeeded in *signaling something* that we suspect holds meaning.

This ability of artifacts and images to carry and signal meaning is useful in the context of communicating The New. Our discoveries and proposed new conceptual spaces are typically abstract and unfamiliar to others, and this is where the limits of language and the false concreteness of words can fail us. Physical representations of the work, by contrast, can be excellent at framing The New because they are visual and concrete. They prompt important conversations, and act as reminders of that conversation long after the words have faded.

How to use an artifact to frame The New? Artifacts can be symbolic or literal. As an example of the symbolic: famed ad agency Leo Burnett offers apples at the reception desk in every office across the globe, as a corporate symbol of its founder's values. Leo Burnett opened his agency in Chicago during the Great Depression, a high-risk move that drew jeers from the local press. "He'll be selling apples on the street," said a local journalist. "The hell I will," Burnett is said to have responded, "I'll be giving them away." Today those apples at the front desk are an enduring symbol of Burnett's determination, his perseverance under tough conditions, and, by extension, the firm's commitment to hard work and success on behalf of their clients.

The high school student's backpack, by contrast, is a literal, functional object lifted from the lived experience of students in a research study. The backpack is also a revealing and representative artifact because it can tell stories of life on the go, the educational experience, individual identity, and the participation in a subculture. The backpack as framing artifact has power because it is authentic to the situation.

In communicating The New, artifacts and images can visually frame the work in useful ways:

- **ARTIFACTS AND IMAGES CAN EMBODY KEY IDEAS**

- **ARTIFACTS AND IMAGES CAN REPRESENT CHANGE**

- **ARTIFACTS AND IMAGES CAN REDUCE COMPLEXITY, CREATE FOCUS**

ARTIFACTS AND IMAGES
CAN EMBODY KEY IDEAS

Work by John Shin, with Professor Kim
Erwin advising; photo courtesy of I-5 Design

For the Most Valuable Spender, checkout at the grocery store is the

VOTING BOOTH.

Elections every week.

The Most Valuable Spender captures the mindset of research participants studied for their belief that **what they buy is an extension of their influence**.

Every week—sometimes more often than that—the MVS's arrive at their voting booths and elect the food providers worthy of representing their values.

These moms believe their purchasing decisions directly influence the people and companies around them. They value the impact they have in their interconnected world and spend more on foods that empower their role as valuable consumers.

Sometimes problem framing and research will center on areas of human activity that involve objects or places of particular importance. These artifacts can be excellent framing devices because they are typically concrete evidence of otherwise abstract concepts, and because they are authentic to the situation. They are derived from the area of study, rather than imposed on it.

Take, for example, the challenge of making visible the mindset of a consumer segment, here dubbed "the most valuable spenders" for their belief

that how they spend their money can influence changes in the world around them. Researchers observed that study participants in this consumer segment consciously bought food brands that aligned with their values. They sought to prop up artisan bakers, local farmers, and small grocery store owners to send a message to big food manufacturers and retailers. For this segment, food purchases equated to power and influence. And for researchers, the grocery store checkout suddenly emerged as a political platform, with elections every week.

ARTIFACTS AND IMAGES CAN REPRESENT CHANGE

The stay-at-home **mom** is no longer home

Work by Miguel Cervantes, with Professor Kim Erwin advising; photo of 1950s woman by Lambert/Archived Photos/Getty Images

Cultural anthropologists know that artifacts can tell powerful stories about the people who use them, how they lived, what they valued, and even their daily routine.

In assessing a complex conceptual space, it can help to play the cultural anthropologist and perform a survey of relevant objects and places. The stay-at-home mom of yesterday does not resemble that of today. The responsibilities of today's mom go beyond meal preparation and

presentation. Much like a businesswoman, today's mom manages, delegates, advocates, and provides for her family from wherever she may be. Comparison of the 1950s mom with her modern counterpart reveals changes in the tasks of motherhood, and the different standards of practicality that govern each one's days. Juxtaposed with these women are the tools and objects that help them accomplish their daily tasks, which show a change of era and adaptation.

ARTIFACTS AND IMAGES
CAN REDUCE COMPLEXITY,
CREATE FOCUS

Sometimes a simple image can bring clarity to a complex problem in ways words and diagrams cannot. Take the image of a 12-year-old girl, presented to Citibank execs to redirect their thinking. CitiCorp had just merged with Traveler's Group, and had hired Michael Wolff and Pentagram to rebrand the new, hybrid organization. As Pentagram's Michael Bierut tells it, the design team's thinking was enmeshed in the complexity of two corporate giants merging into a single entity—while scrutinizing organization charts of both companies, thinking about ways to signal the outcome of the integration. Michael Wolff made an observation: ■ ·······························>

It was a powerful reframe. So the team found an image of a 12-year-old girl and used it to tell the story of a future customer. That future customer, the story went, might be 12 today but in 6 years would be looking to open a checking account somewhere. Ten years after that, she would be looking to buy a house, and in a few years after that, she might need to open a retirement account and have some money to invest. That customer should be the motivation driving not just the brand redesign but the larger efforts of Citi as it restructured. The image—no words attached—became a kind of mascot for the project, and was used so frequently by Citi execs as a way to communicate how the identity of the new entity would play out, that Citi went so far as to get a model release.

Somewhere off in the future there's someone who doesn't care about this merger, and will never care about it. It's just someone who needs a bank and needs what a bank can do. And people in their offices who are reading about this merger in memos and emails and on the financial pages and are worried about their livelihoods, they care about this now. But there's a customer out there who is never going to care about it. What we have to do is somehow remind people about that customer.

Work by Michael Wolff, of Michael Wolff Design, and Michael Bierut and Paula Scher for Pentagram

HOW (AND WHY) TO USE MULTIPLE FRAMES TO GREATER EFFECT

In the late 1960s, Berkeley professor Horst Rittel coined the term "wicked problem," pointing to an emerging class of complex, systems-level problems with characteristics that set them apart from conventional problems. Some of the ten characteristics of wicked problems he identified include:

They defy clear definition at the outset— definition comes through attempts to solve them.

Each is unique and novel—there is no clear precedent to apply.

They are intertwined with other problems—the root problem may not be evident at first.

Solutions are neither right nor wrong—there is no ultimate test to predict consequences over time.

Creating The New is inherently a wicked problem, characterized as it is by ambiguity, complexity, and a perpetual state of "still emerging." Communicating The New is too. This was Al Gore's challenge in his efforts to build momentum and investment around a nebulous "information superhighway." And this is the challenge to a business leader such as CEO Andy Parham in communicating something profound and new to investors, employees, and potential customers. Communicating The New is rarely a single problem, or a "tame" problem, as Rittel terms it. The New brings with it a series of problems, each with its own context and constituents, and each of those constituents with its own language, mental models, and needs. Every communication process, then, needs tailoring to the problem, the constituents, and the context of the moment. Finding a single frame

that can effectively address all these conditions simply may not be possible.

In such cases, it can be advantageous to create multiple frames, each targeting a particular dimension of the proposition. As an example, let's look at how Andy Parham uses a series of frames to explain his cloud-computing proposition to potential clients. Andy, with his team of Jim Fisher as writer and Paul Bussman as designer, targeted the critical issues: Explain the traps of the current IT paradigm; describe the larger wave of change around personal information that will be shaping all information-intensive industries; and propose a credible path forward that both anticipates that change and looks achievable. This generated a series of frames that allowed Andy to unfold his complex story in stages, each with a simple, visual device to anchor each critical issue. What's also valuable about his divide-and-frame approach is that frames can be recombined or swapped out to fit the constituents. For instance, Andy has learned that IT people get the mantra immediately and can then imagine how a cloud-based future might work. Medical practitioners, on the other hand, think in terms of patients, not data, and so find the mantra less relevant. Andy and his team set out to evolve a new framing device to better address their context, and they can slot that into the story with minimal revisions to the rest of it.

The Gulliver metaphor describes the condition of data under the current paradigm: trapped in proprietary, closed systems that limit access and don't support the powerful new tools that consumers want to use to manage their information.

Work by Jim Fisher (writer), Paul Bussman (designer), and Andy Parham, Bick Group

The electrification story tells an analogous story to cloud computing of how a new technology in electricity distribution upended Edison's dominant platform and transformed how power was produced and consumed in the United States. Cloud computing is poised to bring similar efficiencies and industry transformation to IT services, says Andy.

Insull image © SuperStock/Corbis.
Background image © Dan Collier, 2012. Used under license from Shutterstock.com.

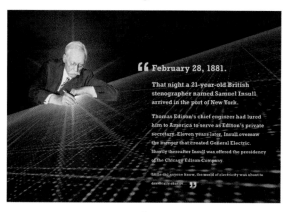

The mantra lays out a staged path through this change, and for each stage offers early evidence of the coming change.

Work by Jim Fisher (writer), Paul Bussman (designer) and Andy Parham, Bick Group

THE TAKEAWAY
Five big ideas when framing the work

At this stage, the work is still in process, and the team is still the primary unit of meaning making. Framing can be embraced not as an end-state, but a means to improve the process. This implies some general principles:

1. Frame early and often.

Ideas evolve and diverge and are sometimes thrown out altogether, a fact the entrepreneurial world embraces. Keep on top of that concept creep by framing early and often. This keeps the team aligned and alive to what's changing and what's staying stable, building that all-important shared basis of judgment.

2. Try a lot of frames; see what sticks.

In my experience, teams advance their thinking more by running through all five framing techniques in a defined time frame, say thirty minutes, than by laboring over just one. Variations test the solidity of the concept: If the variations don't sound as if they are referencing the same concept, you've spotted a problem. Variations also tease out where soft language might actually be covering up deeper misalignment.

3. Test your framing with outsiders.

Framing in close quarters can lead to collective delusion. Especially under tight timelines, teams can become too close to the work, too convinced that concepts are brilliant, and too confident that their explanations are self-evident and compelling. Testing will tell. Take an outsider to lunch, try out your favorite frame, and see if your communications are communicating clearly.

4. Match the frame to the organization.

Although all framing tactics can be effective, they are not necessarily interchangeable. Stylistic differences between them are significant enough that it will be important to consider each against the communication style of the organization, market, or other stakeholder group. An operations-focused organization might respond better to the compact directive of a mantra. A consensus-based organization might gather more easily around a metaphor.

5. Harness the elasticity of language.

Use language as a probe.—Language is imprecise, although it seems concrete. This is an opportunity: Actively negotiating shared meanings of abstract words such as "quality," "risk," or "innovation" can help team members and organizations find a shared set of priorities and purpose. Because meanings are in people, not words (to quote the General Semantics movement), it's best to ask "What do we mean by this word" rather than "What does this word mean?" Early-stage alignment via such "linguistic probes" is about more than just establishing shared terminology; it will build shared mindset and mission.

Use language as a proxy.—If the words to vividly describe a discovery seem in short supply, create or co-opt the ones you need. As discussed in the "Mantras and Catchphrases" section, words can be used to point to, rather than summarize, new phenomena. "Googling," for example, is neither a word nor a particularly accurate descriptor anymore, but it points to something powerful. What started as a product-based behavior has become a broader set of cultural expectations around what's known and knowable, and even the responsibility to know it: "Did she not google it before she stayed there?" we now ask incredulously. Similarly, in the 1990s, "mobile work" and "digital home" were constructs created to explain emerging areas for technological development. Years later, "mobile work" still doesn't have a precise definition—Who *isn't* a mobile worker?—but as a proxy for important phenomena, it still has communicative power.

Use language as a protagonist.—Sometimes the introduction of third-party or technical language can break up an entrenched way of thinking, and do so in a way that is not threatening to existing conversational partners, because the language comes from outside.

Recalling his role as head of research at Doblin, Dr. Rick Robinson recounts an example of this from an early 1990s project he led with McDonald's to reconceive the customer seating area. McDonald's was then a mostly efficiency- and operations-oriented organization. Their goals for seating had been to make it easy to clean, hard to steal, hard to damage, and not too comfortable—since founder Ray Kroc had actively sought not to re-create "hangout" restaurants of the 1950s. The McDonald's team Rick worked with was discovering that there was real opportunity to be had in offering something that encouraged guests to stay and socialize. But for the organization, it was a hard sell. At the time, Ray Oldenberg had just written his seminal book *The Great Good Place*. In it he coined the term "third place" (neither home nor work) and identified it as a very fundamental human need. Rick introduced this term and concept to the McDonald's team, and it became very effective. It was credible because it came from a third-party source. And it became doubly relevant when they learned that emerging rival Starbucks had already adopted the concept to describe their own ambitions. This is an often-repeated phenomenon, as teams have used other third-party-sourced concepts, such as "The Long Tail" or "The Creative Class" as material suitable for framing.

Gail Fairhurst tells us that framing is an act of leadership, and that great leaders know how to consciously use language to create meaning for others. Unlike the political leaders I introduced in the beginning of this section, I do not believe that our role in creating The New is to control the meaning. But I do believe that our role is to exercise leadership around the act of discovering meaning, and to help one another create a shared frame around the content and purpose of The New. And for that we need a command of language and framing that goes beyond conventional communications. The tools in this section should help.

3
Targeting your constituents

THE COMMUNICATION PLAN

MENTAL MODEL AND ORTHODOXY ANALYSIS

THE QUAD A DIAGNOSTIC

THE "ORGANIZATION AS CULTURE" FRAMEWORK

Build a network of collaborators and contributors.

Profile constituents to better tailor content
and engagement.

Surface organizational dynamics that limit
The New.

When the strategic shift requires a big, bold move—a transformative pivot—then the toughest sell may be inside your own organization.

—Andy Parham, CEO of Bick Group

If you resonate with Andy's thoughts, you are in good company. This is the number one identified communication objective among executives and managers in the executive education sessions I've been part of. Other commonly expressed variations include:

"How do I get the organization to buy in?"

"Getting my people to embrace change is a constant battle."

"I gave them a presentation with everything laid out. Nothing happened."

The last quote is particularly interesting because it comes from a high-ranking official in the U.S. Army. He had invested his time crafting a PowerPoint that detailed important shifts in strategy that needed to be implemented. This occurred in the context of the Army, where hierarchy is absolute and orders are to be executed. And yet "nothing happened." How is it that powerful ideas and important information often fail to engage the very people who need it most?

"The biggest mistake in communication is assuming it has occurred."

These words of George Bernard Shaw offer both a life lesson and a clue to engaging the organization. Until now, we've focused on content: *Finding the conceptual center* and *framing* offered approaches and techniques for creating clarity and focus. But great content, like great ideas, is not sufficient. It is at best half the equation, half the effort that needs to be expended. What's still missing is careful consideration of the people whose attention we need, whose support and engagement we must have in order to progress. Having something to say and being heard are not the same challenge.

This section turns a critical eye to the topic of stakeholders: the people you are trying to connect with. We will look at who they are, how to think about them, and why building empathy with those constituents is critical to communicating The New. It also introduces a model for segmenting those people, and proposes a preliminary match between those groups and communication modes. The two sections that follow proceed with this model in mind and introduce methods and techniques to engage those stakeholders.

If you are tempted to skip ahead, do so. But please come back. Even an hour spent thinking about stakeholders can significantly alter your thinking and shape your communication strategy. When testing the approaches and objectives in the following sections with executives, they report that simply spending the time to truly consider their constituents changes how they proceed. Whether writing a grant or presenting a new market opportunity to senior management, executives tell me that targeting stakeholders pays off by opening their eyes to the opportunities to connect.

Before we get started: Stakeholders versus constituents

Until now, I've used the term "stakeholders" loosely and without definition. Most of us have at least a loose sense of how the term is used in a business context and to whom it likely refers; the following Wikipedia definition reflects this well:

Project stakeholders are those entities within or outside an organization which:

1. sponsor a project, or

2. have an interest or a gain upon a successful completion of a project;

3. may have a positive or negative influence in the project completion.

—Wikipedia

But when it comes to creating The New, I think this term has overly narrowed our thinking. I prefer Shelley Evenson's word *constituent*, which she uses to better reflect "those that don't always have an obvious stake" and so might be overlooked. The term "constituent" shifts our thinking by training our attention on a broader range of individuals. It suggests there are people in the organization whose support and engagement we need, but who may have no explicit financial or organizational stake. Going forward, I use the term "constituents" to refer inclusively to broad swaths of the organization who may be very important to the success of The New, but who might never be considered when we are thinking of stakeholders. I use the term "stakeholder" only to refer to a subset of those individuals—those who are most explicitly staked-in and have the most direct influence. For more on who belongs to which group, and how to best target these people, see "Segmenting and targeting constituents" at the end of this chapter.

What to think about when thinking about constituents

So what is it that I ask executives to do when sizing up constituents? Simply this: Pay attention to the reality and needs of the individuals whose time and attention you want. Find out what's on their plate, what decisions they need to make, and the pressures that shape their thinking. When Andy Parham concluded that Bick's business needed to shift to cloud-based IT services, he spent two years just listening to his future customers. "We joined a group of healthcare executives at an event at the Broadmoor that we've participated in for four years with a group of healthcare CEOs or COOs from some of the largest systems. It's like a summit, and the CEOs and COOs bring their spouses, not their IT managers. We have fun together, and we do three roundtable discussions. So I just listened—I asked them questions about IT and I wasn't trying to sell them anything." Andy learned the kinds of thing that read flat on paper but feel powerful in person: These CEOs and COOs deeply felt the need for flexible, upgradable and cost-effective IT. They just didn't know where it was going to come from. Andy not only gained insight into the CEOs, he gained a window into the planning process of IT departments. He knew Bick Group could help.

Paying attention to the reality of others is not a complicated directive. But few people do it. In fact, when it comes to understanding stakeholders, the situation is often the inverse of that in *Finding the Conceptual Center*, in which creators of The New typically underestimate what they know about their "mess." When it comes to constituents, individuals tend to overestimate what they know. This leads to communication misfires or, worse, to the assumption that effective communication has occurred and surprise when sensible action fails to follow.

In my experience, when individuals engage in a more structured evaluation of potential constituents, they surface insights that shift not just their word choice but their understanding of what's needed. This is an important moment. In their awareness of others, *they come to recognize that building bridges, not just having great content or powerful ideas, plays a pivotal role in communicating The New.*

Without relevant bridges and access points, the "new" remains an island in the organization and you, its inhabitants, a people apart.

HOW TO AVOID BEING "A PEOPLE APART"—OPEN MODELS AS ENGAGEMENT PLATFORM

Innovation centers, new product development teams, and similar initiatives in organizations tend to start with a common set of premises: Give us the time and resources to explore the white spaces/blue skies/blue oceans. However, please shelter us from the vagaries of conventional business cycles, fiscal year, and profitability issues. In return, we will invent new value streams that can't emerge from the short-term thinking and inhospitable conditions inside conventionally measured business units.

This operational model for creating The New—often called a skunk works or, more generically, a *closed innovation* process—has an attractive veneer of logic. This logic holds that isolation creates the necessary conditions to allow ideas to emerge and flourish before being hacked apart or distorted by practical issues such as feasibility, revenue potential, relationship to strategy, and the like.

However, the Achilles' heel of this closed model is that, *by its very design*, few in the organization are staked into its success. As a result, dismissal or active resentment of such efforts and of the "special people" involved with them is a common reaction. Isolated innovation efforts tend to get little uptake, disappointing everyone involved. Even efforts that are received enthusiastically at first often fail to take root inside organizations.

Today, many innovation practitioners are embracing *open models* for creating The New and are enjoying greater organizational success for their efforts. Open models presume that the creators of The New are in service of the organization, not apart from it. For this reason, open models prioritize ongoing exchange and engagement with both immediate stakeholders and the organization as a whole. In other words, open models tap into communication, connection, and the value that others outside the immediate team can bring to the work. This orientation toward a broad set of constituents is evident even in the upfront effort to cultivate a productive "mess." As they seek to create an optimal collection of diverse inputs from which something novel and new might emerge, leaders operating in an open model look to others in the organization (and even outside of it) to bring relevant factors to the table.

Engaged constituents are powerful assets

No one exemplifies the transition from closed to open development models better than the McDonald's Innovation Center. The Innovation Center, housed in a suburb of Chicago, underwent its transformation over the past decade under the leadership of Innovation and Design SVP Ken Koziol. Up until then, according to Melody Roberts, senior director of experience design, the center operated more as a skunk works. This allowed for focused, future-oriented research and development, according to Roberts, and the innovation team worked informally, using the space to prototype and test ideas at will. The center was there for doing innovation, not sharing or communicating it.

That has changed. Koziol and his team began to open the doors of the warehouse and invite the Oak Brook executives and international market teams in for a look. He added new types of innovation practitioners: operations research experts as well as designers, like Denis Weil, who is now VP of concept and design, and Melody, formerly of IDEO. He also set a high bar for success, challenging his team to enable great business outcomes in uncertain future conditions. "The change wasn't easy," says Roberts. "We had to somehow make progress on complex systems innovations in new teams. And these teams were conflictive because the problems were really hard to solve and we all had a vested interest in different ideas. And besides that, we were constantly being asked to share the ideas with skeptical colleagues before anything was proven."

But once the doors were open, the value of the Innovation Center took a quantum leap. Operations teams from around the globe began visiting and then: "Every single market came. Most of them had never been out there. It seemed like nobody in the company knew about the place! So suddenly everybody's been there. And once they've used the facility, they start to take a sense of ownership, and they developed new skills while they were at it. The Innovation Center went from being the skunk works for new inventions to a place that everyone could use for continuous improvement."

Today, the Innovation Center is an open facility for prototyping and testing new concepts, whether those concepts are new restaurant footprints, kitchen systems, seating options, or menu offerings. Roberts notes that the facility is now open to everyone in the company. "You can book a week in July and show up with your top operations talent, the marketing folks, your menu people and you start running your menu through the test kitchens and see what happens. If you've added two or three new items, do you run out of grill space? Can you hit your service times? All that kind of thing. We know it's valuable because the markets pay for it—this is not a free effort. So this has been a really big transformation in the role of the Innovation Center and how it functions within the corporation."

The open model has raised the Innovation Center's visibility and value. It has grown from a "tiny team" to a group of over 40, and communicating its vast body of work to stakeholders is a significant part of the job. The team now punctuates its development processes with two high-profile communication events: The *Gallery Walk* targets top leadership across the world, showcasing what's in the pipeline that will be ready to test or deploy within the next year. For this event, "it's all about the audience," says Melody. It's organized around their annual planning cycle—so that participants have time to marshal the resources they need—and it focuses on near-term solutions. "These folks, who run countries, run regions, need solutions to problems they have today. It's can't be pure concept we're showing. If it's not been crystallized enough, they can't really imagine whether it's of value to them. They're very smart people, but they'd rather spend their time talking about, learning about things that are going to be ready the next year." By contrast, the *Futures Booth* targets the roughly 15,000 owner/operators from across the world who attend the biannual McDonald's Convention. Here the Innovation team brings attendees into future-oriented work, using full-scale models and realistic environments that can be experienced. These experiences allow owners to take their stories back to the restaurant teams, priming them for what lies ahead.

Both events put healthy pressure on the Innovation team. The events create a work cycle with deadlines to hit, questions to answer. "In a corporation, R&D efforts can go on indefinitely. The sky won't fall," observes Melody. "But with the Convention, every two years we have to account for ourselves. What are we doing? What are we seeing on the horizon? What do we plan to do next? So it forces convergence, and it forces work to get done."

As the McDonald's Innovation Center demonstrates, communication and stakeholder engagement can make The New everyone's business. It builds relationships, engenders trust, and allows The New to take root through self-discovery and self-persuasion. And, importantly, it puts the "people apart" back in the middle of what matters, where they can simultaneously lead, contribute, and be sought out as a vital organizational resource.

When stakeholders won't come to you

The McDonald's Innovation Center uses artifacts and experiences as a powerful draw, pulling in owner/operators and regional partners with a potent mix of novelty and relevance. They rely on a "show and tell" model that uses space, facilities, and prototypes to demonstrate new experiences in tangible ways that feel real (even when prototyped using foam core sheets and markers) and can be tested. This sets up a powerful dynamic, one whereby stakeholders feel in control, voluntarily engaged, and optimistic that their time is well spent. In short, they are eagerly traveling to you. And they're coming in prepared to listen.

In many organizations, creators of The New do not enjoy this position or visibility inside an organization. It's the creators of The New who must do the traveling. We pack up and head into the constituents' environment: the corporate headquarters, the business unit, the conference room located in a different wing. This is not neutral ground. This is territory in which business must proceed as usual, and day-to-day pressures compete with The New for time and attention.

In these circumstances—and this describes the vast majority of circumstances—it's critical that we extend ourselves to constituents so that we may earn their trust and build the relevant bridges between our New and their everyday responsibilities. To do this requires that we cultivate a deep curiosity about their circumstances. We must spend time actively listening. And, because we tend to overestimate how well we know others, and what we know about them—for those of you who lived through the seventies, think Newlywed Game—we also need methods to organize our listening.

GETTING STARTED

In this section, we look to the social sciences (and your English 101 instructor) to identify four methods for sizing up stakeholders for effective communication. Each method offers a different lens, some tightly focused and others more open, to better address the degree of separation between the creators of The New and stakeholders. They also work well together, so consider doing two or three to create a 360-degree context for communication:

- THE COMMUNICATION PLAN
- MENTAL MODEL AND ORTHODOXY ANALYSIS
- THE QUAD A DIAGNOSTIC
- THE "ORGANIZATION AS CULTURE" FRAMEWORK

The *communication plan* is a simple planning tool for thinking through any impending communication. *Mental model and orthodoxy analysis* is a preemptive framework for stakeholders of all kinds, good for structuring interviews and kickoff meetings. The *Quad A diagnostic* is a versatile tool for teams unfamiliar with an organization or stakeholder base, and is especially useful after any form of organizational discovery. The *"Organization as Culture" framework* offers a big-picture perspective on organizational identity, values, dynamics, and politics; use it to organize your listening and to structure questions and note taking during interviews and on-site tours.

When to start? Now.

Don't let the position of this chapter in the book signal its place in your process: Targeting constituents should begin on day one. It's as critical to the success of the work as the work itself.

Creative and innovative fields often rely too much on the power of The New, presuming that novel, intriguing work will convert the crowd. But social science research repeatedly shows that relationships with people deeply influence how and what is heard—a missive from a stranger is not received or attended to in the same way as a missive from a trusted colleague or friend. Studies show that content exchanged in the context of a positive relationship is heard more accurately and met with lower resistance. Given that The New often entails hard-to-hear realities, tough decisions, and big commitments, it's critical to have those conversations among people with whom you feel connected and respected.

Seasoned practitioners know this, too, and almost all I interviewed have tuned their processes to include stakeholder exploration from the get-go: "Now we do as much research into the client organization as we do into consumers," offers

It's really this simple. On day one, this team grabbed a white board and the Quad A framework and got to work mapping constituents' mental models.

Heather Reavey. "We spend a lot of time trying to get a sense of the roles of everyone on the team, the political situation in the organization, how they communicate, what's their internal style—are they a PowerPoint culture or are they an email culture? We know that the biggest challenge they have is selling this work through the organization, so they're pretty open to spending a few weeks having us interview stakeholders."

It's the human systems that get things done in organizations, and targeting stakeholders is about interacting richly with that human system. It is a short walk to failure when you relentlessly pursue an agenda without acknowledging the organization and taking into account the individuals in it. Performing any of the analyses shared in this chapter will help put you in their shoes, build that empathy, learn their values, show regard for their day-to-realities and—of ultimate utility in communicating The New—reveal the issues and special rules that govern their thinking. Better yet, explore two or three of the methods here to get a fuller picture.

THE COMMUNICATION PLAN

3 Key questions in a communication plan

1 Who's in the room?

identify participants, their pressures + upcoming decisions

2 What's your objective?

what do you want them to do differently back at their desks?

3 What's your key message?

the one core discovery everyone should know

With 10–15 minutes of planning, you can save hours in the execution of communication materials and produce better, more effective results for your effort. Communication plans offer a low-impact but productive structure for thinking through any communication challenge. They are particularly useful in communicating The New, because they force a fuller inventory of all the relevant factors in any communication exchange: the content, the intent, and, most importantly, the participants and their realities. If yours is a meeting-driven culture, communication plans can and should be your go-to tool. More effective than intuition and good intentions, communication plans can help define the conceptual bridge building required to make your work relevant to everyone else in the room.

HOW TO WRITE A USEFUL COMMUNICATION PLAN

Communication plans are not complicated. In fact, I recommend that you set out to create one that fits on a single piece of paper. Brevity is a sign of clarity, and clarity is the goal. If you find yourself composing long paragraphs, you are still discovering what you really think. So keep going—writing is a means of synthesis and discovery. But you aren't done until you've edited your responses to each question back down to one or two essential statements. And don't stop until the plan is short, tight, and sharp.

1. Who's in the room? Identify the participants—all of them.

Participants always have their own agenda, and it pays to think about what that might be. Participants have jobs, roles, and decisions to make. By defining the individuals clearly and with detail, you'll spotlight those agendas and can factor their interests and frame of mind into your plan.

When identifying participants, it pays to be specific. List all participants by name and position, and then consider the following:

- What are their roles, and how do they see themselves?

- Are there upcoming decisions, events, or milestones related to their responsibilities?

- What other efforts are they part of that might complement (or compete with) this project?

- What professional backgrounds or personal interest areas could connect to the project?

- What do they spark to—stories, visuals, numbers, concepts?

- Are there departmental dynamics that might influence their thinking?

- Are there any financial cycles, including end-of-year budget issues, that might be relevant?

2. What's your objective? Define your intent—both practical and emotional.

What do you want your stakeholders to do differently after this experience, as they head back to their desks? What is the course of action you want them to take? Define this in one to two sentences, and you have your practical intent. Again, soft definitions don't help as much as specific ones: "I want the brand manager to understand. . ." is weak tea. What do you want her to *do*?

More helpful: "I want the brand manager to rework the supply chain for her entire product portfolio to allow the brand to claim it is a purveyor of regional food." "I want the company to create a new investment category to nurture women entrepreneurs."

If you are asking for a substantive change from current behavior, it pays to break your larger intent into several smaller pieces, and select the one that seems achievable now. Consider your participants' tolerance for stretch, and remember that inertia and prudent risk aversion take time to overcome. Try to define small, achievable steps that will add up to something transformative.

For additional insight, define an *emotional intent*, or how you want participants to feel. This is highly contextual: Obviously, you want them to feel "good." But beyond that, ask what the group needs emotionally at this stage in the process. Do they need an exploratory session to bring them together and establish team dynamics? Do they need to gain trust in an unfamiliar process? Do they need to be encouraged and motivated? Do they need to increase their sense of ownership and pride? These are human beings we are engaging, and their emotional relationship to the work, the process, and each other is important to consider. It's helpful to contemplate emotional intent as an overlay to the practical intent, rather than as separate from it.

3. What's your key message? Identify the one core insight participants need to know.

Effective communication cannot occur if you don't know what you're trying to say. At the core, what are the one or two critical items your participants need to know right now? Using conversational language—something more like what you might say to a colleague who pulls you aside and asks for your point of view—summarize your key message in one or two sentences. For instance: "To be successful, environmental products need to be good for the consumer *and* good for the environment. One without the other won't be enough to amass a market."

Another: "By enhancing infrastructure and local government policies, the city of Chicago can create a bicycle culture. This will promote a much-needed sustainable mode of transportation, reduce reliance on cars, and alleviate the pressure on mass transit."

Do not aim a fire hose of information at your participants—this is overwhelming and only shifts the job of finding what's important to them.

Whether the message is about findings, insights, or opportunities, brevity is your friend. When you can "tell it short," it means you know what's important about your work. Additionally, once you've isolated your key message, it will become obvious how to organize, edit, and focus the rest of the content. The size of your presentation deck will shrink by 75 percent.

4. What kind of engagement might make sense?

At this point, step back and ask: What kind of experience might bridge participants to the content of the work, while advancing our objectives? Is another presentation-driven meeting the best choice for this job?

We are not yet conscious or deliberate enough about how we engage stakeholders in the process of communicating The New. As veteran communication strategist Tom Mulhern notes, "Adoption of significantly novel ideas requires a change in your psyche, not just your thoughts. This has to come through experience and engagement. A memo is not enough." In Chapter 4, we will look at five different types of experiences you can use to engage stakeholders. Consider browsing these options and asking if there are "culturally compatible" variations that might work in the plan you've just outlined. Stakeholders often neither want nor expect new ways of engaging with ideas, and cultural resistance to unfamiliar ways of doing things can cause us to play it safe. So, if the experience models I propose seem too big a jump for your organization, consider taking smaller steps to make the engagement more relevant and objective-driven.

MENTAL MODEL AND ORTHODOXY ANALYSIS

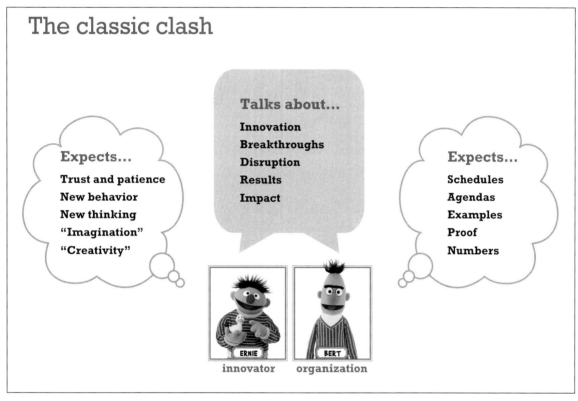

Courtesy of Tom Mulhern and Steve Portigal

Communicators of The New can't successfully engage an organization until they understand its culture and business environment. One way to size up stakeholders and the larger organizational appetite for change is to step back and analyze prevailing mental models and orthodoxies. Mental models, efficiently described by Gail Fairhurst in *The Art of Framing*, are the assumptions and beliefs held by individuals that define for them "how the world works and will work in the future." The mental models

of stakeholders are crucial for creators of The New to understand because, as Fairhurst notes, these assumptions can make certain aspects of a situation look hard and fast, and can therefore limit the new space for thinking. Mental models are problematic because they typically operate unconsciously. This means that they influence behavior and structure thinking in ways that individuals do not recognize and therefore cannot easily articulate. This makes certain kinds of exploratory conversations difficult or impossible, and causes even reasonable propositions to be rejected out of hand. Given that *everyone* has mental models, leaders of The New would do well to find and observe the ones at work in the room, if they want to avoid triggering a rush of organizational antibodies and concept rejection.

Similarly, every culture has orthodoxies—*there are some things we just don't do*—that are understood by members of that culture. Organizational orthodoxies are often transmitted tacitly, not through spoken agreement, so that they are "in the ether" and are presumed by insiders, rather than easily identified and articulated to outsiders. It's useful to think of orthodoxies as mental models that operate at an organizational scale— these are the broadly understood rules and values that guide acceptable behavior and thinking inside an organization.

The hazards of our mental models

Mental models create misery-inducing communication traps when individuals who don't hold those models engage with individuals who do. Creators of The New are especially vulnerable to this, as illustrated by innovation consultants Steve Portigal and Tom Mulhern with *Sesame Street*'s Ernie and Bert. Speaking at the Design Research Conference in 2004, Steve and Tom addressed the classic Creative versus Suits mental model clash: In the kickoff meeting, everyone in the meeting rallies around key words such as "innovation," "deliverables," and "transformations." For Ernie (the creatives), these words presume a process of exploration, discovery, and deliberation. But Bert (the suits or the clients)

assumes a process of steady progress, project milestones, proof—the stuff of Gantt charts. Soon enough, enthusiasm turns to frustration, and that rallying cry of all failed communicators is uttered: "They just don't get it!" Mental model mismatches can turn great teams into dysfunctional factions, draining precious energy away from the productive, problem-oriented conversations required to create The New.

Mental models come from personal experience. This makes helping others to "get it" a tough proposition when their experience base is significantly different. Melody Roberts sees plenty of this in her work at McDonald's:

Intra-team communications around mental models are the biggest challenge right now. Marketing and IT are very critical partners in anything we do. They're great to work with and they enjoy the work we do together. But it's challenging sometimes to cast things as experimental or learning-oriented versus deployment-oriented because they don't have that practice . . . they almost always think that they're getting ready to scale it on a mass basis, whereas we often think, among the Innovation practitioners, that we're trying something out. We're testing it out. The other thing we do a lot of is try out things in markets. As soon as something's testable we have to partner with somebody in the market, and there's only a handful of people globally . . . less than a handful even . . . who are close enough to this practice that when you talk to them about partnering you're both on the same page: Ok, we're going to try this in one restaurant. We're not going to make a lot of fuss, we're not going to ask a lot of permission, we're not going to advertise the results. We're going to learn for ourselves and then keep going.

As Melody notes, when mental models are aligned across stakeholders, we experience working together as efficient, productive, and even effortless and joyous. These are the collaborative dynamics we strive for. They create a high-functioning environment where individuals feel engaged, productive, and personally empowered. These are the conditions for creating The New. The ability to preemptively align mental models to better nurture these conditions, then, seems a useful skill to cultivate.

Taking on organizational orthodoxies

If mental models create interpersonal minefields, orthodoxies create disabling blind spots about what's possible and what's desirable for an entire organization. They can lead to rigid thinking and myopic vision—barriers to The New that are difficult to dislodge from the outside. Ben Jacobson states well the danger of orthodoxies: "When I hear people say we will never be in the business of X, Y, Z, that's always a warning flag for me because I think things migrate so much. Everybody likes to use Apple as an example, but back when they were making computers and the first personal desktop computers, they never knew that all of their money was going to come from phones and music. The path that got them there? Well, they didn't say 'we're never going to be in the music business.' They would have missed the boat, right?"

Larry Keeley has long made exposing orthodoxies a core part of his firm's practice: "Organizational orthodoxy is extremely important. Doblin uses robust methodologies to tease out orthodoxies, and what's great is [that] if you get the client

themselves to identify, externalize and even laugh at their own orthodoxies, it accomplishes two things. It gives clients the habit of understanding that they will tend to look at literally everything unfamiliar through a filter of what is familiar and tend to reject the things that are unfamiliar. Separately, it gives them the sense that this is actually a discipline—that to innovate they're supposed to consciously flip around."

Rejection of the unfamiliar is one of the great ironies of initiatives designed to create The New. Every leader of The New has encountered the invisible threshold that separates "blue sky" from outer space, by inadvertently stepping across it. One client of mine, having enthusiastically signed up for a ground-up rethink of their product category, clued us in early with this hallway comment: "This company needs change . . . [pausing] well, as long as it's not *too* different." It was a telling moment—more candid and self-aware than most. The client's limited appetite for risk and disruption was revealed, and we began to think from day one how to stretch them past it.

"We make cash registers, not software"

Orthodoxies are often tied into the core identity of an organization, which can make them particularly difficult to penetrate, and make proposals that run counter to them seem as if from Mars. At NCR, Tom MacTavish recalls trying to explain to senior management that the future of cash registers lay in software, not hardware: "I went into my boss at NCR and said, 'You know, NCR is in transaction processing and you keep thinking about it as cash registers, but electronic payment systems are the future. People are going to sit at home and buy stuff.' And he said, 'Tom, you're an idiot, get out of my office.' He grew up as a hardware salesman. He sold cash registers. He didn't even understand software, per se. And so when I tell him the future of his company may be all software and the product may be something people interact with, he's like, 'But, where's the hardware?'"

Research told Tom that the future of payment systems lay in laptops, but organizational orthodoxies forced him to work on the wrong product. This is a common frustration voiced by R&D leaders who know that the transformative New lies outside of the current offering and resides instead in a world executives often don't know and can't conceive of. And so leaders of The New receive a perplexing message: Call it big and bold, but it'd be great if the future could resemble the past. We're good at the past.

The two faces of orthodoxy

Orthodoxies are more than vestigial beliefs that have yet to be updated or reimagined. That would be fairly easy to fix. Rather, they hold power because they have been legitimate keys to success. Melody Roberts observes that "there are any number of orthodoxies that guide my work. We could call them orthodoxies, but you might also think of them as things that are central to the brand identity or to the experience promise, or to the business model. So do I question the real estate model? Not when I'm trying to redesign the service system. Do I question the service time? Well, only if I'm totally re-architecting the customer journey. So many of the orthodoxies constrain the work in a useful way. And the art

of it is figuring out which ones to retain, and slavishly and devotedly follow, and which ones to open up to experimentation or to eliminate later."

There are some things we just don't do. What happens when orthodoxies correlated with past success become barriers to the future? This is what every leader of The New must contend with when she recognizes that a way of working or thinking is past its expiration date. This is what Andy Parham faced with his internal stakeholders, the hundred employees of Bick Group who'd spent the better part of their career finessing a business proposition that was less and less relevant. This is what Tom MacTavish faced in his R&D role at Motorola, when his manager told him the U.S. market would never accept touch screens on their phones because they need the tactile feel of buttons ("nobody wants a misdial").

Orthodoxies are not just about an industry's or a profession's mindset. Sometimes they can be quite particular to companies. Innovation consultant Jonathan Vehar tells the tale of two apparently similar consumer packaged goods companies, both established players in their category. At jam-making Smuckers, the main focus is what's inside the jar (as its slogan says, "because with a name like Smuckers, it has to be good"). At mustard-making Plochman's, the discussions revolve predominantly around packaging (since it introduced the squeeze-barrel container for mustard). Jonathan calls persistent values like these "cultural currencies"—a belief that a core part of the business is responsible for its success, and, to extend its success, the organization should stay with the formula that got it there.

Explicitly examining orthodoxies and other mental models is an excellent early-stage stakeholder strategy for senior management, who often find it cathartic and invigorating to put words to what's constraining their organization.

HOW TO DISCOVER AND DEFANG MENTAL MODELS AND ORTHODOXIES

As already discussed in this section, existing mental models and orthodoxies are not necessarily the enemy of The New, but if unacknowledged and un-named, they can prevent it from ever happening. For this reason, the most important tactics I can offer aim to create detail and spark reflection. Some of what I recommend can be quite informal, but when you're trying to tackle the true, deep orthodoxies, you'll need bit more rigor and structure. The following are five tactics to try when seeking to reveal mental models.

Pay attention to language; ask for stories

Misalignment hides in abstract language. Sometimes that misalignment is evident: Steve Portigal was hired to unpack the word "quality" for an organization that discovered one of its core values was ill-defined. "They said, 'Look, this term is coming up in conversations in the hall, and we know we all have our own idea of what quality means. And we have clichés or proxies for what it means for our users. But we need to get a fresh perspective on that.' So our clients are warning us about how stakeholders are talking about this stuff—they know they're disconnected internally in their vocabulary. But the current notion of quality is well rooted in their culture,

it's rooted in all the things that have made them successful. They have to figure it out." As part of his inquiry, Steve solicited stories from employees, providing prompts, such as: "Tell us about the best experience ever . . ." that would provide clues as to mindset. You can follow Steve's lead, and use stories to promote conversation around known hot words such as "research," "innovation," and "risk," by asking for "the most successful research project" or "the biggest risk that paid off." The details of these stories will reveal mental models at work better than direct questions, such as "What does innovation mean to you?" which typically generate unfocused and abstract answers.

Seek out patterns in experience that generate mental models

Gail Fairhurst encourages us to train our attention on the situations or beliefs that created the mental models in the first place. People's day-in and day-out experiences are what builds enduring beliefs such as "how things really get things done around here" or "what happens to people in this company who invest in new initiatives (that fail)." Attitudes like "why rock the boat" and "don't expect to be listened to" are *learned*. With a little probing, leaders of The New can reveal the experience base that feeds these cultural norms. It's critical to success, says Fairhurst, that leaders explicitly surface the existing models and contrast them with those needed to go forward.

Identify the mental models for others, and identify your own

We have to become sensitive to the mental models of stakeholders, to better bridge our work to their reality. However, to do so, we need to be conscious of our own mental models, too. This level of consciousness breeds an important set of behaviors: It helps us stop asking the nonproductive "How can they think like that?" and start a new mental habit of "What causes them to think this way?" and "How can I help them hear this in a way that makes sense to them?" And don't wait to be a reflective practitioner. As Fairhurst notes, it's important to think through your mental models in advance of when you'll need them. This way, you'll be better prepared to spot the problematic mismatches in the moment, to discern whether others are even aware of their own mental models, and to better articulate them for everyone.

Directly engage the stakeholders in the conversation

Unlike the observe-and-share approach to mental model analysis, orthodoxy analysis will be more effective and persuasive if, as Larry Keeley points out, it is a process of self-discovery led by stakeholders themselves. Creating a hypothesis or two in advance of such a session is not a bad idea, in case stakeholders demonstrate difficulties getting to the more problematic biases in the organization. But conducting the hard work of self-evaluation in a more open session where others can contribute will increase the "stickiness" of what emerges.

Listen carefully; provide structure

Worksheets and questions should be organized to allow individuals to both reflect and share. Reflective exercises ask individuals to consider questions independently and to arrive at hypotheses or insights in an uninfluenced manner. This produces richer results and provides interesting stimuli for shared conversation. But reflection does not need to be fully open-ended. It's a good idea to provide structure that encourages your constituent group to consider all kinds of orthodoxies or assumptions, including biases around identity, behavior, finances, or accountability.

QUAD A DIAGNOSTIC

4 Factors to consider

Activities

projects, efforts, and work streams

Ambitions

longer-term, bigger-picture goals

Anxieties

what keeps them up at night?

Attitudes

relevant perceptions and opinions

The Quad A—activities, ambitions, anxieties, attitudes—framework is a structure teams can use to organize observations, stories, and insights and to more richly interact with constituents. I originally developed this framework as a way to describe segments of consumers on the basis of qualitative research data. Today, I also use it to help organizations describe themselves.

Quad A looks at behavioral, emotional, and cognitive factors equally in sizing up human beings. The output of the analysis is a broad snapshot of the current constituent context. This snapshot can then be helpful in all communication efforts, but especially when considering how to bridge The New in ways that will be most relevant to your constituents. In early stages, the four "A" categories are simply buckets in which to arrange what the team is discovering. In later stages, teams can revisit the four buckets to understand which bridges have been built, and which have not.

Activities

Activities are the projects, efforts, and work streams that dominate constituents' attention and time. When you inquire about activities, you will understand your constituents' realities that exist outside of your project, as well as the pressures and expectations they are likely to bring into the room. Activities are *behavioral*, and so are open to documentation. In general, any formally defined (i.e., job-related) or recurring activity is worth noting. It's also worth noting any routine informal or social connection activities. These might include "the meeting before the meeting," where decisions really get made, or "hallway rituals" whereby regular social exchanges help keep personal networks healthy.

Ambitions

What longer-term, bigger-picture goals do your constituents have? These can either be in relation to or completely unrelated to your area of concern. I define ambitions as distinct from short-term motivations. Motivations are often highly unstable and open to change in response to minor shifts in conditions: "The VP is coming to the meeting, so this needs a real wow factor to get her attention." Ambitions, by contrast, are more enduring; they are about who we want to be in the future, how we want to live, what we want to lay claim to: "I want innovation to get a regular seat at the strategy table and to be recognized as vital to the company's success." And I have heard: "I'm retiring in two years, and I don't need or want to rock the boat." It's extremely useful for development teams to get a bead on the larger ambitions of stakeholders. And it's also a reasonable topic for inclusion in interviews, as many individuals are open to talking about their desired future states. While it's best to have ambitions explicitly stated by stakeholders—their language choice can shift meaning in important ways—it's also acceptable to infer ambitions from conversations if stakeholders are reluctant to share their larger agendas.

Anxieties

What keeps your stakeholders awake at night? Anxieties can be a powerful psychological force. What constitutes an anxiety can vary: from low-level worries (I don't think we're really prepared for the future) to vague suspicions (something unseen and potentially harmful is lurking) to a looming sense of doom (we will all be fired after this product launches). Often, factors filed under this heading are the result of an interpretive act on the part of a team member—reading between the lines to surface a constituent's unstated but

implied sense that something is amiss or failing. Asking about anxieties directly is a reasonable course of action, but can produce evasive answers. However, with some care, the answers will come, and then you will have built a level of trust that will open other channels of communication, too.

Attitudes

This is a loose category that I tailor to the inquiry at hand. Its intended use is to capture relevant constituent perceptions or opinions or judgments. These can be of the industry, the organization, or the topic at hand. It's different from ambitions because it's the present tense we're looking for—capturing how constituents feel *now*: "Management doesn't care about anything but profits." "Innovation teams don't get the realities of the business." "Our scientists don't know as much as they think they know." "Sustainable practices are the future because transparency means consumers can see everything we do." Attitudes are often based on past experiences and so offer a signal about their receptivity to the future. This is often the category in which "orthodoxies" or other shared mental models lurk: Big companies can't act responsibly, innovators can't survive here, and the like.

THE "ORGANIZATION AS CULTURE" FRAMEWORK

3 clues to organizational culture

Vocabulary	Stories	Customs + conventions
metaphors shorthand special expressions	corporate stories personal stories collegial stories	conflict resolution rites of passage rites of affirmation rites of degradation rites of integration rites of renewal

Quad A and mental model analysis help us identify potential barriers and opportunities as regards immediate stakeholders, the people we know are going to be in the room. What's missing from the methods and tools so far is how to think about the organization itself. The "Organization as Culture" framework turns our attention to these other constituents and intelligences in the organization—the people we may never meet, but who will be using our work.

Why use a cultural lens?

This requires a (very) quick step back into academia. Historically, scholarly investigation into organizations looked at productivity levels, lines of authority, channels of communication, and the like, with the goal of making organizations work more effectively. For example, Frederick Taylor's time-motion studies on factory line workers, in the early 1900s, are one example of this approach. The metaphors underlying this approach were "organization as machine," "human as machine part," and "organizational study as science."

Then, in 1973, cultural anthropologist Clifford Geertz published a seminal work, *The Interpretation of Cultures*. It is hard to overstate the impact of this work on academic traditions of all kinds. In *The Interpretation of Cultures*, Geertz powerfully questioned the use of methods from the natural sciences—with their focus on prediction, accuracy, and "law"—as relevant to studying human beings: "The concept of culture I espouse . . . is essentially a semiotic one. Believing, with Max Weber, that man is an animal suspended in webs of significance he himself has spun, I take culture to be those webs, and the analysis of it to be therefore *not an experimental science in search of law but an interpretative one in search of meaning. It is explication I am after*" (emphasis added). The methodology for looking at human systems, he proposed, should be interpretive and focused on how meaning is constructed and communicated, rather than on predictive laws like those of physics. This radical reframe was ultimately taken up by those who studied organizations and gave rise to a new operative metaphor: "organization as culture."

I propose that all creators of The New take a moment to act as cultural anthropologists and look for clues as to the culture of your sponsor organization. Whether operating from inside an innovation center or from outside as a consultant, we all become visitors when we step outside of our milieu and into a new context. As innovators, consultants, or researchers, we should familiarize ourselves with the systems by which that group makes meaning, so that we may operate smoothly and successfully inside its culture. This will help bridge our work to others (people we may never know very well as individuals) in ways that acknowledge and respect their circumstances.

THREE CLUES TO LOOK FOR WHEN LOOKING AT ORGANIZATIONAL CULTURE

Many academics have adopted and helped build a cultural perspective for looking at organizations. Here I offer the work of Professors Michael Pacanowsky and Nick O'Donnell-Trujillo, with elaboration by Harrison Trice and Janice M. Beyer. Together they form a simple framework within the reach of everyone—no PhD required.

Vocabulary

What are the standout expressions, references, or jargon used by organizational members? Shared language offers an immediate window into a given culture. Pacanowsky uses the example of the army, where standardized expressions such as "chain of command," "salute," and "yes, sir" are intentionally leveraged to affirm army values of rank and status. This language not only

affirms the status of others, it also confirms *your* membership in the army.

Unlike army language, most language used by subcultures is voluntary, not dictated. It emerges and evolves to reflect the values of its people, and serves to build identity and bind members together. In other words, language not only expresses a culture, it also *reinforces* the culture.

When sizing up an organization, what should we look for? In general, pay attention to language that stands out. In many organizations, as Professor Karl Weick pointed out, metaphors and analogies offer clear information about organizational style. Sports and war references signal a competitive mindset and reinforce the notion of winners and losers. Metaphoric expressions such as "management track" and "moving up the chain" signal a structured, hierarchical organization with strong boundaries that typically limit the actions and decision making of individuals.

Cognitive linguists tell us that metaphoric language is more than a rhetorical flourish— metaphors in our language are evidence of how we think, and they signal the conceptual structures that organize our thoughts. Word choice can also signal conceptual frames at work: Are the people studied in qualitative research *customers* (typical term used by market researchers seeking an economic relationship) or *users* (used by designers and usability experts seeking behavioral insights) or *informants* (used by social scientists seeking specialized information)? We tend to use words that provide clues to our context.

Specialized language is also worth noting. The heavy use of acronyms, which require that one be "in the know" to understand them, can signal operationally oriented cultures that like to launch initiatives. This not only speaks to an execution-oriented mindset, but may also signal that your initiative is one of many. Additionally, more organizations are investing in training to teach team skills and interpersonal skills to employees, and so mandate the use of facilitative expressions such as "let me build on that" or "yes and . . ." These suggest an expected way of working, and it pays to acknowledge and temporarily adopt these rules as your own.

Stories

There is a good reason management consultants kick off projects with stakeholder interviews. Theoretically, they conduct interviews in pursuit of corporate facts. Organizational culture theory holds that they should simultaneously be in pursuit of stories. Stories, say cultural anthropologists, are a very powerful way that groups create and transmit meaning. Stories are heightened descriptions of events and individuals, and so provide a way for members to dramatize organizational life. Organizational stories are useful to communicators of The New because the stories often typify what's worth emulating and what's not, defining the heroic and the misguided. The way in which individuals talk about their work, themselves, or their colleagues is always revealing. When we head into a new organizational context, or conduct a round of interviews, Pacanowsky suggests that we listen for three kinds of stories:

Listen for *corporate stories*, typically told by management to new employees, outsiders, or others who need to be socialized into the culture and its history. These stories (and here Pacanowsky references the work of Brigham Young University's Alan Wilkins) are repeated to convey the managerially favored values, ideology, and customs of the organization. Every new McDonald's franchisee, for example, heard about the late Ray Kroc, who, even as chairman of the board, picked up trash in the parking lot when he came to visit a new store. The message is clear: In the McDonald's universe, the customer experience of the brand is paramount, and no one is too important to pick up the trash if it helps achieve excellence. Not all corporate stories are spoken. Some are illustrated or performed. For instance, Google—famous for its explicit statements of values, such as "Don't be evil" and "Work should be challenging and challenge should be fun"—communicates its emphasis on speed and fun through whimsical but functional workplace design. A slide communicates the story "We move so fast around here we don't have time to take the stairs or the elevator."

Personal stories, on the other hand, are told by individuals about themselves, in an attempt to influence how others see them. For example, a new employee might be greeted with a line of chatter: "I'll be in charge of your first meeting, and believe me, I don't believe in wasting time. I walk in with a clear agenda, and everyone walks out with tasks." Translation: I'm competent and know what I'm doing (unlike others here), and my teams are productive and focused. So you will be, too.

The rumor mill is a repository for *collegial stories*, or stories that portray others in the organization. These stories reveal how others are seen or "how things really get done." When I started my first job, I was told to pay attention to the receptionist if I wanted to be in the know. She tracked who came and went, who met with them, how long they were here, and whether they were shown the good conference room or the bad one. That receptionist had a surprising amount of knowledge and power inside the organization.

Customs and conventions

What are the predictable, planned activities that organizations orchestrate to bring members together? Annual picnics, award ceremonies, and board meetings are all patterned activities that reveal an organization's culture. In social science circles, these activities are referred to as *rites and ceremonies*, and Pacanowsky in particular characterized them as *organizational performances*. The social science terms are interesting for their framing of activities as performative events with distinct social scripts that temporarily engage members in a shared conception of the culture. In other words, these are more than just functional procedures—they are communications designed to synchronize members and reinforce an organization's cultural life.

Put more plainly, the customs and conventions of an organization offer useful clues to the observant visitor. Here is a list (from researchers Harrison Trice and Janice Beyer) that we can use to find out what's valid and valued in an organization:

- What are the prescribed means of *conflict resolution*? Do they vote? Look to senior management to make the call? Bargain and negotiate? Or ignore and deny problems?

- How do they mark changes of status or role in the organization? Look for *rites of passage*, such as hazing or retirement dinners, or parties.

- Every organization formulates clear ways to disavow and punish members who act outside of the organization's value system. *Rites of degradation*, like the Army's dishonorable discharge, are public statements of disapproval.

- How does the organization publically reward those who strongly demonstrate organizational values? Best teacher awards, employee of the month, and top sales awards are all *rites of enhancement.*

- How do they reinforce the sense of community? *Rites of integration* can include the softball team, annual picnic, or community service events.

- How does an organization invest in its culture? Training, retreats, and even English language classes are all *rites of renewal.*

The "Organization as Culture" framework supports a holistic look at organizations that can powerfully inform creators of The New. As Pacanowsky and O'Donnell-Trujillo note, "Organizational culture is not just another piece of the puzzle, it *is* the puzzle." If an organization is to accept and help nurture The New, it must be considered as more than the sum of its parts. This analysis may not uncover specific tactics, but it will help your team grasp the relevant cultural intangibles (values, identity, ideology) and the means (expected language, decision-making processes) to bring The New into widespread acceptance.

SEGMENTING AND TARGETING CONSTITUENTS

As creators of The New, we have a tendency to under-include stakeholders and constituents in our development processes. We do this for a variety of reasons—all of them reasonable but not good enough to continue this practice. In the course he teaches at the Institute of Design, strategist Tom Mulhern lists common excuses for under-including constituents:

- It's more work, both for us and for them.

- They don't have the time to be engaged; that's why they hired/tasked us.

- Exposure to the organization will corrupt the "beginner's mind," polluting the effort with everyday business baggage.

- Early inclusion violates cultural norms—that's not how we do things around here.

- We risk involving the wrong stakeholders.

- We risk engaging too intensely too early.

- We don't have the skill set or training to engage others.

Without a doubt, managing constituents adds complexity to the already challenging process of creating The New. So it's tempting to limit the number of people we consider and include. However, connecting the right constituents to the work—especially early in the process and with greater frequency—increases the odds of our success. It's an effort we must make. What's missing, then, from our toolkit is a more strategic way to target constituents for communication and more diverse and effective ways of connecting with them, so that our time and effort produce better results.

GETTING ORGANIZED: PEOPLE, OBJECTIVES, AND COMMUNICATION MODES

As we set out to communicate The New, we need to pick and choose which constituents to engage when. And for each type of constituent at each stage, we need to make deliberate choices about how to engage. For simplicity's sake, constituents can be thought of as clustering into three concentric rings.

Development team—core stakeholders

It's easy to overlook the development team—the ones responsible for catalyzing, creating, and communicating The New—as a stakeholder group. Yet they are important individuals to consciously consider. Communication is central to the creation of The New, and conscious communication across the core team is essential. This team is defined as active participants who have continuous involvement in, and a formal responsibility for, producing The New. A good team is typically cross-disciplinary and has a solid base of subject matter experts. It's critical that the primary communication mode of the core team be highly *collaborative*. Many of the communication techniques presented in the first half of the book are intentionally selected for their support of collaborative communication and development processes. These methods also advance the overall communication needs of this stakeholder group: achieving clarity of vision and alignment around that vision, in addition to developing the work.

Larger working team—the inner ring

The larger working team typically includes organizational representatives whose expertise

Segmenting constituents for The New

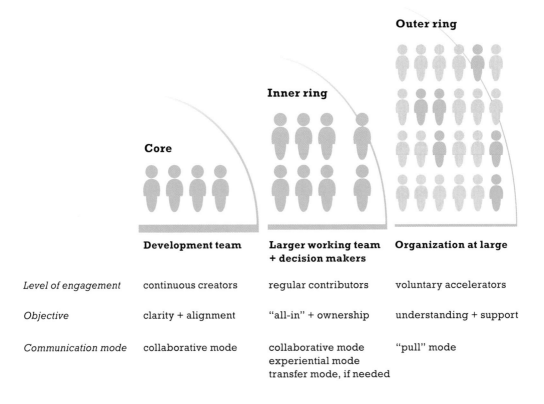

	Development team	Larger working team + decision makers	Organization at large
Level of engagement	continuous creators	regular contributors	voluntary accelerators
Objective	clarity + alignment	"all-in" + ownership	understanding + support
Communication mode	collaborative mode	collaborative mode experiential mode transfer mode, if needed	"pull" mode

should be included or will be required by the project at some point. Take a page from the innovation experts interviewed for this book and think expansively about this group. Our objective is to make them active participants and ensure they have skin in the game. We want their energy, experience, and commitment. If they touch the product or

could touch parts of the product at any point, they should be included in the larger working team:

- Sales people (they won't sell what they don't know or understand)

- Supply chain people (critical sources for tips and reality checks on what's possible)

- Brand, packaging, and retail people (they know what's out there and will need deep knowledge to help your New appear—well—*new* in the world)

- Marketing and IT (these are propagators and enablers of The New)

To achieve our objectives, the dominant communication mode should be a measured mix of *collaborative* and *experiential* (see Chapter 4 for ways to do this), to allow for engagement, investment, and self-persuasion.

Funders and sponsors—also inner ring

It's an unfortunate and common reality that funders and sponsors, who are essential to The New, are typically treated as passive and peripheral to the process of creating it. They tend to be included only occasionally, typically later rather than earlier, and positioned as consumers rather than producers of the work. Given their stature as gatekeepers, their role as financial stewards, and their formal responsibility for The New, this dynamic is a problem. Our communication objective is to have them all-in, with deep belief in the work, and connected emotionally and intellectually to its promise. In other words, treat funders and sponsors as you would members of the inner ring, or the larger working group. This suggests, in contrast to current practice, that funders and sponsors also be connected to the project primarily through an *experiential mode* of communication.

Organization at large—the outer ring

It's important to consider that the organization at large has little overt stake in our New, and yet we need them. There are individuals in the organization who have expertise we need, or passion and energy we want, or connection to other projects and individuals that relate to our work. They are also de facto gatekeepers: Many of them have, directly or indirectly, the power to say no to our New. Our communication objective for these constituents is not to have them "all-in"—that's neither essential nor practical—but rather to entice them to be partially in, partially engaged. This means we need ways for these people to self-select as stakeholders. This requires a different communication mode, one leaders of The New such as John Seeley Brown have characterized as a *pull mode*. In pull mode, we seek to be worth someone's time and to draw him or her in by being relevant and interesting (see Chapter 5 for ways to do this). In the context of communicating The New, this means we communicate and share information and artifacts of possible interest to the entire organization, and use them to attract individuals with relevant experience or with social networks that might accelerate development and acceptance of The New.

1. Think EXPANSIVELY about who might qualify as a constituent for The New.

Economic and political realities can cause us to privilege decision makers and funders over the myriad of others who are required to make The New work. This is shortsighted. Birthing The New can be a solo act, but raising it to maturity takes a village. It pays multiple dividends to alert and engage a broad set of constituents early on, if possible even on day one. Don't presume they will care—it's our job to establish the relevance of The New—but do take care to think expansively about who might provide relevant inputs to the process and who might be a carrier of The New later on.

2. Connect to your stakeholders: Who are they, what are they up against, what's relevant to them?

At a minimum, invest an hour, alone or with your team, thinking in an orderly way about the circumstances of the people whose time and talent you need. Put yourself in their shoes, and think about their roles and pressures. Better yet, get out and talk with them directly, using semi-structured interviews—open-ended enough to learn that which you don't know to ask, but also structured enough that you use a few key questions that allow for comparison across stakeholders. Or take a page from Andy Parham's book and invite them to a neutral place to talk to you in a more collaborative context. In all of these efforts, setting aside your agenda and listening to others not only shows regard, it also opens important channels of communication and exchange that you will need later.

3. Size up biases, orthodoxies—including your own— and don't presume these are all problems.

Everyone operates from mental models, biases, and assumptions that often go unrecognized or unquestioned, and can limit new ways of thinking. So even an hour spent in a structured evaluation of mental models and biases can put these invisible barriers in the foreground, allowing teams to reckon with them in a more deliberate fashion as they create and communicate The New. Not all orthodoxies are problematic or worth challenging. In fact, operating standards or areas of obsessive focus inside organizations are often critical to success and coherence, and are not always barriers to change. As Melody Roberts notes, one art of bridging The New is knowing which orthodoxies to build from and which ones to challenge. But you can't figure out which models are useful if you don't know what they are in the first place. Invest the time to size up the "givens" that stakeholder and organizations rely on.

4. Target stakeholders and constituents with the best communication mode

Not all stakeholders are alike, nor do they all need the same connection to The New. It pays for every communicator of The New to learn to operate fluidly across diverse communication modes, in order to create the optimal level of engagement for each constituent group. Most communication is focused on only one mode—the "transfer mode," which depends heavily on presentation. Presentation is a blunt instrument, and seldom well suited to the kind of engagement we need with our constituents. As Tom Mulhern observes, "Presentations require us to talk before we have listened. It is hard in a presentation to avoid the metaphor of selling—an idea, a story, a belief. This is the least powerful position to be in." In the first two chapters of this book, I have introduced a number of approaches that I would characterize as "collaborative mode." These are best suited to the core and inner-ring constituents. In the next two chapters, I will introduce specific ideas for how to function in "experiential" and "pull" modes, which are particularly well suited to middle- and outer-ring constituents. If there is one thing you take away from this chapter, I hope it is that the constituents and related communication objectives should drive your communication mode, not the other way around.

4
Introduce
new thinking

EXPLORATORY EXPERIENCES

IMMERSION EXPERIENCES

INTERACTION EXPERIENCES

APPLICATION EXPERIENCES

EXTENSION EXPERIENCES

Create emotional and intellectual engagement with the work.

Incubate new thinking in others.

Build belief, conviction, and ownership.

Establish relevance, potential of The New.

It's never enough just to tell people about some new insight. Rather, you have to get them to experience it in a way that evokes its power and possibility. Instead of pouring knowledge into people's heads, you need to help them grind a new set of eyeglasses so they can see the world in a new way.

—John Seeley Brown

It's time to step away from the projector. Slide presentations are standard operating procedure in most organizations, and their ubiquity is one of several reasons we should strive to limit their role in communicating The New. To wrap new thinking in conventional communication practices diminishes the novelty of the work because the experience model is too familiar and overused. It invites others to slip into a correspondingly conventional mindset, and it encourages them to engage in *their* conventional behaviors around presentations, including managing their e-mail instead of paying attention to you. It's time, instead, to get people out of their seats and into an experience of the work—an experience that reveals detail, showcases novelty, and *earns* their attention.

Our mission at this stage of communicating The New is both to demonstrate new thinking and to incubate that new thinking in others. We do this because we need to expand the network of people who believe in our work. We need others to add to our work to bring it into reality. We need to move our concept through the organization, and we need to do so in ways that build alignment and create "all-in," not buy-in. We need to preempt the power of no, because, as Michael Winnick notes, there are many more moments and reasons to say no to an unfamiliar and possibly challenging proposition than there are reasons to say yes to it.

But to conceive of this moment, as so many in industries often do, as "delivering" the work or as "selling" the work, is to misidentify the challenge and to court failure. The path to success is not to persuade others—persuasion often dissipates in the face of new facts or hard decisions. The path to success comes from experiences that allow others to persuade themselves.

This is the moment when The New can start to diffuse into the organization. To do so, it needs to break out of the everyday and to foster not just intellectual but emotional connection. Active experiences have the power to demonstrate new thinking in ways that are fresh (but not phony) and that enlist and bridge (rather than deliver) others into important aspects of the work.

HOW TO DEMONSTRATE NEW THINKING? BREAK WITH CONVENTIONS AND CREATE EXPERIENCES

In this section, we explore ways a team might break with convention and demonstrate new thinking using a *design for experiences* approach. Experiences turn audiences into participants and bridge them into important aspects of the work, in ways presentations and conventional reports cannot. Michael Winnick sums the difference nicely when he notes that "One of the big challenges in our work is that deliverables don't really matter that much. It's not about having a prototype, it's about *prototyping*. It's not about having a research deck, it's about *researching*. It's not about having an idea but *ideating*. I believe that everybody learns experientially. But I think particularly adults learn through experiences. And so I would rather figure out a way for you to make the connections—including some that I want you to make—than for me to make those connections for you. That will build your conviction around what to and what not to do."

The notion of experiential learning is not new, and educational theorists tell us it's unarguably an effective mode of education. But the practice of experience design in organizations has not yet matured into a set of methods and techniques. For this reason, even teams who value the concept of experiences as communication don't always know what experiences to create, how to create them, and when to roll them out. In research I have pursued with my Institute of Design colleague Anijo Mathew, we have developed a preliminary typology of five experience models that we believe will help fill this gap. In this chapter, I offer examples and suggestions for applying each of these five models for experiential engagement with The New:

- EXPLORATORY EXPERIENCES
- IMMERSION EXPERIENCES
- INTERACTION EXPERIENCES
- APPLICATION EXPERIENCES
- EXTENSION EXPERIENCES

WHY—AND WHEN—TO STEP AWAY FROM THE PROJECTOR

Conventional practices in communication are not up to the task of communicating The New because they were never designed to do so. Conventional practices, such as presentations, emerged out of the academic context and were the tools experts used to communicate with audiences of a similar background. I use the term "academic" here in a general sense, referring to experts who share a similar frame of reference, level of knowledge, language, and professional objectives. In this context, the role of the presentation is to expose primed audiences to new information, transferring knowledge from one expert to another.

Today this technique is used by nonacademic presenters in an expanded number of settings, with greater frequency and to much more diverse audiences in terms of their shared frames of reference. While the context for presenting has clearly changed, our communication conventions have not. Why is this?

Often heard but not seen: The "transfer" model of communication

Lurking beneath the presentation format is an unexamined, but problematic, model of communication. Communication theorists tell us that we all act according to implicit models of communication that direct our behavior and shape our expectations. The most common of these is the *transfer* model, in which we presume that knowledge can be packaged up and transferred to others through exposure to carefully selected (by us) words, diagrams, and maybe images. Our receivers, then, will unpack or decode our meaning and reconstruct it with high fidelity as we intended.

The myth of information "transfer"

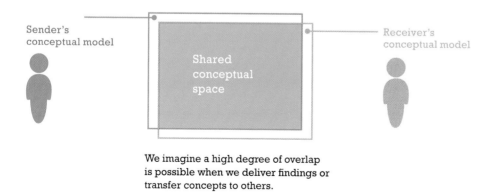

Sender's conceptual model

Shared conceptual space

Receiver's conceptual model

We imagine a high degree of overlap is possible when we deliver findings or transfer concepts to others.

The reality of information "transfer"

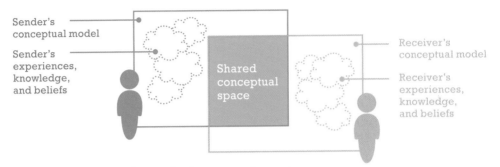

Sender's conceptual model

Sender's experiences, knowledge, and beliefs

Shared conceptual space

Receiver's conceptual model

Receiver's experiences, knowledge, and beliefs

The overlap in conceptual space is always partial and limited, as individuals reinterpret information in light of their own experiences, beliefs, and objectives, and ideas are not independent of the people who hold them.

But both our everyday experiences and extensive research across fields—educational theory, psychology, organizational learning—reveal that accurate transfer of knowledge is not just difficult, it is impossible. Our individual experiences, objectives, biases, and beliefs strongly influence how we take in new information. As a result, we do not "receive" information. We process it, interpret it, and integrate it into our own conceptual model of a given topic. In the end, the conceptual models that "receivers" have of any given topic may be quite different from what the "sender" intended.

If the transfer model has misled us to believe we can pour our knowledge into the heads of others, it has also generated a set of communication conventions that now dominate many organizations. Four of these conventions are of particular interest to us:

1. Content

The transfer model assumes a one-way information flow and suggests that we reduce information into bite-sized chunks that can be sent and received more easily. Working in this paradigm, we fall into conventions that work against clarity, relevance, and even the reality of how we use information today. We produce content that is linear in structure, and that requires participants to be present from start to finish to gain full access to the work. We reduce complex thoughts to bullet points, with the implicit assumption that shorter is better. We compress rich ideas into loaded-with-meaning words, such as "convenience" or "easy-to-use," making our ideas sound indistinct and ambiguous. We rely on abstraction representations, such as frameworks and diagrams, which require context and firsthand experience to interpret. And we include "special code," such as acronyms and abbreviations that require familiarity and shared expertise to decipher.

2. Materials

To "deliver" information we use "containers" such as slide decks, handouts, and reports. These all are designed for one-way information flow, and so encourage a fire hose of information. When we conceive of communication as a one-way affair, we must create a self-contained story that starts at the beginning and continues to the end, and include all the evidence to support the logic. As a result, decks and reports (often the same thing today) swell with content and overwhelm audience members.

3. Interactions

A one-way model presumes an active sender and a passive receiver, with interactions to match: The sender is standing, and the audience is seated. The pace of the story is set and controlled by the speaker. If audience members start to ask questions, they disrupt the flow of the narrative, and speakers attempt to take back control with statements such as, "We're getting to that," or, "Hold that thought."

4. Environment

Our conference rooms and even peripheral workrooms have been adapted to our presentation conventions. The projector occupies the central position, with the rest of the space optimized to support the projector/screen dynamic. Seats face the screen, creating a lecture-style context. Rooms are outfitted with a single projector, with a single wall as focal point for projection, and other fixtures in the room are oriented around the screen.

Over time, the reflexive use of these four conventions has generated predictable outcomes: "Receivers" have learned to pay partial attention; they come and go during presentations, they limit their input, and their passive role has allowed for selective investment in the content and the outcome. Communication conventions, then, and the underlying paradigm of delivery of information, combine to form a low-bandwidth channel with an unpredictable outcome. Although this may continue to be the only practical model to employ when exposing a mass audience to information, it is strikingly ineffective when we need to bind people to information in ways that will lead to collective conviction and action.

THE EXPERIENCE MODEL: EXPERIENCES AS STORY PLATFORMS

Experiences are a more effective model for learning because they allow participants to bring their own varying knowledge, experiences, and agendas into an exchange with new information and individuals. Adding the new experience to their existing experience allows them to exit the process with a stronger sense of the potential trajectories of the work. But just as importantly, the shared experience has created a story platform for all participants.

A new communication model
Constructed experiences to expand the shared conceptual space

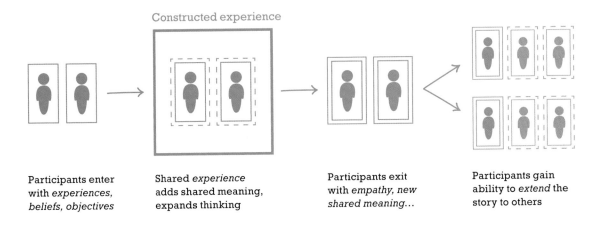

Constructed experience

Participants enter with *experiences, beliefs, objectives*

Shared *experience* adds shared meaning, expands thinking

Participants exit with *empathy, new shared meaning...*

Participants gain ability to *extend* the story to others

What is a story platform? In the context of communicating The New, it's useful to think of a story platform as the stimuli and experiences that allow others—people beyond the core group of content creators, people who in the transfer model might be considered "receivers"—to construct their own stories of the work. Because in creating The New, having passive receivers just won't do; we need engagement and "all-in." The nature of a shared experience is that participants engage with *one another* to make sense or to build on what they are seeing and doing. This dialogue typically involves participant-supplied stories, either by bringing in past experiences to connect the new work to what they already know, or by creating new narratives that integrate the new work into a new conceptualization of the topic. In communicating The New, both kinds of stories serve to bind people to the information in ways that are both logical and emotional. These stories help us internalize information in a new way, one that is more native to how we learn. These stories feed our intuition, a core source of decision making. They leave us better prepared to act on the information, to contribute to the work, or to implement some of the ideas.

And, of great use to us in communicating The New, participants can extend those stories to others in the organization who were not part of the experience. This addresses a significant issue in the experiential approach to diffusing work into the organization: Experiences have an upper limit in the number of people that can be included. To include more people requires that the experience be repeated. But there is an echo effect if participants leave the experience with strong stories about what they learned. A second-hand story does not substitute for the original experience, but it can begin to build organizational interest in and knowledge of The New, potentially adding to its uptake and reducing its rejection.

How experience models break conventions

	1 **Exploratory**	2 **Immersion**	3 **Interaction**	4 **Application**	5 **Extension**
Content	non-linear, free-form			self-organizing content	non-linear, bite-sized random-access
Materials	3D artifacts, visual and varied in scale	multi-media, multi-sensory props	3D artifacts, games	artifacts, worksheets	visual artifacts
Interactions	self-directed or small groups		self-directed, tactile, experimental	facilitated	self-directed or small groups
Environment	full-room, large-scale installations	full-stage, technology-aided	stations and work spaces	collaborative work spaces	
Good for …	rich learning spaces for iterative, self-paced discovery	simulations of user experiences or proposed experiences	experimental experiences to build new mental models	build familiarity with data via problem-solving	extensible learning experiences to help data go viral

Expanding the number of experience models

The experience models presented here were derived from three years of experimentation with graduate students at the Institute of Design. Professor Anijo Mathew and I asked our students to deliver project findings while breaking at least two of the four conventions—content, materials, interactions, and environments. Much of the work presented in this section is theirs, but we found variations of these models increasingly in use by practitioners in industry. It's also worth noting that practitioners I spoke with are using these approaches earlier in their process and more frequently throughout a project, sometimes to onboard new team members but largely to keep an expanding number of constituents staked into the project.

With an increased emphasis on experiences will come a need for more models and variations. The experience summary chart demonstrates how breaking existing conventions can produce meaningfully different experiences. If you are persuaded, as I am, that the transfer model of communication is inadequate for brokering the deep connections necessary to create The New, then we will need to advance this preliminary typology into one that is more robust, better defined, and larger in its offerings.

EXPLORATORY EXPERIENCES
Use your environment to your advantage

I think the best case scenario is that we're all in one room, and we can start at one end of the room and walk through the story on the wall, so that people can look back and see how it's all adding up. Compare that to PowerPoint, where every slide is new. PowerPoint is the worst tool for any story that needs to add to itself.

—Heather Reavey

This first type of experience uses physical environments and artifacts to create meaningful information experiences. Exploratory-oriented experiences often make use of the whole room to build a rich learning space, and can involve large-scale installations and displays of key artifacts connected to the work. The environment might be a replica of an important user context that is not easily accessible, such as a user's bathroom or a scientist's lab. Or the space might include a series of stations—zones in which one can explore and compare distinct customer segments, for example—to make abstract information tangible and touchable. Or, as Heather proposes, maybe it's a simple, spatially arranged sequence of information that's useful because it's additive and always visible, so participants can track (and backtrack on) an important narrative.

Exploration-oriented experiences break the power relationship of the conventional single-presenter/multiple-audience format. They invite participants to stand up and get out of their chairs, prompting them to negotiate the space and the information with others. This is an important contrast to the presentation dynamic. As Ben Jacobson notes, "The minute that you see somebody lean back in

their chair and take that 'I'm going to critique whatever I see in front of me' mode, it becomes unproductive. And it causes not only that person but all the other people around the table to behave differently. But it's harder to be in an assessment, pontificating kind of mode when you're standing up and shoulder-to-shoulder with other people, and it's people engaging with other people and with information, rather than people around a table. It's just different."

Artifact-rich environments are excellent alternatives for shared sense-making. They are especially useful for heterogeneous groups of stakeholders who may not be equally familiar with the project, because these environments foster group engagement with content. They generate spontaneous conversation among participants, and act as ice breakers for important conversations. Discussions around artifacts are a great way to negotiate the meaning of the content, shape opportunities for applying the content, and make enduring connections to the work.

Large-scale environments are particularly effective at helping others understand the work because they encourage browsing and self-directed learning, which is why people at Continuum and the McDonald's Innovation Center invest in spatial experiences to engage their constituents of The New. Exploratory environments allow participants to build their own story of the information. Participants can progress at their own pace, instead of having a presenter set the pace for them. Participants can stop and dwell on elements of interest or revisit information again as their understanding evolves. While exploration-oriented experiences lend themselves to guided tours by the team, the self-guided experience can also be nonlinear, free-form, because there is no set in and out point for participants. Given our Internet-driven information culture, in which information comes in bits and bytes and is ingested on an as-needed basis, this is much closer to how we use information today.

Environments built for exploration can also extend the experience across the organization.

Since the information and intelligence are embedded in the artifacts, rather than a single presenter, the environment can be used as a traveling road show. Using scale and drama, these environments also function as attractors, drawing attention to projects inside hallways and offices, and helping disseminate information and create buzz across the organization or community.

LARGE-SCALE INSTALLATIONS CREATE FOCUS, DRAMATIZE PROGRESS

■ Experiential environments support self-directed exploration, but also guided tours.

Courtesy of Continuum

Artifacts and large-scale installations invite casual browsing.
■ They don't need to be expensive productions to create a rich learning environment.

Continuum relies on full-scale environments made of low-cost foam core to help clients experience a future in a realistic way. The environments allow Continuum to experiment with ideas in a flexible way and help clients to learn, role-play, and "feel the future." The low-resolution finish reminds participants that the outcome is still emerging. Taken together, the scale and the "sketchy" quality invite feedback and contributions, inviting participants to have a say in their future.

SEQUENTIAL ENVIRONMENTS
SUPPORT A RICH NARRATIVE

Artifacts act as attractors, drawing attention to projects inside the organization.

Small, focused stories are easy to sample and digest, and add dimension to the overall experience.

Participants can explore at their own pace, build their own story of the information.

This fifteen-foot installation tells a research story of ideals versus realities for mothers, in getting dinner on the table every night. Every artifact on the wall is double-sided. The black and white side offers information on how study participants perceived their role in cooking, which often referenced 1950s ideals of motherhood.

The colorful side shows the actual behaviors and conditions of study participants around dinner. The whole installation showcases the language, artifacts, and tactics of the mothers in the study, putting participants in contact with the raw consumer voice so they can draw their own conclusions.

Work by Jim Horner and Miguel Cervantes, with Professor Kim Erwin advising; photos by Miguel Cervantes

MODULAR ENVIRONMENTS LETS PARTICIPANTS "NIBBLE" AT DATA

Removable "fact" panels can be brought into meetings and ideation sessions.

Large-scale panels invite groups to engage together, and can generate spontaneous conversation among participants.

Participants can dwell on details when they need to.

Each of these portable panels defines a weight management strategy observed in research participants around food preparation. Put all panels together, and they offer a new behavioral segmentation model. Life-size photos keep the people real, while smaller, removable summary panels put facts and insights into one place. Summary panels can be taken off and into team meetings for ideation. They also allow participants to compare and contrast weight management strategies, putting all the information in view at once.

Work by Amanda O'Grady, with Professor Kim Erwin advising; photos by Miguel Cervantes

IMMERSION EXPERIENCES
Use technology to transform the experience of your content

Immersions leverage conventional technologies in new ways to create high-sensory experiences of the information. Projectors, laptops, whiteboards, prototypes, and speakers—standard equipment in most office environments today—can all be repurposed to heighten participants' experience of the information. Immersions can also create intense, shared experiences that drive work deep into the collective memory of the group.

Immersion environments are particularly useful for their ability to simulate experiences that are important to grasp but can be hard to record or participate in—a mother's nightly guilt and pressure around feeding the family, or the delight at finding local information while on a commute. Conventional technologies, when combined with powerful content and a bit of set design, can bring participants into a visceral, not just an intellectual, experience of discovery.

Immersive experiences depart from the conventions of bullet points, presentations, and reports by transforming the materials into multisensory media and props: Two projectors side-by-side can tell stories that one projector cannot. Images can be informative and intriguing on their own, but combined with sound and print they can be even more so. Using a projector on a whiteboard, so that others can "write" on the pictures, can open up new ways of playing with information. All of these work by bringing together multiple media and multiple technologies to flood the senses with parallel channels of information. The objective is to activate the memories, emotions, and senses participants instinctively use to navigate the rest of the world, but which are so rarely engaged in organizational life.

Immersive environments are useful when trying to bring constituents into a future state that does not exist yet—simulating the use case for a new mobile technology, for example. Immersive environments can also reconstruct a state that stakeholders cannot experience firsthand: negotiating emergency room care or shopping for a car online in between shepherding kids to their activities. In both cases, participants in immersive reconstructions of events can project themselves into the situation, building empathy, because the environment triggers their own similar experiences. And, in both cases, the resulting intensity of experience can be a powerful transition to understanding.

Simulations and recreations also have extended impact. They become story platforms for participants who've experienced the immersions together—the shared experience becomes a concrete, shared reference point for later conversations. This is useful in binding people together in ways that conventional presentations often don't. In addition to this, participants will also have their individual story of the experience, one they can share with others inside the organization. Immersion experiences can build word of mouth, a powerful primer as new concepts start their journey into the organization at large.

MULTIPLE PROJECTORS CAN
BUILD A DEBRIEF ENVIRONMENT

Work by Alisa Weinstein, Helen Wills, Russell Flench, and Jeff Hsu for WorldWatch's Nourishing the Planet project, with Professor Patrick Whitney advising; image by Russell Flench

If you can't step away from the projector, why not use two or three? For this team, the topic was the state of crop management innovations in developing countries. For data collection, the team asked researchers with extensive experience on the ground in the developing world to bring their photos and tell stories of time spent with local farmers. The development team used three projectors simultaneously, projecting onto large white sheets of paper, on which teammates took notes about the stories, discussion, and insights around that image. The result was a visual history of the conversation. The projections allowed images to persist and to be referenced, even as the storytelling moved forward. The large paper notes became visual, portable transcriptions that captured the discussion for later use by the team.

MULTIPLE MEDIA INTENSIFY
THE EXPERIENCE

Even low-resolution set design can add emotion and intensity to the experience.

Sound, print, and projection come together to create a multisensory experience.

Work by Tim Miller and Scott Mioduszewski, with Professor Kim Erwin advising; images by Miguel Cervantes

Presentation-as-theater is an existing paradigm that can lead to overblown and awkward experiences, largely because it's used to inflate weak content or, worse, it has nothing to do with the content. In communicating The New, this is not our typical condition: Our content is rich and full of stories that need to stand out in a busy organizational environment. In this context, a bit of theater can be of use provided it's tied to the information (no dry ice or dancing girls). In this case, a design team used multiple media to create a more realistic context in which to present its research findings: large printouts of quotes from study participants; simultaneous voice recordings of those participants describing their guilt, anxiety, and frustration around meals and motherhood; and a projector to layer on facts and focused information. This multichannel delivery is also useful in creating visual and auditory reinforcement, which is helpful to people encountering new or unfamiliar information.

MULTIPLE SCREENS HELP PEOPLE EXPERIENCE THE FUTURE

<----------▪

Concepts designed for use in a special environment come alive when that environment is shown.

Work by John Vollmer, Jared Allen, and Jennifer Lee, with Professor Anijo Mathew and Oscar Murillo, Microsoft, advising

Prototyping new solutions is a great way to bring others into the future. But looking at a prototype without the context of use tells only half the story. These design teams used multiple projectors to create a low-resolution, theatrical set in which to show their proposed ideas in use. The sets, composed of real images of the people and places they designed for, helped the team inject much-needed reality back into their simulations of the future. The added concreteness also helped participants to imagine themselves in the proposed situations of use, permitting more

engagement with and evaluation of the concept. Simple additions like this help advance the logic of The New, creating clarity and believability.

Sometimes what makes a concept great is the rich interplay between components and people. This experience let participants witness that interplay: On the right, we see three live video feeds of different types of users. In the middle, we see a demonstration of the concept as a user might see it. On the far left screen, we see a system diagram showing all the technologies used in the concept and the current position of a target user in that system.

Work by Keta Patel, Diego Bernardo, and Adam Panza for Memorial Sloan-Kettering, with Professor Anijo Mathew advising

INTERACTION EXPERIENCES
Use tools and games to bring hands-on learning to the experience

Hands-on interaction experiences permit participants to get familiar with new information by physically interacting with it, and with one another. The interaction can come through games, tools, or prototypes—all of which encourage experimentation and give participants the chance to get comfortable with information in stages. Self-directed experiments establish a deeper connection to the content, as participants are building their own mental models of the subject area.

Using hands as a means to learning and thinking can be a powerful alternative to linear, analytic reasoning. Learning experts call this kinesthetic, or tactile, learning, whereby learning comes through doing. "It's the kinesthetic that actually has the greatest memory associated with it," says Dev Patnaik, who consciously sizes up his clients' learning styles when working with them. "Kinesthetic experiences are inherently tied to moving your body and therefore tied to your emotions, so you'll remember the emotions that you had at the time you learned that lesson." By playing with information and ascertaining what might go where, participants can develop personal models of where a concept is heading or should go. The experimental nature of interaction also allows participants to test and refine their understanding, evolving a complete enough picture so that they might also evaluate their own role in the future of the project.

Interaction-driven experiences are also highly social. Because they occur in a shared space, these experiences bring people together in ways conventional communications don't— experimenting with tools and games in a

group setting or at stations helps get the right conversations going, and lets participants engage in shared sense-making. This is useful when the goal is to spur plans and actions that require shared vision and shared effort to execute.

Interactions can also be used to build empathy with users. For example, Gravity Tank designed an experience for a client team that was mostly men. Martha Cotton explains:

We were trying to help them understand the experience of women's shoes—not only how high heels feel, but the role that heels play in how women "perform" themselves. For example, one woman we interviewed was a teacher in Moscow, who wore 5-inch stiletto boots on her commute but then changed into flats for work. Commuting in Moscow is tough, can take up to three hours and involve many modes of transport. So we bought pairs of size 11, 5-inch strappy sandals and had our mostly-male clients walk around for a half hour. It was instructive for them to see how they changed their posture and gait wearing heels and, of course, experience the pain. Now they know how Russian women's feet feel.

TECHNOLOGY CAN SUPPORT
HANDS-ON EXPERIMENTATION

A dry-erase marker with a projected image can demonstrate the results of a simple decision, such as how a one-dinner shopping list plays out in the store (in this presentation, the next image showed the circled items in the context of the store aisles—demonstrating that it's a long walk to dinner!).

Work by Tim Miller and Scott Mioduszewski, with Professor Kim Erwin advising; images by Miguel Cervantes

Putting stakeholders inside an experience through hands-on interactions can create a different path into important work: one that is more concrete, delivers more nuance, and can be welcome relief from highly verbal, analytic reasoning. Experimentation puts participants in control, and tends to prompt questions and open-ended thinking, rather than criticism. It invites participants to imagine with you. A simple whiteboard with a projected image can become a dynamic medium when combined with a dry-erase marker. An interactive PDF can simulate what it's like to use a complex information system or a new device.

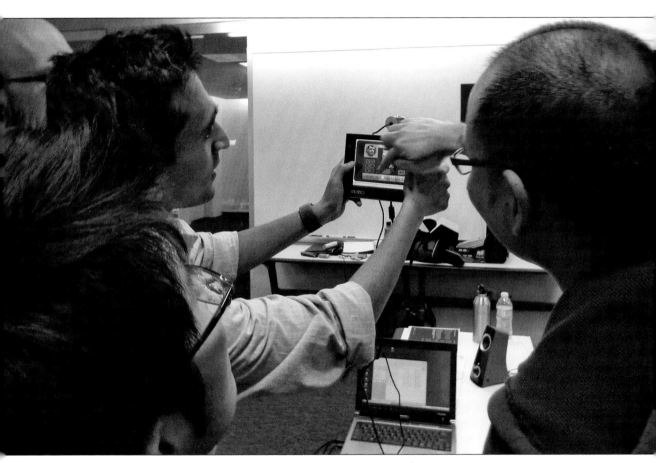

Work by Thom van Der Doef, Kshitij Sawant, Mo Chang, and Jerad Lavey, with Professor Anijo Mathew advising

Even a rough technology demonstration can feel novel and cutting-edge. Here the demonstration shows off the most important interactions of a proposed design, including how augmented reality—the real-time combination of virtual and physical worlds—might enhance the user experience.

GAMES CAN DRIVE STAKEHOLDERS
DEEPER INTO THE DATA

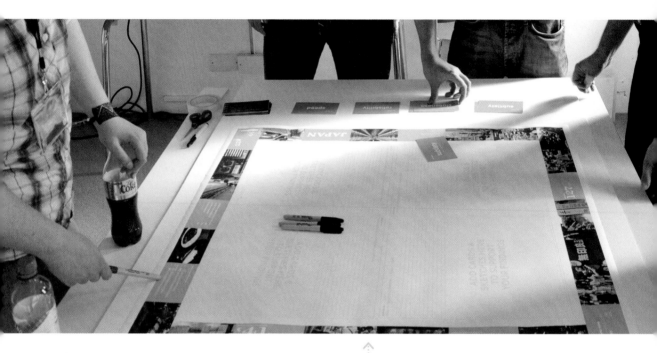

For stakeholders who need to understand core discoveries but can't partake in the research phase, games are a way to catch up. Games create contact points between stakeholders and the work by asking players to make decisions or plan their moves. To solve even simple games, like the matching game shown here, participants must head into the data for guidance. This drives participants to internalize information in ways a presentation cannot. And because games are typically played in groups, the structure provides a platform for discussion and dissection of the information that becomes a shared perspective. While not everyone may be in agreement with each other, everyone leaves better informed, more connected to the project and the team, and better prepared for later stages of the work.

Games build familiarity with large amounts of data—this is one of five game stations, each of which addressed the facts of a specific market—and let players teach themselves about what's meaningful in the data.

Photo courtesy of Gravity Tank and © Skype

A simple matching game can drive participants into data in ways a presentation cannot. Short stories introduce each user, providing context about their lives and mindset. ■ ·······················>

Players must match the quote to the user, getting familiar with their stories. ■ ·······················>

Once quotes are matched to the right user, the stories are complete and participants know just a little more about their customers as individuals. ■ ·······················>

Work by Katherine Gabel, with Professor Kim Erwin advising

CONVERSATION SPACES CAN
OPEN UP NEW THINKING

Every table has content to
stimulate and focus the dialogue.

The World Café™ concept is a simple, flexible conversational technique for engaging large numbers of people in dialogue. That dialogue can include topics that are highly exploratory, such as cultural trends relating to a project, or highly focused, including internal organizational issues that might be standing in the way of change.

The process rotates participants through a series of conversation tables, each of which presents a topic or question to address. Tables may have additional stimuli, such as product or consumer behavior examples. Or they may hold question sheets that every conversation group adds to. Such sheets are engaging and fun to read, and ultimately become a useful visual record of the process.

The design principles for the World Café™ format, which can be found at theworldcafe.com, set the context for reflective conversation

that engages everyone equally in the process. Principles include:

. . . create a hospitable space

. . . explore questions that matter

. . . encourage everyone's contributions

. . . share collective discoveries

How to plan a World Café™-style interaction to communicate The New

World Café™ is a flexible format, but I have evolved it somewhat to suit the challenges of creating The New. For a fuller perspective of the method, please see the website for World Café™.

Topic: Identify project challenge areas or research insights or opportunity areas that need attention.

Participants are rotated through tables, finding new topics at each station and new partners, too.

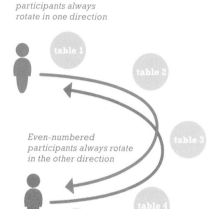

Odd-numbered participants always rotate in one direction

table 1

table 2

table 3

Even-numbered participants always rotate in the other direction

table 4

table 5

Break these into separate but related subtopics to fit the number of tables.

Timing: Conversation takes time; plan for 10 minutes at a table; six tables will take 60 minutes, plus at least 15 minutes for a group debrief.

Number of tables: Calculate tables by the number of guests. The power of World Café comes from small group rounds, with new conversational partners at each table. I prefer two to a table, but four works as well.

Materials: Each table needs a conversation guide. I often use a large worksheet with four to five questions. Each group reads what's been written by other groups, and then adds their own thinking. Broader, opinion questions are more effective at eliciting dialog.

Process: Assuming you have twenty people and five tables, each small group will have four at a table. First ask all participants to count off 1- 4 (tell them to remember their number). Ask all the "ones" to pick a starting table; ask all the twos to pick a starting table, etc. When every table has a one, two, three, and four, direct their attention to the materials and start the timer.

When the timer chimes, have the odd numbers—ones and threes—rotate right; ask the even numbers—twos and fours—rotate left. While pairs of people will move together from table to table, they will always have fresh conversation partners.

Task-oriented experiences allow individuals to engage with new content through problem solving. Workshops and toolkits are both good examples of such constructs. The strategy here is to direct participant attention to the utility and potential of the content, rather than to build familiarity or general knowledge. This is a "kick the tires" experience, where participants can test the relevance of the data to their responsibilities, and develop a point of view about its relevance to the organization. They can also begin to see what role they might play in a future state built around this new thinking.

These experiences break every communication convention at once: The content needs to be chunked and organized, rather than in a linear sequence; the process uses worksheets and artifacts, rather than slides; the environment requires collaborative spaces, not a conference table. In fact, information is not really delivered at all; rather, it is embedded into the design of the experience and the artifacts, accompanied by guidance and explicit objectives to generate new insights or concepts. The net effect is that the experience is both novel and practical at the same time.

Application experiences can be a welcome change of process because they put participants in control. Rather than designing the outcome, workshops create a context that encourages participants to interpret and apply existing information to create new opportunity areas or design ideas. This way of working shifts the participants' role from consumers of information to producers of content. As a result, participants feel greater ownership over the project and staked into its success. They

also internalize the information more deeply and are better prepared to act on it at a later date, as it moves towards implementation or funding.

This way of working can build energy and optimism, which will transfer from the working team to the larger organization. Because they helped build something with the project materials, adding to the output, the project becomes more personal to more individuals. Michael Winnick notes that workshops may not produce brilliant ideas, but they do bind people to the information, making them a powerful way to build belief. This is also a more human way to engage the collective intelligence of all stakeholders, including the core team. As Ben Jacobson says, "I get a lot more joy out of rolling up my sleeves and getting involved with people, and really understanding what they're trying to achieve, than 'here, go do this work and send me the report.' That's not the work that I really like to do, and I think a lot gets lost that way."

TOOLKITS CAN PUT DATA TO WORK

Turn interesting data into productive data by taking it out of reports and presentation decks and into a usable set of tools. Toolkits for exploration or ideation help organizations see the potential of the research and problem framing. Toolkits structure insights into bite-sized chunks that are ready to use, and they organize the content in ways that demonstrate how to use it. Toolkits also signal that the hard work of creating The New is not a one-time effort limited to a few individuals, but a repeated effort that can involve many. Toolkits can be novel and tangible demonstrations of a new way of working.

← ·········■

Test-drive the data: These three sets of rotating cards, each based on research findings, show how family objectives can be matched to family members and eating occasions to produce new product concepts.

Work by Jessica Striebich, with Professor Kim Erwin advising

WORKSHOPS CAN PUT EVERYONE ON THE SAME SIDE OF THE TABLE

Large-format posters deliver the research; removable cards provide additional findings and illustrative starter concepts.

Workshops use collaborative problem solving to create a shared mission for groups of people who may not otherwise find themselves working together. Great workshops leverage physical space and designed artifacts and tools to bring participants into a new way of thinking. Large-format work can make important information visible and accessible for ideation; structured worksheets can provide guidance and keep teams working at a productive level. Well-architected

Cards propose design challenges connected to the research; they can be mixed and matched for ideation.

What if Trader Joe's created a modular system of bases and add-ins that moms could mix and match?

Work by Jennifer Lee, with Professor Kim Erwin advising; photos by Miguel Cervantes

workshops do more than problem-solve; they build team skills and break down walls between organizational silos, creating long-term capability and organizational capacity for innovation work.

EXTENSION EXPERIENCES
Use artifacts to keep information alive

Extension experiences stretch the learning experience past any project end or presentation. These experiences might include toolkits, comic books, information cards, videos, and posters, or other artifacts that keep the information alive and usable. As such, extensions allow for *data persistence*—information collected over the course of a project can be referenced as the work progresses into implementation. They also permit *data reuse* for future projects. Extensions are excellent tools for keeping teams in touch with the initial insights and information, and for providing high-fidelity decision support as projects head into implementation or funding.

Extension experiences rely on artifacts that provide access to detailed information—research data, insights and concepts—and open up multiple entry points into that information. Traditional linear presentations are often designed to orient and organize the thinking of people who are new and unfamiliar with the work. These presentations have to start at the beginning in order to make sense. By contrast, extension materials don't presume a single narrative or a single point of view, and instead use bite-sized data loosely organized to support random-access, nonlinear browsing. Data broken down into bite-sized chunks can be "nibbled at" easily over time, aiding ad hoc moments of discovery by individuals or groups who may not have been part of the initial project. This is particularly helpful as projects progress, new questions are raised, and more detailed decision making is required.

Because they are visual and often attract attention, extension experiences make it possible for information to "go viral" inside an organization. Participants can not only carry these artifacts back to their desks, but also bring them into meetings or work sessions for wider dissemination and use.

Extension experiences are physical reminders of a project. They keep us connected to what has been learned and make it harder for us to revert to previous behavior and assumptions. As Chris Rockwell notes, "By using these more visual communication techniques, these large format techniques, these storytelling techniques, we can change a culture. We can change the culture of innovation for a company and help it make decisions that are more customer-centered. And the work can become more sticky. Insights that support innovation and strategy need to be sticky so that it changes your way of thinking every day."

BIG PROJECT TAKEAWAYS
KEEP WORK VISIBLE

■ Interesting project artifacts, such as summary posters, draw attention, keep work visible, and start conversations.

Work by Yixiu Wu, with Professor Kim Erwin advising; photo by Philipp Böhm / boehmphilipp.de

Large-scale, visual summaries of projects keep important insights out of file cabinets and in view of the team. These artifacts remind teams of what they've learned, which can prevent them from regressing to what's comfortable and familiar. Visual summaries also help teams align decisions with findings, as concepts progress into implementation. They act as evidence of The New, prompting conversations that can help new thinking diffuse organically into the organization—no presentation needed.

Project takeaways do not need high design to be effective—in fact, some organizations view all-out production efforts as wasteful, while other cultures, Nike for example, expect it. Most important are scale (for attention), authenticity (for credibility), and detail (for reference value).

DATA REPOSITORIES TO CAPTURE THE FACTS—AND THE SPIRIT—OF THE NEW

The "big binder of everything" is a low-cost, high-value reference book that helps teams put their hands on everything a project generated, from raw consumer data to insights to behavioral frameworks.

Work by Conifer Research

Finding engaging and expressive ways to communicate project data can make the work more accessible to others, and keep teams in touch with important but intangible aspects of the work.

Extension artifacts can use novel variations on traditional archiving means to preserve the context and to offer a visual memory of processes, insights, and concepts that have been a part of the development process. These can serve as important reminders later in the project or when the original vision starts to fade and compromises threaten to undermine The New.

With a bit of thoughtful design, these artifacts can get others to "feel the work," as Heather Reavey would say. While business presentations focus on evidence-driven communication, extension artifacts work to pair analytic and business issues with emotional content to remind

Unconventionally designed reports can preserve the user's and analyst's voice, and bring everyone back in touch with the human elements of the case.

Digital repositories that capture a little spirit of the project, like this one to store insights around food shopping, can keep the details—and the energy—of a project alive.

Work by Margaret Venema, Jared Allen, Junyoung Yang, and Jaesung Park, with Professor Anijo Mathew advising

Work by Shlomo Goltz and Eunkyung Kim, with Professor Kim Erwin advising

stakeholders, too, of the need for business concepts to fit the human beings who might use them.

Extension artifacts are also closer to the way we use information now—nonlinear or searchable data, chunks of information that can be targeted as needed, and compendiums that mix images, stories, frameworks, and other inputs that held promise.

To reframe "the report" as an extension artifact to support continued learning allows us to rethink the output. If the objective is rich reference material, we can consider sidestepping the long, linear presentation and ask, "What will help teams stay in touch with the raw data needed for decision making?" The answer may be something more pragmatic, or more delightful, than we can imagine today.

1. Stick to the content and skip the shtick.

Dev Patnaik talks about having witnessed an experience design for a client that included dry ice and thumping music. Hugh Dubberly recounted dancing girls and a float as part of a "brand experience." Dry ice and dancing girls are not only irrelevant, they are "lean-back" experiences that put participants into an audience mode. This might impress your colleagues—maybe—but it won't advance The New. So be scrupulous in designing your experiences to drive participants into the content, and be obsessive in avoiding shtick that is not connected to creating knowledge.

2. Expand the number of people invited.

Think ahead when considering whom to include. On the basis of his experiences at Motorola, Tom MacTavish advocates for a very inclusive approach, looking at the entire value chain to understand all the people involved, and inviting a representative from each of those functions. This is a two-way street, he says: Those individuals often introduce information and points of view that could be barriers later on if not explicitly addressed by the work. Additionally, those individuals carry away with them seed ideas that you can connect to later. Tom specifically counsels the inclusion of salespeople early in product development work, because if they can't (or won't) sell The New concept, it won't survive.

3. Low production design can offer high impact.

A common response to advocating experiences instead of simple presentations has been skepticism around the skill and money involved in creating highly designed materials. But experiences don't require costly materials to be effective. One vocal skeptic in an executive education session approached me four months later at a conference, excited to tell me that she had given up presentations as a routine team communication mechanism. Instead, she was interacting with ideas and teammates around big sheets of butcher paper, and finding that more productive and more satisfying. Ben Jacobson talks about a low-tech, low-budget "big binder of everything" that Conifer gave to a client—it included primary data, photographs, imagery with call-outs, "really just doing our best to capture all that detailed information about product interactions, packaging interactions or at-the-shelf interactions, and the higher-level stuff that basically only a marketer could love." Months later, he was called down to present again, only to discover the entire team was new. One person had inherited the binder, which "was the most dog-eared, thumbed through, Post-it-noted thing that you've ever seen in your life. She called it her Bible, and said she used it every day." The point is that both of these solutions departed from conventional practices, and neither is particularly edgy or pricey. There are practical, low-cost ways to shift your practices toward more human-centered, experiential models of engagement. What matters are the fundamentals: interaction, nonlinear exploration, task-orientation, and the creative and on-point use of artifacts and environments as repositories of information.

4. Conversation counts.

Much the way the list is overlooked as a simple synthesis tool, conversations are equally overlooked as a simple means of creating shared mindset and building knowledge. Conversations are low-budget, low-tech—and they still work. Even the associations of the word "conversation" are more accurate in their description of the collaborative interaction model required to create The New. Hugh Dubberly, in fact, advocates that we replace the word "communication" with "conversation." "Communication," he believes, is too intertwined with the transfer model to be an effective descriptor of our interactions, whereas "conversation" is more versatile in explaining the many productive forms of interaction we engage in: "Conversation is always interactive. Conversation also can take place within one's mind between two points of view. Conversation can take place with materials. And conversations take place between groups. All these scales and types have a place within design. While it may be necessary to separately describe the 'work' and the 'conversation,' in practice, the two are one. Whatever is done or made aids the conversation. Whatever is said aids the doing or making." Conversation, then, is a powerful framework for the process of creating The New.

5. Don't. Wait. Until. The. End.

Communication is not an event; it's a process. The best practitioners know this, and this is why they use experience models to engage people in the work from day one. And they keep going, adding more and different experiences around the work as it evolves. There is a cumulative effect of multiple experiences that can't be replicated in one or two larger events staged toward the end of the project. Experiences involve, engage, and invest the people you need, so bring them in early to help bring The New into the world.

5
Expand
the
conversation

COMMUNICATION SYSTEMS

PERFORMATIVE PRESENTATIONS

DEMONSTRATION ARTIFACTS

Diffuse The New within the larger organization.

Signal new thinking that is both under way and upcoming.

Help others in the organization self-identify as relevant players.

Stimulate broader organizational pull for The New.

In any creation of The New, there are moments when we need to build interest and awareness across large numbers of actual and potential constituents—for example, leaders of related business units, relevant industry partners, the salespeople, distributors, or back-office employees. These constituents are different in nature and number from the larger working team that, up until now, may have been the sole focus of our efforts. Experiences are an ideal and workable communication vehicle for the larger working team and for project sponsors because their relationship to The New and their roles in making it happen are clearer and knowable from the outset. But the wider constituency for a new idea is more diffuse, harder to identify at the outset of a project, and is generally a more mixed group in terms of their interest in the work.

When expanding the conversation, there are two main groups of constituents to target. The first are inner-ring stakeholders whose active participation and engagement are critical to success, but whom we somehow missed including earlier. This can happen either because we don't know exactly where The New will take us and therefore did not know whom to include, or because efforts to explore The New tend to begin in one organizational silo and we don't have immediate access to people in other silos who may be key players down the line. The second group to which we need to expand is those who might simply have valuable information or significant energy to contribute. These are classic outer-ring constituents. The relationship of these individuals to the work could be characterized as interest-based, rather than need-based. Even at this stage, we still may not know precisely who these stakeholders are, and they may not either. So it's important that we expose other parts of the organization to the work in ways that will help them self-identify as relevant players who need access and inclusion.

Creating organizational "pull" to attract new constituents

In open systems, such as the Internet or Twitter, expanding the conversation is always a good idea because it attracts people who have dimensions of knowledge greater than one's own. These people not only bring in their expertise, they bring their social networks and communities of practice that increase the number of parties interested in the work. This is why savvy entrepreneurs and researchers start blogs or hash tags. Doing so attracts others who *might* want to be there and *might* have something to contribute and *might* be important to the future of the work. Large organizations often have similar conditions but lack the "bat signal" to attract others when needed. As a result, leaders of The New are on their own to discover the unidentified stakeholders who might be surprising allies and beneficial in unknowable ways. Our job, then, is to create a series of bat signals to attract both of these hard-to-spot constituent groups, and to stimulate broader organizational pull for The New (for more on the concept of a using "pull" model to attract interest, see *The Power of Pull* by John Hagel III, John Seeley Brown, and Lang Davison).

And here we confront two problems with the "experiential" approach to communication that this book has been advocating so far: First, experiences are very hard to scale up—they have an upper limit in terms of the number of people they can reach simultaneously. Experiences are powerful modes of exploration and self-persuasion, but they don't scale well. And sometimes scale is what we need. Second, experiences ask a lot from others—they require participants' time and often require them to engage in behaviors that are unfamiliar and sometimes hard, and can sometimes feel intrusive because they are designed to change how participants think.

Our new communication objective, then, requires a different approach and set of communication methods.

Back to the future: Using "transfer model" tools to package The New

I've been swinging hard at the transfer model because it's so ingrained in our conception of communication that I believe we need to break its hold. And my reasoning has been this: Packaging and delivering ideas is not the route to *all-in*, or to serious participation and commitment to The New.

But, in this section, I'm going to double back to suggest a modified version of the transfer model, because some parts of it are useful. Additionally, we are not in need of "all-in" from these participants; what we need from outer-ring constituents is for them to be *partially-in*, partially engaged. Tools of the transfer model—presentations, reports, and polished packages of content—are well suited to this objective. These tools ask very little of others. The engagement, time, and attention of others are voluntary and at their discretion. And transfer tools scale well, permitting content to travel great distances and hit a large number of eyeballs simultaneously.

We can encourage and entice engagement by reconceiving "the old tools" as compelling mini-experiences or as self-propagating artifacts that are desirable and confer status on the owner. Done well, these can open the route to awareness and curiosity. They can give people something to talk about and share, and can act as a precursor to more complex experiences or decisions to come.

We can start by introducing broader themes and findings from our work into the organization. We can take interesting information streams—discoveries, trends, or problem reframes—and turn them into self-contained nuggets of knowledge. We can package and diffuse these nuggets throughout the organization separately from the solution stream, so that they have independent value. For example, on a project in the mid-1990s regarding the potential for audio distribution via the Internet, part of the communication toolkit was an unconventionally designed, pint-sized document that simply asked people to contemplate the changing nature of doing business in an Internet-connected economy. This was broadly useful in introducing others to a critical shift in business conditions. Creating multiple information streams from the work not only seeds the organization with interesting, future-oriented knowledge— getting important findings into circulation and into the minds and hearts of decision makers—it also creates multiple value streams from the work. If solutions fail to hit the mark, the team has still succeeded in diffusing a new way of thinking into the organization, and in identifying themselves as leaders and sources of The New.

How to expand the conversation to those inner- and outer-ring constituents? Here are three "old tools" that can be rethought and repurposed with new vigor to attract attention, build interest, and begin to create the organizational pull we need:

- **COMMUNICATION SYSTEMS**
- **PERFORMATIVE PRESENTATIONS**
- **DEMONSTRATION MATERIALS**

COMMUNICATION SYSTEMS:
Give them something rich and relevant

Every "new" is made up of many stories—stories of discoveries, of problem reframes, of opportunity areas, of potential user experiences, of potential strategy trajectories, of novel applications of technology, of fresh business models, and so forth. In other words, if we chose to be thorough in our thinking, we would acknowledge the obvious: There is no single "new." More accurately defined, The New is a composite of multiple "news" that comes together into something truly novel, rich, and worth talking about.

The communicator's dilemma

This multifaceted complexity, this powerful network of ideas that underlies The New, is what makes communication so tough, especially when the objective is to expand the conversation to include more diverse constituents. Knowing which facet of The New will have the greatest impact at what time and with which constituents is the communicator's dilemma. But too few individuals address this as the complex problem it is. So they fail to allocate the attention, time, and talent it requires to do well.

In communicating The New, there is no such thing as the big deliverable that does everything for everyone. But we proceed as if there is. "I think clients need to be brought along in this a little bit because I don't think they really get it," says innovation strategist Brianna Sylver. "They want one deliverable to do everything, but then find themselves ripping and tearing decks apart for different audiences internally. They're not going to the VP with a 150 page deck, you know. There they need five pages. A lot of people

don't understand that there are lots of ways to tell the same story, or that they can have multiple deliverables targeted towards different audiences."

Single deliverables are satisfying because they put all the stories in one place and typically have a story line that is chronological and so easier to organize and deliver. The problems with this approach are myriad: It doesn't think at all about the recipients of the work—what matters to them, how to make best use of their time, how to give them something that fits their objectives. And it doesn't actually save time because the One Big Deliverable isn't really relevant to anyone. So it always needs work.

And here we come to the relevant question: How do we create materials that deliver a rich but more relevant experience of The New? How can we be more strategic and effective when the stakes are high and the constituents are not well known to us? The answer is to place multiple bets. Rather than creating a single communication deliverable, create parts and pieces of the story that work together simultaneously or can be combined and recombined over time to create more effective, more focused communication events. In other words, create a kit of parts, each focused on a part of the story or optimized for a subgroup of stakeholders. And this is what communication systems do: They address the communicator's need to have a greater range of materials to tell the many facets of The New, and to do so in ways that better fit constituents.

Two ways communication systems can expand the conversation for diverse constituents:

• Create multiple paths into the work at once.

- Tailor the work for multiple audiences over time.

Communication systems as a transition step for changing how organizations communicate

Taking a systems approach to communication is merely acknowledging a reality that seasoned communicators of The New already know: To draw others into the work, we need to entice them with aspects of the work that are both novel and relevant. This requires both tailoring the content and diversifying the materials we use to engage others.

It's worth pointing out that this approach may be sufficiently novel inside an organization that leaders of The New might consider starting any change in communication practices here. It can take time to transition an organization to experience-based communications. Communication styles that are too different, or too unrelated to how an organization already operates, are likely to be perceived as disconnected from that organization's reality ("those crazy new people in R&D have no idea what we're about"). As a transition step, the communication systems examples shown here can prime organizations for larger changes in behavior, because these systems contain many of the same principles of experience-based modes of stakeholder engagement. But the experience of these ideas is smaller in scale and therefore "less different" or foreign to traditional organizational cultures. For highly traditional, meeting-based organizations already stressed by the need to respond to new market realities, or by internal innovation pushes, the communication systems approach may offer the best stretch without triggering the organizational antibodies that cause rejection of new ideas and behaviors.

This approach may be particularly well suited to organizations that have invested in innovation groups, but have not yet situated those groups in a collaborative relationship with the rest of the organization. As Brianna notes, "For an incubator-type model communication becomes immensely harder because, if they don't have that collaborative process, then it is very much a push. It's like 'hey, we've learned this really great thing and now, Business Unit A, you should really make this.' And Business Unit A is saying 'are you kidding me? I've got tons of other things on my plate, you know?'" Experienced leaders of The New know that innovation in the context of a business unit is more likely to succeed internally than innovation generated from a standalone innovation unit, because the collaboration builds important connective tissue between the work and the organization. But when that collaborative model is absent, or is under way but not yet fully realized, communication systems can begin to demonstrate new thinking in ways that get attention and at least temporarily breach organizational boundaries.

Create multiple paths into the work at once

To pitch the investment in streaming audio, Doblin created a kit of parts that told multiple stories of the potential. Each piece was optimized to explain one facet of the proposition:

The slideshow outlined the general logic of the concept.

The brochure depicted the potential product hardware and software.

The video demonstrated the potential user experience.

The planning document illustrated a strategy roadmap for development.

The "Nature of the Net" booklet acted as a white paper to educate funders on the new business conditions and behaviors of Internet-based players.

The CD was the proof repository, containing all the industry research behind the investment.

Photo by Philipp Böhm / boehmphilipp.de

Here's a common enough scenario: A team has completed its work and reached a conclusion about what's possible, desirable, and feasible to pursue. They've thought through the market, technical, and business issues, and have developed a concept that shows promise. Now it's time to secure funding and support from decision makers who have had no exposure to the work.

It's at this point that communicators of The New, rattled by the complexity of the proposition and high consequence of failing to make the case, are tempted to turn on the fire hose of facts and drown their constituents in proof-based data. This was certainly a live option for Steve Leeke, as a director at Motorola New Enterprises, when he was seeking funds to invest in a startup company called Broadcast. But working with consulting firm Doblin convinced him to take a different tack.

In 1995, innovation consultancy Doblin worked with Steve to help create an investment strategy for fledgling information technologies, particularly those that could be incubated into Motorola-sized firms 15 to 20 years out. It was an ambitious program. Together, Steve and Doblin customized a *user-centered* investment strategy—based on a massive secondary research, trend, and precursor scan—to identify what users might be willing to do in the future, and how Motorola could invest in and accelerate that future state.

One vision of the future that emerged from Doblin's work was a concept called Internet Digital Audio—a vision that became the reality known today as streaming Web content. To pitch the work to Motorola financiers, Doblin created a suite of materials that addressed multiple aspects of the proposed investment. Each piece focused on a different facet of the proposition. "It was brilliant visual storytelling," recounts Steve in an interview for this book. In addition to the core presentation, "we had a spiral handout called The Nature of Nets. We had an 8.5 × 11 fold-over brochure describing Internet Digital Audio. We had a video showing what the user experience

might be like. And we had a [strategy] brief, which I put on par with a children's book for grownups, because it was a visual as well as a textual narrative."

After the presentation, Steve received his funding: "That became a $20 million plus investment in Broadcast.com and produced, I think, somewhere in the neighborhood of $400 million, maybe $500 million in subsequent value to Motorola. And that was pretty profound. I mean we did a few other things: we did Netspeak, which was a voice-over-IP company that did Ok. I think we made two or three times our money, but we didn't make, you know, 20 times our money like we did with Broadcast.com."

Tailor the work for multiple audiences over time

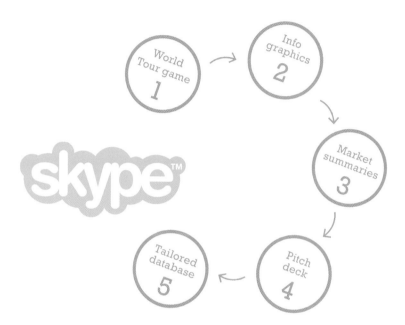

Here's another common scenario: A team has completed its work and has been given the green light to roll it out to relevant constituents inside the organization. Again, most of these constituents are seeing the work for the first time. They are a highly diverse mix—engineering teams, business managers, executives—and will be using the findings inside their silos in ways that are quite different from one another. You might conclude, as Dave Sonders and his team at Gravity Tank did for their Skype client, that the information needed to be repurposed and repositioned in meaningfully different ways, if it was to be taken up by the organization.

Gravity Tank was hired by Skype to "map the fit of Skype into the communication tool landscape," as Gisela Gier characterizes the project. At the

time, Gisela was a senior researcher in Skype's Experience Research group, based in London, and was responsible for providing insight and direction around customer needs for the Engineering group. She was also the internal project lead. "We wanted to understand what people valued about their communications tools and how the mobile experience was fitting into their communications routines." Given Skype's utility in bringing people together over large geographic distances, the team took the research global, looking at communication practices across international markets.

The output of this global investigation was "illuminating, as you might imagine," says Gisela. But how to get these insights to take root inside Skype was the pressing question.

Targeting diverse constituents

Work by Gravity Tank for Skype; photo courtesy of Gravity Tank

The World Tour game provided experiential, collaborative interactions between the design team and the research data.

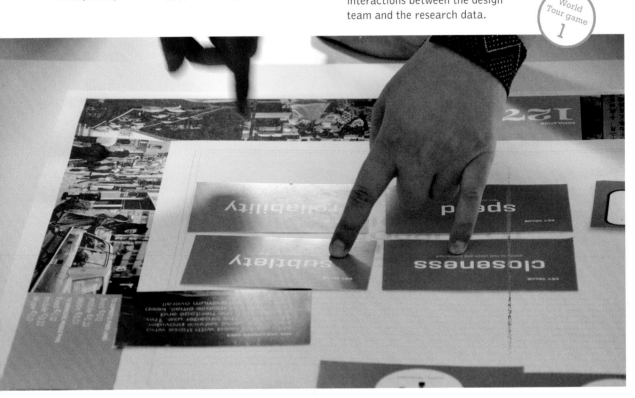

The experience design explorer (XDX) compiled all the raw research data—field notes, images, etc.—from three projects with Gravity Tank into a single digital binder for Skype's design team.

Info
graphics
2

Infographics offered focused, standalone market snapshots that made data visible, viral, and portable for marketing people.

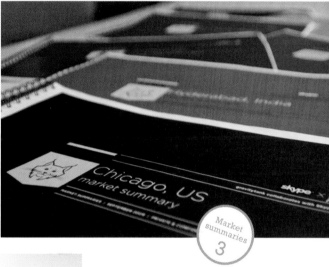

As an organization, we see the world through **Skype-colored glasses.**

Market
summaries
3

Market summaries trained regional teams in aspects of the information directly related to their domain.

Pitch
deck
4

The pitch deck framed organizational implications and opportunities at a high level for Skype's senior executives.

Stage one: The world tour game for the working team

To get the organization's feet wet, Skype flew in its design team—24 people in all—for an immersion in the research findings. To support self-directed learning, Gravity Tank designed the World Tour game, a series of game boards and question cards for each country, to drive the Skype designers into user-research data. "What I loved about [the game] was that we never had to present anything," observes Gravity Tank partner Martha Cotton, "they taught *each other* what was meaningful, and right away started them thinking 'what are we going to do about it?' And it was physically active, which I feel is a better way to learn. Nothing would have filled me with more dread than standing up there and giving a three-hour PowerPoint on each country."

Gisela agrees this engaged the group in a new way. "The World Tour tool was wonderful because it really helped discussion," she notes. "We had different tables, and we switched around so we weren't only assembled around one table. You got to sort of globe trot, if you like, throughout the whole experience, and we had conversations and we had ideas and we got to answer the questions. When you're trying to distill information and put information to teams that have not been through the process or rigor of the research or listening to respondents with you, this was a wonderful way to contextualize and to bring people into a new space—a new *cultural* space—and allow them to learn something new and fun."

Stage two: Market infographics and market summaries for regional business teams

Gravity Tank recast the core information from the World Tour game into a series of posters—or "infographics," as Gisela calls them—that depicted research findings by country. "That was wonderful because it gave us immediate, movable objects to send to regional teams. So suddenly we could involve the Business Strategy team and the Business Development teams and the Marketing teams from those specific countries, which they found phenomenally interesting. It came at a perfect time within the organization as well, as those teams were looking for budgets and they're looking for reasons, they're looking for opportunities . . . those inspiration pieces were very important as assets."

The market summaries expanded on the content of the infographics, narrating key research insights and painting a picture of how Skype's customers used Skype in each market.

Stage three: The pitch deck for executives

"After the workshop," continues Gisela, "the Design leadership team came in and said, 'Hold on, there is a bigger story here, another story we can tell the organization. There are some myths internally that we now understand through [studying] the Skype users and the Skype experience.' We used this as a pitch deck to communicate to the executive teams." What the Experience Group was pitching was an expanded role in the organization's strategy. The work had built deep knowledge of how customers were using Skype and, more importantly, how they wanted to use Skype, that could be transformative for the organization going forward.

To that end, Gravity Tank helped formulate five guiding principles for experience and design (sorry, gentle readers, those are proprietary) that could drive new products and services and help Skype achieve a stronger fit with customers. "This was our pitch to the executive team," summarizes Gisela, "We matter, you need to engage us more, this is why we matter, because we understand these things."

Gisela found herself reusing this presentation a year and a half later with a larger group of engineers, explaining again the gap between "the experienced internal reality versus the experienced reality with our product in almost 200 million connected users. It was a real eye-opener [for the engineers]. They asked a lot of questions."

Skype was purchased by Microsoft in the fall of 2011. Priorities changed, and Gisela and the project team have since moved on to other companies. But Gisela maintains that this way of working was critical to diffusing relevant project information to important constituents inside Skype: "It created the basis for many conversations and dialogues about product and product reform or product innovation. And it gave everybody who was involved in that process either the ability to push back or take forward ideas—push back on ideas that may not have been great and push forward on ideas they believed

in—because they had some basis for it. Gravity Tank's productions could direct the content to what it needed to be, to the level of information we should look at, to how we should contextualize it. They came up with the goods. And their acumen and understanding of what was of interest to Skype really showed in the work."

PERFORMATIVE PRESENTATIONS:
Give them something to talk about

Peer-reviewed studies confirm . . . before the first quarter-hour is over in a typical presentation, people usually have checked out. If keeping someone's interest in a lecture were a business, it would have an 80% failure rate.

—John Medina, *Brain Rules*

Today, most presentations are more accurately characterized as oral reports than as presentations. They are recitations of facts, analysis, and insights, and maybe recommendations—essentially written reports read aloud. And yet, presentations remain an indispensable tool for reaching a large number of individuals. The weakness of presentation as a communication method, as offered in the last chapter, is that it is a "lean back" experience—it creates a passive dynamic between the presenter and the individuals in the room. Presentations are a lot more like television in that they move individuals from active participants to a passive audience.

By contrast, performative presentations can take important content—insights, problem frames, solutions—and create an experience of them that is not necessarily participative, but is nonetheless experiential and attention getting. Think of performative presentations as a lean-back experience with a twist that makes them worth talking about when participants leave. The objective of a performative presentation is:

- To seed organizational conversations

- To create exposure (not deep knowledge)

- To offer discovery (not persuasion)

How does this work? Performative presentations inject a bit of drama or otherwise heighten the experience of the work by adding a variety of techniques to the *content*. Such techniques might include demonstrations, intriguing stories, content-driven props, or even not using a projector at all. Success in performative presentations comes in attracting attention, piquing the curiosity of others, and building interest in the knowledge. The time and attention of others is, arguably, the most precious resource for everyone involved. If we are given the gift of someone else's time and attention, we should not waste it. We must make the most of it, and earn the right to more of it.

News they can use in a form they can remember

The objective in performative presentations is to offer new knowledge that may be of interest and use to individuals in the organization, and to do so in a way that fuses the knowledge to a compelling emotional experience. Cognitive neuroscientists and psychologists (LaBar and Cabeza in 2006, and Kensinger in 2004 and 2006, among many others) have studied and validated what likely seems obvious on the face of it: Human beings have greater recall of events that are associated with heightened emotions. A wave of emotion, such as fear or anger or sadness, opens our perceptual system and sharpens our ability to focus. This was a particularly useful response in the distant past when confronted by a tiger in the open grass or even today after a close call with a bus in a crosswalk. But our emotions do not have to be extreme in order to heighten our perceptions or lock in memories. Novelty, a bit of mystery, and even anticipation can foster focus and, by extension, engagement and recall of the event. In communicating The New, successful performative presentations find ways to use emotional gateways to bind people to key information.

Intel's Tony Salvador has a passion for performative presentations. Tony is a veteran communicator of The New: He leads the company's prestigious Experience Insights Lab, which is tasked with investigating how cultures are responding and adapting to technology. This is a human-centered, data-gathering mission that takes him all over the world. At Intel, he spends much of his time explaining his findings to engineers and business units to help them form a point of view about what capabilities should be embedded in Intel's chips. Tony is also tasked with explaining his findings to industry partners to help inform a collective dialogue and vision about where technology might go and to "give them an imagination they might not otherwise have had," he notes, in considering their role in that future. Not surprisingly, Tony's job involves a lot of explaining, often in large groups, and often in the context of presentations. Given this, he thinks deeply about how to give audience members news they can use and in a way they can remember:

There's a thing around Intel where people start off a meeting by saying, 'Ok, laptops down, you've got to close your laptops.' And I refuse to say that. My rule is I hope I'm interesting enough that you will put it down. I know you all have jobs and have things to do—you have decisions you have to make. You have to make use of this information in some way. If I can understand how you are going to use the information,

then you will pay attention because it's going to be intrinsically valuable to you. I actually work pretty hard to figure out what it is that the audience wants or needs to hear, and then I try to balance that against what I need to say. And if I can actually get that information across in a way that it can get through their heads, then more power to me.

To "get through their heads," Tony thinks not just about what he's going to say, but how he's going to say it. Tony uses a variety of performative techniques to engage his audience, such as building stories around individuals known to the audience, handing out relevant artifacts, or acting out small roles to set the stage. He knows, though, that such techniques have an upper limit. "I can't do the over the top stuff. It has to be something that suits me. Nothing too schmaltzy or slick. *I try very hard to be authentic and just stick to the data, stick to the stories of the people, stick to the meaning, to not go hyperbolic, but to have a perspective and make a point."*

Tony's rules for himself create a useful rubric for all communicators of The New who might be considering a performative presentation as a path to building interest and gaining attention within the larger organization. To build on his advice, I add my own:

Be authentic to yourself.

The performance has to feel true to you, or you won't carry it off.

Stick to the data.

It's tempting to introduce false drama into a presentation—but leave the fog machines and charismatic animals at home. Drama that is not content-related may grab attention, but it is unlikely to further the work or to build credibility.

Offer a perspective.

Articulate meaning and significance, not just facts. Do the hard work of drawing out and making explicit what's relevant to the people in the room, and why.

Have a key point.

Choreograph your presentation and messages around a few specific points, rather than the whole project, and then expand on those key points. If you open up too much information to people at once, they can't make use of any of it afterwards. If individuals can resonate with one point of value, they will come back to you for more. And that, after all, is the objective!

Five ways to add something performative to your presentations:

- DRAMATIZE A KEY POINT
- MAKE THE CORE IDEA TANGIBLE
- BECOME THE MEDIUM
- CREATE A DEMONSTRATION
- USE THE PRESENTATION TO PRIME A CONVERSATION

Dramatize a key point

As a skilled communicator of The New, Al Gore has a history of elevating his message, but maybe never more so than in his presentations on climate change in the 2006 movie *An Inconvenient Truth*. For this presentation, Gore swaps his usual rhetorical strategies for a performative one. While making the case that CO_2 levels in the atmosphere are surging, he walks the audience through a full-stage line graph representing 600,000 years of carbon dioxide levels, and the correlation of those numbers to average global temperatures. When he comes to twentieth-century data, Gore hops on a hydraulic lift that slowly elevates him to the top of the screen, where the new and steeply higher CO_2 numbers peak. With this performative gesture, he makes his point—the current century's numbers are so dramatically different from those of a hundred thousand years ago that he can no longer reach them from the stage floor.

As we consider performative techniques, it's worth noting that this tactic, while theatrical, was built around fact. It was designed to dramatize one crucial point to create a larger call to action. In the course of elevating himself, Gore also elevated that CO_2 number in the audience's consciousness so that it stood out from the litany of science and other numbers. Of course all the numbers in his presentation were telling and important—but none more so than the one that required a lift to reach it.

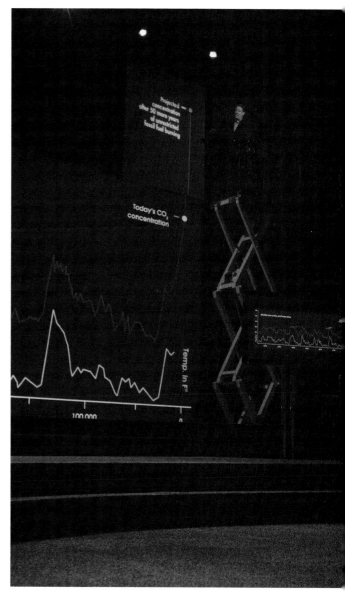

Image courtesy of Paramount Pictures

Make the core idea tangible

"Spain is a daisy"

When giving a presentation, sometimes a carefully chosen prop can open minds and hearts *and* deliver a deep idea. This is what Intel's Tony Salvador was hoping to do when he handed a daisy to every individual attending his research presentation on home life in Spain, and then declared "Spain is a daisy."

Why a daisy? In the late 1980s, Intel sought to develop a point of view about the future of technology in the home. Intel recognized that home life might be different outside the U.S., and dispatched Tony Salvador and his research team to study home life in Europe and South America. What they discovered was that home life in countries such as Spain is very different indeed:

In our observations in Northern Spain, people didn't hang out in their apartments very often. It was uncommon for people to gather at each other's homes. Yes, there was a sense of the home as being a central place that people came back to on a regular basis, and it was a center of family life, of individuals and the collected family unit itself. But people would go away from the home and then bring back to the home in various ways. That was the pattern we saw: they'd go off to school, they'd come back, they'd go to a café, they'd come back, they'd go to a little store, they'd come back. The notion of the daisy formed out of this flow of people coming and going and returning to a hub. The daisy shape itself came from modeling this behavior.

At his presentation on home life in Spain, Tony Salvador gave over 100 attendees a daisy as they entered.

Image © April Cat 2012. Used under license from Shutterstock.com

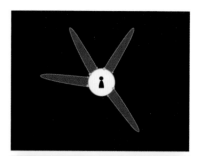

That the behavioral model for northern Spain looked like a daisy was a useful metaphor—the team had experimented with a clock metaphor but didn't feel it captured the more organic spirit of Spain—yet the giving of the daisy held more meaning than that.

In giving the daisy itself, I was also trying to give a sense of Spain—that it's a welcoming place. It's definitely a warm place, a family place. It's a place where people know each other in the street. We would look at the images that we had taken—of the sidewalks and the way the cobblestones are laid and architecture that was very flow-y, and there was definitely a gentle sense of movement that was very different from, say, Brazil. We also wanted to describe Spain in a way that had mutual resonance. We wanted the people we visited to be able to see themselves in our abstraction, and we wanted the engineers and technologists to be able to use that abstraction to generate ideas and ways of thinking about technology. And so we just sort of put the whole thing together and said why not.

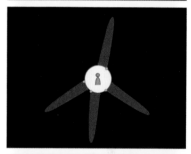

As Tony implies, using a dramatic element to better communicate the substance of your point is more than just creative—it can also be strategic. The introduction of a tangible element or prop, like a flower that represents a core discovery, is sufficiently unexpected that it can encourage the suspension of disbelief and lower the defense systems in an audience relegated to a lean-back, and typically critical, role.

Tony's slides explain the behavior patterns around home life in Spain— very different from the "nest" metaphor of the United States.

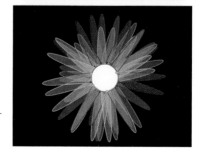

Photos by Chris Royer

Become the medium

Rick Robinson was "just responding to that really deadly tiredness of PowerPoint at conferences" when he chose to deliver his presentation via a stack of t-shirts—t-shirts he was wearing—and then strip off layer after layer to make his next point. It may help to know that Rick is a leader in the design research field respected for his quiet thoughtfulness—not the kind to take off his shirt for idle effect. His decision to disrobe on stage was not for kicks; it was driven by conviction that slides were not up to the task.

Rick was preparing to speak at the 2010 Design Research Conference, and knew he would be delivering a message that would be tough to hear. His point—that the field had been in a "methodological malaise" for 20 years as a result of seeking design inspiration in the needs, motivations, and drives of individuals at the expense of understanding the larger, dynamic systems at work—was a strong critique of the field. Coming from a person many in the room saw as a leader and founder of their field, it needed careful articulation. And Rick decided it would be most effective if he were to walk his audience through the evolution of activity and insight that led him to this radical criticism.

"In the course of working out the idea, I was thinking about that metaphor of stripping down to the basics of that idea—what's underneath it? How to show that progression? Louis Menard talks about how hard it is to simply *talk* about things that evolve or change. You really need to see them animated and in motion. Straightforward slides don't have that dynamism, and anything I could do would be really awful looking. So I decided to try something else." With

his layers of t-shirts, Rick set up a progression of ideas and showed how they evolved through a metaphoric "shedding" of the outdated ideas to reveal the newer thinking that took their place. In the process, he kept everyone's eyes on him.

He knew it was a gamble: "I think if I'd gotten two minutes into it, and everybody was dead silent, I would have been completely abashed and walked off the stage. But it started to work, and everybody was going with it. It was actually fun to do."

Sometimes conventions such as PowerPoint slides don't serve us well: They compete with us for attention, they constrain rather than enable our content, and they can shape expectations beyond our intentions about the content and thus generate a lack of engagement. Sometimes—especially when the idea is truly meant to challenge conventional thinking—it may be useful to become the medium, putting yourself fully into the story and acting out the discovery or insight that led you or your team to where you've arrived.

Create a demonstration

When it comes to describing the future, especially a future that is truly unfamiliar and substantively different from the present, a demonstration can be worth 10 presentations. Take it from Tom MacTavish, who found himself in the early 1990s as leader of the NCR lab explaining a wireless future to executives who had only known wired data communication. "We will be eliminating the data communication wire that connects cash registers to each other," Tom said, "and will instead be sending data through the air." Confusion ensued.

They said, "How are you going to do that, with light beams?" We said, "No, it's going to be radio signals." And they said, "But how can your computer interpret that? Are you going to send tones through the air?" Their only metaphor was radio—radio as transmitting sound. And we said, "No, we're going to transmit ones and zeros with a new technique." And we spent a couple hours going through the theory of what's called spread spectrum technology. But they weren't getting it.

So we asked them to come back in three months for a demonstration. We used a cart, and on the lower shelf we put a series of car batteries. And on the upper shelf we had a large circuit board and series of circuits that included a radio transmitter. We showed them the cart, and said, "Imagine this is your mobile computer." Then we pushed the cart up the hallway and transmitted a message, keystroke by keystroke, from our "mobile computer" on the cart to the desktop computer being projected in front of the executives. It was a simple message: "This is a test message from our cart." And then they got it.

That was a whole new step in our dialogue because they had literally seen us push data through the air in a way that they could understand. And it took significant engineering effort, you know, to put together this huge cart to get them to viscerally understand what we had been telling them for several months. So the experiential element allowed them to go to their buddies throughout the corporation and say, "I just saw the damnedest thing. I saw some kids transmit a text message from a cart in the hallway." But it gave them a story to tell, and it was a story based on their experience. That helps get the electricity going. That gets you your evangelist in your corporation.

Tom followed the simple rule taught to countless generations of people in creative writing workshops: "Show, don't tell."

Use the presentation to prime a conversation

What if the presentation is just a warm-up instead of the main show? This is the approach the design team at Gravity Tank took with a retail client who didn't really know who its customers were. Introducing the client to its customer base was a crucial first step, before the client could even begin to evaluate new information about those customers. Michael Winnick explains:

Looking at their own data, we found out that the vast majority of their customers were women. They were office managers and assistants. So we decided that we would bring women to life as an example of a customer group the client could focus on. In our workshop with executives, we set up a simple storytelling line: what does it mean to be a retailer focused on somebody versus anybody? We took that data and made simple slides, delivered in rapid fire, shock and awe style. Then we presented a very high quality video documentary we had made on six or seven women talking about their careers, their work lives and on caring for others. It was pretty emotional stuff, but it wasn't about the category at first. It was about their lives and expectations.

After watching the 14-minute video, the lights come up and reveal six of the women from the video sitting at the front of the room. We didn't tell them the women were going to be there. It was great because these women felt special. They were on the screen and in the room, and the clients were really curious. So then they just start talking to the women directly. It worked out really well.

Conceiving of a presentation as an introduction, or as stimuli, or as a shared experience, to inform a subsequent activity is an effective use of an otherwise narrow medium. In this example, the Gravity Tank team engaged the client executives in that conversation in person, but there's no reason that the conversation couldn't reach more people across an organization, if it were enabled online or in a series of town-hall style meetings or workshops.

DEMONSTRATION ARTIFACTS:
Give them something to show and share

Tom MacTavish's theatrical demonstration of wireless data transfer in the previous section illustrates a simple but enduring principle when it comes to communicating the "unfamiliar new": Whenever possible, show, rather than tell. Entrepreneur Judd Morgenstern, who is constantly thinking about attracting stakeholders, knows the power of making the intangible, tangible. "The best alternative I've seen to the X meets Y model is a show-not-tell model, where you start off by saying, 'Here's something interesting about what we do,' and then show them a mockup or a prototype or a screen grab. I'm told my prototype is why I, out of 1200 companies who presented, was invited back to TechStars. There were fifty ideas there that I think were very similar to *Wayla* [his project]. They told me, 'We've seen lots of competition and lots of submissions around this product space, but this was the best communicated and designed. And that's why you're back.'"

Ideas you can hold in your hand

If performative presentations are about being memorable and emphatic in driving home a core message, demonstration artifacts are about being concrete and experiential. They deliver small tastes of big concepts, and do so in ways that are physical and portable—posters, booklets, cards, and brochures. Demonstration artifacts become an idea you can hold in your hand.

What might a demonstration artifact actually demonstrate? As Judd Morgenstern points out, concepts come alive in persuasive ways when embodied in a prototype. But every project is capable of producing multiple information streams that are relevant to more areas of the business than ever get exposed to them. This is a moment to selectively package key discoveries or nuggets of information and to open a channel to the rest of the organization.

Five information streams of enduring value:

- CULTURAL CONTEXT
- TRENDS AND FORCES
- CONSUMER INSIGHT
- NEW PROCESSES OR TOOLS
- POSSIBLE FUTURES

There is an additional benefit to unbundling content from an initiative or project. It's a form of insurance for the intellectual capital generated in a project: Even if the project fails to move forward, the insights and evidence of a new way of thinking can continue to reside inside the organization.

Creating demonstration artifacts takes forethought and investment, but if your organization is not ready for experience-based communication, demonstration artifacts can promote The New in ways presentations and reports can't:

- Artifacts start conversations. In offices and hallways, artifacts attract comment and do their part to act as beacons for the work.

- Artifacts play well with traditional communication modes. Bring them into meetings or hand them out at presentations to reinforce important content that's otherwise trapped in words.

- Artifacts inspire new thinking. They often "act as triggers for innovation," says Heather Reavey. "Once you are all in a room together, you can have a conversation about them."

- Artifacts persist over time. They can stand alone because project intelligence is embedded in the artifact, not just in the people. This helps ideas endure and can start to seed changes in organizational behavior and thinking.

- Artifacts allow others to tell stories of the work, expanding the conversation even further.

This last point is important and worth expanding on. The New is best understood by the individuals who worked on its development. Members of this group own the ideas, and can use their firsthand experiences and data to communicate effectively. But when the time comes to expand the conversation beyond the working group, we need not only to expand the audience, but also to prepare and support the next tier of communicators—those outside the working group—with communication tools that they are excited to own and that help them spread the word.

Little experiences with big pull

To draw in this next group of communicators, we need artifacts and tools that are distinctive, visual, and interesting. We might call it creating *walk-by impact*, whereby individuals are temporarily drawn in by a distinctive visualization or object and, for their effort, learn a little something. And if they like what they learn, there's more there to reward their investment and time. When we draw

others into our project with interesting artifacts, we begin to create the next tier of communicators.

But to attract attention, these materials need presence. This does not mean that their presentation has to be fancy. In fact, simple and portable tools tend to be more useful. But the impact has to be big. It has to have a cool factor, so that others will not only inquire what it is, but ask if they may have one. The best of these demonstration materials become things that individuals are proud to own and so proudly display where others can see them. In short, this is the time for design.

Skilled communicators of The New already understand the impact design brings to these moments. Kathleen Brandenburg says her clients are learning, too, and are increasingly asking for it: "I know that the power of really great, smart, visual communication isn't just that it's pretty and attractive, it's that it's inspiring. Clients increasingly recognize the value in having these deliverables—not only for gaining the investment from their superiors to spend the money and invest in the project, but also for their own personal portfolios. Because it is a mobile world, and it's useful to have something amazing in your portfolio."

Kathleen, a skilled communication designer by training, knows that to successfully advocate the work internally, artifacts have to fit the organization. "In our work, those tools are co-created considering a culture's brand language and communication channels. In other words, we might make a pre-loaded, multi-language video synced to an iPad, an online and interactive project blog, and a physical campaign that inspires an internal culture to take a strategy forward. These are strategic communication decisions—getting the message and medium right is key to making ideas happen."

Good designers know that different manifestations of information allow for different kinds of interactions and learning moments; form, in fact, directs thinking and shapes experience. Done well, even traditional forms such as posters can offer fresh ways to engage others in The New—building awareness and priming others for what is to come.

Showcase cultural context

Creating The New often requires a broad and varied look at a given market for potential fit. Cultures and subcultures in those markets are critical contexts to understand. But how does one depict the findings? How do you share something as abstract and layered in meaning as the nature and values of a culture?

American clothing manufacturer LL Bean originated in the tiny town of Freeport, Maine, and desired to strengthen its brand connection to Maine's unique sensibility and way of life, as the company grew in size. In an effort to identify the DNA of the LL Bean brand, with its myriad products and services, Continuum packed up and headed out to see for itself what it's like to be a "Mainer."

What's it like to be a "Mainer"? Research into cultures or subcultures can have enduring value to an organization and inform decisions in surprising ways. Cultural context can help create coherence across offerings from different divisions, drive product selection, or tie marketing efforts or pilot programs to that target over time. Emotionally rich, large-scale posters like these can be an enduring source of value to people who were not in on the research, but need to make decisions that are deeply connected to customers.

Work by Chris Hosmer and Continuum for LL Bean

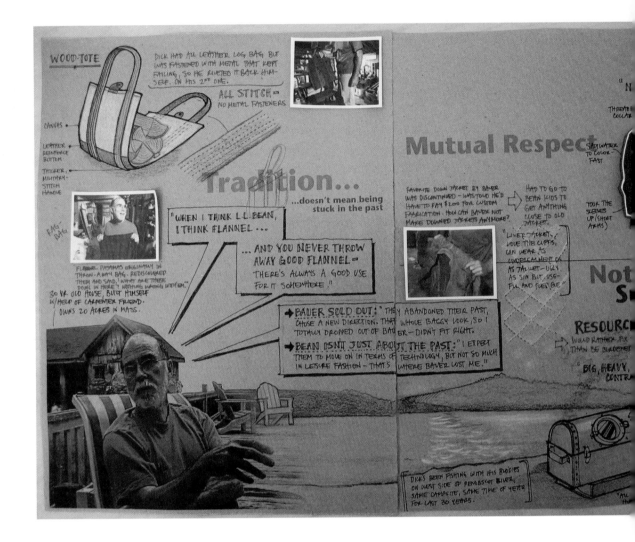

Describing a culture is not something that lends itself to bullet points, slides, and logic. To bring its field experiences to life, the Continuum team created murals that depicted facets of Maine's cultural and physical landscape—the activities, environment, homes, local ethos, and aesthetic of living in Maine. Instead of deconstructing the scene and rationally describing it, the team chose to go holistic, emotional, and visual. "Not all projects benefit from that sort of emotional sketch. Often a framework is more useful to make business decisions. But in this project it was important to communicate a feeling—a state of mind, a state of living—that you can only communicate with something like these posters," says Mike Arney, a principal at Continuum and the project manager for the Bean work. "Looking at it makes you realize there is more there than spreadsheets and PowerPoint presentation can deliver. We were asked by LL Bean to develop products that were more on-brand, and we told them to do that we had to really understand and codify the brand. In the end, because the work was communicated in a way that everyone could understand, Bean was able to use it far beyond product development. They could use it for a

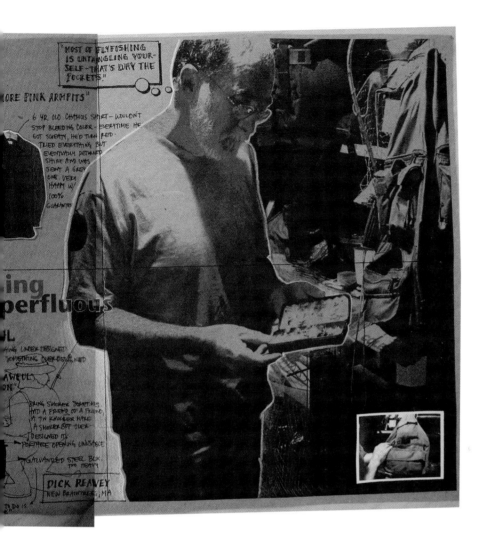

magazine layout. At one point they talked about using it to help them with hiring, and certainly for orienting new hires. The utility turned out to be much broader than they thought originally."

"We are very focused on the goal of helping our clients to engage in the research on an emotional level," says Heather Reavey. "They don't need to know everything we saw and heard, but they need to *feel* it. So a lot of [what we deliver] has some aspect of hand-drawn humanness to it. I think people are drawn to this way of experiencing information—it's so different to what they are used to looking at every day at work. And I think the hand-drawn inherently communicates emotion better than a lot of digital tools."

Capture trends and forces

© Arup; work by Arup's Foresight, Innovation + Incubation group

Creating The New typically requires that teams take a big step back from the everyday to evaluate the factors, forces, and hotspots that are likely to generate change or chaos in a given market. It's common practice to fold these discoveries and insights into slides describing the context for a proposed concept. Relegated to bullet points and background information, this valuable research stream quickly disappears from view.

What else might one do with those larger discoveries, insights, or facts that collectively create the background for The New? Arup, a global design, engineering, and consulting group, knows the power of contextual research in informing strategic practices and projects. "Change has always existed and there will always be change. It is the shifting contexts which we need to better understand—the contexts in which we have lived, are living, and will be living. The deep understanding of context is the focus of all our work," writes Chris Luebkeman, global director for Arup's Foresight & Innovation group, in his introduction to the *Drivers of Change* card set.

The Foresight group turned their powerful secondary research engine into the *Drivers of Change* program and card set. "The *Drivers of Change* program started as a way for our teams to help groups of professionals articulate what they felt was driving change in their sector. Over time, dozens of workshops were held around the world asking the same questions in the same format. The results were quite fascinating," continues Chris. What the Foresight group did with the findings is also quite fascinating: They culled recurring themes—climate change, demographic change, urbanization, water, waste, and energy—

and looked at them through the lenses of social, technical, economic, political, and environmental factors. And then they focused their powerful research capabilities on filling in this structure with stories, facts, and issues. The output of this is their *Drivers of Change* cards.

The *Drivers of Change* cards deliver macro-level research in concise and bite-sized chunks—easy to "nibble at" and learn from. The content is mind-expanding: Arup uses the cards externally with civic leaders and clients, such as mayors from growing global cities who are investing in infrastructure projects, to enlarge the conversation space and generate systems thinking. They also use them internally with their staff, to challenge their understanding of the forces that are, and will be, affecting their projects.

Macro trends, forces, and hotspots are often frame-shifting insights. They benefit from being the kind of information that is easily translated into visual, tangible, and bite-sized expressions. Card sets such as Arup's turn linear reports into modular and reconfigurable units, making complex information easier to understand and tailor to the challenge at hand. Card sets allow information to be reused, allowing discovery to become a longer-term organizational asset. Used in the way Arup does, cards can deliver small but powerful injections of raw data and insight into conversations, to expand the new space for thinking.

Keep consumer insight visible

Few organizations today need to be told to get closer to their customers. Some industries, such as technology and consumer packaged goods, have been scrutinizing customer's lives in one form or another for years. But even the most forward-thinking firms typically plan, execute, and package their consumer research at the project level, rather than at the organizational level, even though the discoveries often have implications for other projects or for the organization as a whole. As a result, valuable insights into consumers—their behaviors, values, attitudes, and mindsets—stay locked in reports and PowerPoint decks,

This insight map summarizes five recurring criteria that study participants applied to create healthy eating options. What's notable is that many participants ask questions beyond the nutritive content, including broader issues around growing practices, economics, and "soft" benefits, such as how the food made them feel after eating it. ■ ······················>

Work by Lauren Braun with Professor Kim Erwin advising

4 Does it meet my standards?

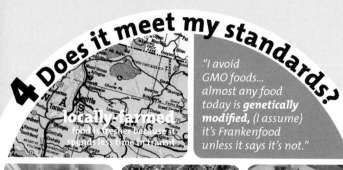

locally-farmed food is fresher because it spends less time in transit

"I avoid GMO foods... almost any food today is genetically modified, (I assume) it's Frankenfood unless it says it's not."

antibiotics and hormones are not natural

free-range chicken is better, but organic and free-range is best

plants that are *alive and growing* are the healthiest things you can eat

USDA ORGANIC

"In general, the less processed foods are, the better they are going to be for you."

While the women in this segment are concerned with the environment, their standards and values for food relate more to "is it good for my body?" than "is it good for the planet?"

Many of the study participants were busy, working moms and the chief food providers to their families. In response to this burden, they've developed rules of thumb to help them shop for groceries efficiently. For example, some described "skipping" the middle aisles of mainstream supermarkets that offer packaged and boxed items. This default mode limits their decision set to the healthier foods on the store periphery.

5 How will it make me feel?

energetic and ready to seize the day

exercise and wise food choices makes me feel *balanced*

"Before I became a vegetarian, I used to feel tired and lethargic after I ate."

When unhealthy foods occasionally sneak into their diet, the women report feeling "bad" both physically and emotionally.

3 Is it nutritious and wholesome?

after a childhod visit to a farm I stopped eating *red meat*

"I avoid crackers, cookies and fried foods for the same reason: partially hydrogenated oils. Your body doesn't know what to do with them because they're so artificial. They're supposed to be cancer-causing and heart-disease-promoting."

tofu is my other go-to protein, after fish

I look for bright-colored *fruits and vegetables*

"To keep my good bacteria level up, I keep live-culture yogurt in the house."

soda even diet, has no redeeming qualities

fish is a great source of protein and healthy fats

" I deliberately buy all-wheat breads. My daughters don't even like white bread."

2 Who makes it? Who sells it?

"The whole middle of the grocery store is a very interesting place. There are entire aisles of

never to be seen again. And as a result, research of similar topics and markets is commissioned over and over again.

Consumer insight maps put that information out where it can be seen by others in the organization. The large format allows for the inclusion of details that slides can't carry, an important benefit when projects progress, and team members need a refresher on the nuances of the work. The physical presence of posters also keeps the findings top of mind: They support casual browsing, informal review, and spontaneous conversation. Consumer insight maps act as good reminders of whom The New is for and the context into which it must fit. Insight maps can foster organizational alignment and important collaboration by attracting the attention and participation of others who may be engaged in similar areas of investigation.

To engage others, consumer insight maps and posters work best with a mix of content: the raw consumer voice for veracity, a narrative voice for orientation and meaning, structure for clarity, and visual material for context and emotional connection. To compose all this content into a coherent experience of the new data, you'll need an information designer. While this adds time and money, consider that quality consumer research is expensive and time-consuming, too, and too potentially transformative of The New to bound into yet another pro forma slide deck.

Studying the home cooking practices of 30-something mothers reveals that they alternate between "planner" and "improviser" strategies. In planning mode, study participants use their larger goals and aspirations to guide food choices, connecting cooking to objectives such as caring for family and community. In improvising mode, study participants listen and respond to their environment, adjusting their plans and working with whatever is on hand to produce the healthiest food option.

Work by Thom van der Doef with Professor Kim Erwin advising ■·····················>

Connecting through tradition

How do people plan for finding personal fulfillment through home cooking?

Observing dinner rituals

How do people plan around taking care of family and their community through home cooking?

Following the rules

How do people plan around eating and preparing healthy food?

Using what works

How do people plan around getting food on the table?

Planning time

How do people plan around their resources?

I grew up with parents who cooked at home ... we never ate out, so it is a lifestyle that is common to me.

I usually bring a vegetarian entree so that my family can eat like everyone else without being bothered for our food choices.

We really bond over the cooking process and having a hot meal together is the best.

She uses Gonnella Bread Crumbs because they are the ones her Mom always used.

Now that Blake and I have moved into together we have made an effort to learn how to cook.

Visit local farms. So many of my values are wrapped up in that one experience: female-owned, organic, rural, socially conscious, community.

It allows us to spend some time together and relax.

Sarah mentions how typical it is for her to be sitting alone and eating.

And as a wife and mom, I love providing fresh, local, organic produce for my family.

They are pretty much silent; they stay around for a few minutes and then leave Sarah to eat by herself.

While sitting at the table we give each other appreciations.

"Loose dinner times"

Sarah says she feels it is important to eat as a family - but it is really dependent on her husband's and kids' schedule.

I love this meal. I put time into it and serve with love. We normally always sit down together.

I'm from Chicago and when home this past Christmas it was crap foods galore!

I ate about 45.5 of them and killed myself at the gym to make up for it when I got back

She says she tries to offer them healthy things, but they give them hot dogs and stuff that isn't good for them to eat.

I'm not a fan of frozen foods, they creep me out...filled with chemicals.

I have control over whether or not food is organic and free of egregious chemicals that I believe harm our bodies

Sometimes labels can be deceiving.

I read labels!

substitution!!!!

I don't put anything into my shopping cart without reading the label first. Period.

I'm the most health conscious out of my friends, they are usually pressuring me to eat bad.

He says he looks at the fat content, but now it is so predictable what they buy, that they don't have to anymore.

Also, some fresh produce and other things I buy goes bad before I have time to eat it all.

Before I ever go on any vacation I always go Super healthy and crazy exerciser before the trip.

Frozen veggies: This means that whatever I make for dinner can be supplemented by a bowl of veggies that I just toss in the microwave.

They usually don't know who will be home for dinner until the last minute.

Variety. Would like to claim this but since she and her kids are busier, it's difficult to think far enough in advance.

One of the daughters is in a stage where she doesn't like meat

I think organic food tastes better, and I believe eating should be as pleasurable as well as practical.

Cooking for myself - it always ends up with me eating the same thing for like 5 days straight.

She doesn't try new things out on her family very often, because she likes to use what works.

There have been many times that things have gotten tossed because they were supposed to eat in and no one was home to eat.

Home cooking: It is important because I can control portion and money.

It really gives her peace of mind to know what they are going to have night-by-night.

Getting so crazy that she goes to McDonald's.

It's cheaper to cook at home, and I have more control over the ingredients.

Sometimes she has to stall dinner, especially when Steve doesn't call to say he's going to be late.

He says the goal on the weekend is to prepare stuff that they can eat all week long. Basically they just want to save time

Really the motivation for eating out is that I just want a night or morning off every now and then.

...prepared frozen foods that are natural and quick to prepare for the times when I don't have time to prepare something from scratch or haven't been able to plan ahead.

Maybe this is cheating, but I have learned to spend money in the right ways to make me feel better.

The Planner

In planning mode, users operate according to their goals and aspirations. They compose elements of their lives, setting the rules and structure.

Key: Women's roles

Key: Women's roles

Mom | Wife

Daughter | Single

Friend

What roles do women play as they plan and improvise for home cooking?

Key: Plan or improvise

Activities | Barriers

5 Identity: Finding fulfillment

The final stage is about finding fulfillment. Home cooking is an expression of your personal faith, and gives identity and tradition.

4 Wellbeing: Sharing the love

The next stage deals with the social aspect of home cooking. It's a way to take care of your family and community, and a way to show your love.

3 Health: Food that's good for you

Stage three is about creating food that's good for you and your family. Health, ingredients and physical well being.

2 Nutrition: Getting food on the table

Feeding yourself and your family. This stage is about nutrition. Taste, portions, energy, and preparation.

1 Resources: Managing time, money

The first stage involves managing the resources at your disposal. Shopping, saving time and money.

As vegetarians, if we went to his family's house for a holiday, like Christmas, they had steak and lobster and we were given a baked potato and a side salad

You shouldn't deny yourself, it just makes you angry. [...] But if I feel fat forget it, I won't go near anything bad.

They throw out a lot because they just aren't a family who eats lots of leftovers.

"OK, WHAT do you guys wanna have?"

She talks about making her husband a bowl of salad to keep in the refrigerator. She says there is a good chance that he won't eat it, but at least he knows that he sees she made it. It makes him feel 'more a part of the family.'

The "Dad twist" to mac and cheese by adding fried ham.

Ava gets a call from a friend wanting their picky 6-year old to spend the night. The rest of the family eats one thing and she eats hardboiled egg, peanut-butter crackers, apple and carrots.

She makes them eat at table, they eat on TV trays when she is tired.

I can buy the big size bag of carrots etc at the store and then measure and pre-bag a weeks worth of veggies into these small bags! Then its just grab and go.

Sarah doesn't think that the kids watch what they eat; but she doesn't try too hard to influence them because she doesn't want them to rebel

substitution!!!!

The family eats turkey tacos and turkey burgers because it is healthier for the family and the kids don't care about the difference between beef and turkey.

Vegetables and kids: it would be a huge battle to get one bite.

Little Alexis and Ariana are given "hold-over" snacks (fruit) to appease them until dinner is served.

"But Arbys really isn't that bad."

Lack of freezer space

"If he doesn't eat what I've made, he'll make easy mac."

The kids get antsy before the food is ready, and begin to hover around the table and complain.

She says she tries to offer them healthy things, but they give them hot dogs and stuff that isn't good for them just to get them to eat.

They "lied" to their oldest daughter and told her that it was chicken

Fast food is if they are already out and don't have plans for dinner.

She doesn't usually do last minute stops to the grocery store, but her husband occasionally will, especially when he is craving something.

Money

She says if she hasn't thought of it ahead of time, she has a block.

For breakfast every morning, Sarah has a zone bar with water. She likes them because they taste good, they're cheap and they fill you up. She says she'll have them for dinner when no one is around.

"If you don't eat what I cook, you don't eat."

She says she's a picky eater [...] She'd prefer to make what the kids want because she knows she can always add something for herself.

She will try to make the salad when the kids are napping

How many ways can you eat chicken? After a while it gets boring.

He wishes they could get more stuff in the repertoire, they both acknowledge that they have to make what the kids like.

They often have "backwards dinner" which is breakfast food for dinner. i.e.: waffles, eggs, bacon, etc.

Spend money to save a little time.

Usually she'll have to go back once or twice during the week.

I like to cook, but I cook as easy as I can during the week

I'm the only one who cooks

She said she should "figure out the defrosting thing" because it would make things easier.

Shopping: Feels like I go every day

Dinner time: She refers to it as a "meltdown".

The Improviser

In improvising mode, users listen and respond to their environment. Go with the flow and make it work. It's an ongoing conversation between them and their surroundings

Mis-connections

What are barriers to finding personal fulfillment through home cooking?

Making small gestures

How do people improvise in caring for family and community through home cooking?

Having tricks up the sleeve

How do people make adjustments in order to eat and prepare healthier food?

Making it work

How do people improvise to get food on the table?

Buying time

How do people improvise with their resources?

Two strategies for finding fulfillment through

HOME COOKING

Two strategies, five stages

When it comes to home cooking, users will alternate between two modes or strategies: planning and improvising. This map shows users' activities and barriers as they implement these strategies.

Vertically, user data is organized according to five stages relevant to home cooking. They illustrate concerns and aspirations ranging from managing resources through health issues, to fulfillment.

Demonstrate new processes or tools

Many organizations now elect to integrate ethnographic methods for studying customers into their innovation processes. But the folks at Conifer Research, who do that kind of work for a living, could see that far fewer individuals understand what they should be looking for when they head into a customer's world.

To help out, Conifer's Megan Fath took some of their own processes and packaged them for use by clients. Shown here is a tool that explains the "5E" framework—an analytic framework for evaluating any user experience as unfolding over five stages: entice, enter, engage, exit, extend.

"Originally this tool was part of a workshop to walk clients through the 5E framework and how

to use it. We'd have a presentation that walked people through examples of the framework using real world experiences. Tabletop posters would act as guides to help participants roll up their sleeves and start playing with the framework themselves. The tool itself was a takeaway to help them apply the framework back in their own work lives," explains Megan Fath.

But the tool started to take on a life of its own.

Then we started giving it away to clients outside of facilitated workshops. A lot of our outputs are experience maps, but those final maps never look like the 5Es. This tool helps explain how those maps were created. One of our clients saw it on someone's desk, had a "light bulb moment," and began to

Design by Megan Fath and Jerad Lavey for Conifer Research. The framework itself emerged from social science research and was converted for use in innovation planning by Doblin and Conifer. Photo by Conifer Research.

think about how the 5Es could help organize all the library of customer research sitting in databases across their units. This was a means of helping them understand what they've learned about their customers' journey. Now we get frequent requests from people who've seen it for 50–100 copies, sometimes asking for it in poster format. They want to use it to advocate a different way of thinking inside their organizations.

For such tools to work, they have to strike a balance between being fully self-explanatory and unstructured enough that people in different contexts can find value in them. "For it to be economical for Conifer, we knew the tool would have to have utility beyond a single use. As a result, it was designed to be a stand-alone piece, so that people can pick it up and apply it to their own work without firsthand experience. But we also tried not to be too prescriptive in it, so that it could be used in many different kinds of kits and by many different kinds of clients."

The single focus, small package, and open structure allow this tool to be taken up by individuals across divisions and industries. Megan notes that this brochure has ended up in many different hands, and seen many different levels of leadership—engineers, designers, researchers, project managers, division heads—helping to make small advances in how an organization thinks and operates.

What happens when collaborators just don't speak your language? Members of the Design Practice Research Group at Loughborough University in the UK determined that industrial designers and engineers often experience disconnects with each other around language and work processes, especially when it comes to new product development methods. For example, both disciplines rely on prototypes to advance their work. But the term "prototype" not only has different meanings to the two groups, each uses prototypes to communicate different information, adding to confusion when collaborating. To help bridge this gap in language and practices and enhance collaboration, the researchers undertook 129 interviews with industrial designers and engineers in the UK and Singapore. This process enabled them to identify what design representations were used for what types of information—they discovered nine forms of prototype, for example—and to standardize the language.

At first, the findings were translated into CoLab, a Web-based tool (www.colab.lboro. ac.uk). This tool presents 57 "iD cards" that identify how industrial designers use visual representations, and another 57 for how engineers use visual representations. Then the Industrial Designers Society of America, who recognized the collaborative and professional value of such a tool, commissioned 5000 copies of a physical variant for its members. The portable, credit-card-sized foldout contains the information for industrial designers only, but has succeeded in turning a PhD-level inquiry into an instant success in industry. The portable foldout went on to be a finalist in the 2011 International Design Excellence Awards, and a PDF version of the iD Cards is available from the home page of the Design Practice Research Group at Loughborough University.

Artifacts like these are important tools for expanding the conversation. More than just a repository of methods and process, the cards bridge processes and people so that they may work more effectively together, and with less friction, to produce the innovations essential to their business.

Tabs on the left indicate which stage of the product development process the tactic best fits.

Color bands on the right indicate whether the tactic best informs design (red) or engineering (blue)

PhD research supervisors: Dr. Mark Evans and Dr. Ian Campbell. PhD
researcher: Dr. Eujin Pei.

Depict possible futures

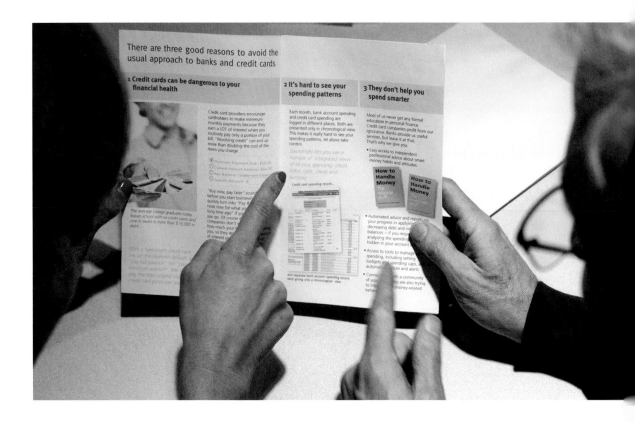

In his 20 years of innovation work, Peter Laundy has observed that with clients "concepts are being discussed at such a high level of abstraction that you might not be sure what the ideas are. But you can be quite sure that the words being used to describe the concepts have different meanings to various team members, especially those from different professional backgrounds. In such cases, perceived progress toward alignment is illusory."

To sidestep this condition, Peter has evolved a useful form of prototyping that he calls a *business*

concept visualization. These visualizations use writing, design, diagrams, and images to create physical manifestations of possible businesses or offerings that can be discussed and evaluated by the client and the working team. Business concept prototypes are created before any commitment has been made to any particular concept. Instead, the prototypes help a business "stand in the future," says Peter, "as if the innovation already existed, and as if it were already developed by the client for the eyes of the prospective customer." This helps clients evaluate more fully the appeal and fit of a new business proposition, and consider whether it's a future state that senior leadership can embrace. This also helps leaders to more accurately gauge the stretch required to implement it.

For Peter and his teams, a business concept visualization doesn't come at the end of a development process—it is a means to developing the concept itself. "It's the process of creating concept visualization that helps development teams uncover decisions that need to be made, issues to be resolved and barriers to overcome. It fosters a more detailed imagining—forcing a fuzzy concept down from a 40,000-foot level of abstraction to, say, a 30,000-foot level," says Peter.

How do his teams make a business concept prototype? Peter kicks off the prototyping process with a description—a one-page summary of the problem to be solved and the various factors that need to be resolved with it. Teams then use this to drive ideation. As an idea takes shape, they use the business concept visualization template to define and tighten the idea further into.

- A concise description of what isn't working in the world

- A set of visuals and depictions of the concept itself (rather than the customer experience)

- A list of benefits and a call to action

Peter delivers all this in the pages of an eight-page brochure—a simple but powerful format that seems to give just the right amount of space. "We also simulate finished production values because we want to convey the illusion of a future reality, and make it as enticing as possible. And because we want the visualizations to convey an overall sense of the concept, we make them into actual brochures or simulated interfaces. These typically accompany a presentation to key client decision makers about what the concept is and why it would make business sense to go ahead with it. But, unlike the prototype of an artifact, a business concept prototype is not about any of the design decisions I'm showing you—it's not about why I chose yellow or why I didn't. It's about giving potential funders a sense of the business being proposed."

In this hypothetical example, "We created this simulated concept pitch for a hypothetical client we dubbed Forefront Financial, an investment services firm. The fictional assignment is to develop a financial services offering for young adults that attracts prospective customers before they have investments, and to earn their trust by providing value that also creates barriers to switching. One of the questions we asked was whether there was an opportunity to rethink the dreaded credit card, changing it from a vehicle that gets people in debt to one that gets them out of it."

HOW TO DEVELOP A BUSINESS CONCEPT PROTOTYPE

According to strategist Peter Laundy, "The intent of a business concept prototype is to be illustrative about a proposed future state and to do so with enough concreteness that we can have a conversation and explore the concept together."

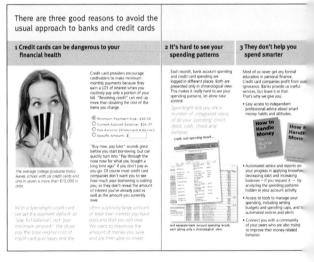

Next, develop a two-page spread to state what isn't working in the world.

Start with a provocative cover— here, the confusing jargon used in marketing credit cards—to whet interest and launch the story.

Work by Peter Laundy for Doblin; images © Edyta Pawlowska 2012, © Khamidulin Sergey 2012. Used under license from Shutterstock.com; © Rubberball / Masterfile

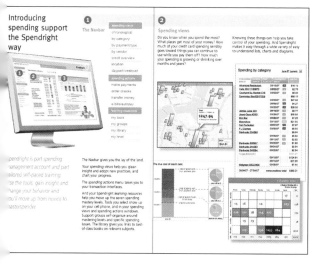

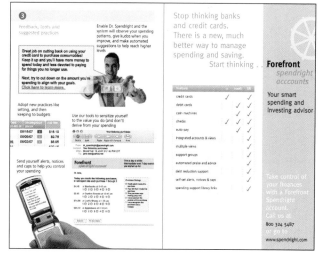

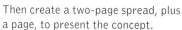

Then create a two-page spread, plus a page, to present the concept.

Close with a page to identify the benefits and provide a call to action.

THE TAKEAWAY
Five big ideas when expanding the conversation

1. Don't be shy about sharing.

If you are learning something powerful, find ways to share that knowledge with other would-be constituents. And think broadly about whom else might care about this work. It's a bit of a fishing expedition to find other previously unidentified constituents and coax them into the inner ring, but throw out a line using the tools mentioned here, and see what comes back.

2. Create a stream of focused messages, sharable nuggets of knowledge to attract attention.

Take those small but valuable nuggets of content out of the project and into the organization, before the project is over. Package them into presentations, artifacts, or other small, self-running experiences to attract others and build visibility for the work. This moves communication of the work away from end-of-project presentations for approval by a few key constituents. Instead, it directs communication into a series of smaller, exploratory contact points that diffuse content into the organization, so that it may be more broadly owned and understood and anticipated. Be judicious but open about what content might have impact: Send it out and see what you attract.

3. Make that content relevant to others.

Why should anyone care about your discoveries? What deserves the time and attention of others? Any editor can tell you that great content doesn't sell itself, and neither will your "new." To succeed in being heard, tailor your information to the needs, roles, and activities of the individuals likely to encounter the work. Or take a page from Tony Salvador's thinking: Figure out in advance what kinds of decisions those participants are engaged in making, and focus your message on informing those decisions. Content can tell many stories—tell the one that is important to them, not you, to demonstrate the utility of the work to the organization. They'll be back for the rest of it.

4. Design content and forms that can self-propagate.

Physical realization of work is important. Not only are these communication tools useful to the working team to help them engage others, but, done well, they can also be reused by those others to bridge to still more individuals in the organization. Yes, you can build a powerful story around the work, but why not create many messengers? Build ownership and diffusion by letting others tell stories of their own, and give them the tools to do so.

5. Deploy those "transfer" tools when the conditions are right.

For communicating The New, presentations, reports, and other one-directional media all have a place in the communication toolkit. But rather than reach for them reflexively or regularly, use them selectively to solve particular communication objectives (attract attention or build awareness of the work) or to draw in particular constituents (individuals who can be hard to identify at the start of the work—those who can help advance the work with their expertise or social network, or who need to be connected to it for other organizational reasons). For best results, combine the transfer-based tools with other tools that compensate for their weaknesses: Add an interaction experience to the presentation, or include a demonstrative artifact along with the report. But don't presume that these tools are effective on their own. As Hugh Dubberly puts it, "Sometimes 'delivery' is important. A client needs work done. That's delegation. It assumes we've discussed and share goals—if I have a heart attack, I want treatment, ASAP. In that moment, I do *not* want to discuss my wellness goals. But if I don't have that discussion sometime, I will very likely be back with another heart attack."

Conclusion

Let's take a step back and take stock of what has been offered here by the numbers:

- 1 framework for including communication methods in the innovation process

- 3 kinds of "new" — complex, unfamiliar, still-emerging

- 4 communication modes—collaborative, experiential, "transfer" (presentation or "delivery"), and pull

- 20 methods and tactics

Many people whose jobs are staked into creating The New have stopped relying on intuition or numbers and started investing in development processes and methods that can more reliably produce success. These processes and methods are designed to speed the discovery of new ideas, new opportunities, new strategies. But these methods address only half the problem. The other methods—the ones that are years behind in development because we didn't know we needed them—are needed to address the human beings involved in this process.

These methods help us engage others in our work, clarify our own understanding, and frame The New in ways that feel novel but sane, exciting but achievable. These are the methods we need to adopt and advance. And we need to do so quickly, because experience shows that these methods make all the difference in the outcome of our work. *All. The. Difference.*

FIVE BIG SHIFTS IN THINKING (AND DOING)

1. Believe and invest.

It's a pattern: Seasoned practitioners who regularly and reliably create The New target communication for formal investment. They hire people, build things—*they make time.* They do so because they see communication as integral to their success and to the *creation* of The New, not just the "selling" of it. The practitioners included in this book were chosen because they employ communicators at a high level in their organizations and use communication to drive their processes. For example:

- Conifer Research, a small shop of 20 employees, invests in a director of design, whose job is to help teams distill their discoveries into models, visualizations, and workshops.

- At innovation firm Gravity Tank, the lead communication designer, Robert Zolna, is a partner in the firm, even though its business is not "communication."

- As part of its global strategy capability, Continuum invests in "envisioners"—five in Boston alone—whose role is to find, shape, and tell strategic stories of the work in an "experiential" or visual way. Heather Reavey is one of the original envisioners, and now leads the strategy group in Boston.

- Communication thinking is omnipresent at IA Collaborative through co-founder and principal Kathleen Brandenburg. Kathleen is a trained communication designer who factors her clients' communication needs and style into every project.

- Bick Group CEO Andy Parham, in his address to executives at St. Louis University, closed his presentation with four pieces of advice: Accept that change is inevitable; know that customers light the path to your firm's future; rethink your strategy as often as necessary; and *communication is key* (emphasis added), by which he means necessary for both internal and external constituents.

2. Treat communication as a process—not an event.

Don't wait until the end of the process to open up The New to others. Instead, engage the intelligences inside (and outside) the organization starting on day one. The successful creation of The New requires a sustained focus on communication at every step of the process—from the first fuzzy conversations, through the early exploration, through detailed development, to widespread implementation. Conscious communication at every stage leads to ideas that are clearer and more relevant. It also builds widespread ownership and personal commitment well beyond the reach of conventional final-stage idea packaging.

3. Don't be "a people apart."

Treat constituents of The New like the true partners they are: Engage them, listen to them, include them in the creation of the work. To do so, you'll need to cultivate a curiosity about their circumstances, priorities, and objectives. This shows regard and provides insight to build more relevant bridges between them and The New. Then you need to engage those constituents, using a communication mode that supports the objective of the moment. It is in your strategic interest to add new modes of communication—the collaborative, experiential, and "pull" modes—to your "presentation" mode, so that you can connect others into the work in ways that are productive, meaningful, and fundamentally more human.

4. Think broadly about who might be constituents for the work.

It's tough to know on day one whose intelligence, energy, and social network will matter to The New. But it's a mistake not to try. Use the four concentric rings of core team, larger working team, decision makers, and the organization at large to ensure that you are being expansive and holistic in your conception of the constituents for The New. Think downstream to implementation and sales. Look upstream at materials, processes, and distribution. And cast the occasional fishing line to see who else in the organization might have something to offer—most organizations are sitting on significantly more talent and insight than their org charts reveal.

5. Don't "simplify" what is rich and nuanced. Demonstrate, symbolize, experience, and model.

The complex, unfamiliar, and still-fuzzy need special care—special techniques to protect what makes them novel from those who wish to make them more convenient. So use language, prototypes, frameworks, experiences, spaces, and demonstrative artifacts to communicate richly and compactly what an elevator pitch cannot.

6. The New is not a problem. It's a class of problems.

It's productive to consider that communicating The New is not one problem but a class of problems, each leading to a different set of communication methods. For example, the complex, the novel, and the still-emerging are three meaningfully different challenges that point to different interventions. In broad terms:

If you are challenged with *complexity*, meaning that the issues are multidimensional but still definable, create a model or framework to sort it out. It will be maximally effective if you do this with others. However, even as a solitary endeavor, a visual model that puts all the parts and pieces in one place is a valuable service when the factors are too numerous for any one person to hold in her head.

If the problem is true novelty, or the "unfamiliar new," the danger is that others are likely to reduce it to something they know (the Hollywood pitch again) or misinterpret it entirely because it's ahead of the cultural conception of what's possible. In the case of the former, control the frame with a metaphor. This allows for a less simplistic, reductionist comparison. But it requires spending the time to find a metaphor that is generative. This means it must have the ability to bridge others from the conventional way of thinking to the new territory. If The New is truly ahead of the cultural conception of what's possible, make a prototype. *Show—don't tell.*

If you are staring down the still-fuzzy or still-emerging, you are wrestling with something that isn't defined—*or maybe isn't even definable* (yet). The *undefinable* is a particularly tough communication challenge because you are also probably living at the edge of language. The words and constructs needed may not exist yet. In these cases, opt for a conversation. Conversations allow you to discover what others know, and to bridge from there to where you are. Conversations allow you to negotiate language and concepts together, to create shared meanings from those fragile things we call words. Conversations can proceed without a fixed destination in mind, and people tend to be more tolerant of that in dialogue than in a half-finished presentation. That said, you will probably have a better conversation if you have a clearly defined point of entry—a quote that reveals an issue or a story that spotlights a transformational moment in your thinking.

Can it be that simple? Anyone testing out the logic in this list intuitively knows that the challenge of communicating The New is more layered and dynamic, and that the mix of problems shifts over the duration of the project. Communication is always a highly contextual act, and there is no formula. But a bit of structure and a strategy can help us consider the options in a more robust, orderly fashion.

ADVANCING THE METHODS BASE

I'm energized by the commitment and contributions of everyone who participated in this effort to build a book of communication methods. But we need more. We need a robust toolkit of methods and a strategy for when each might be employed. We need to solve the case of the missing methods.

The next wave of methods can and should come from two places. The first, dear Reader, is you. Let's tap the collective intelligence and experience of those on the front lines. Do you have a method you can share? Principles that light your way? A telling story that might be instructive to everyone? Help advance the conversation and the practice by adding your voice at www.communicatingthenew.net.

The second source of methods should come from academic study. The careful reader will have observed patterns across the methods on these pages. The raw tools of communication are not that numerous. In short, we have:

- Language
- Models and frameworks
- Prototypes
- Artifacts and images
- Experiences
- Spaces
- Systems

This is the raw material of the New Communication. As a collection, it offers a fertile mix of tactile and cognitive, intellectual and emotional, 2D and 3D. It has the potential to create rich experiences and new modes of communication that better fit how we learn, think, and in turn, act. These tools would benefit from deeper exploration and further definition in the context of communicating The New.

Organizational life has never required this level of richness in its communications before. But neither has it encountered today's highly dynamic, hotly contested markets with shortened product life cycles, uncertainty of customer base, and technology-enabled business models. The New is essential, and the communication around The New must advance to the next level.

Under
the hood

THEORIES, WRITERS, AND REFERENCES

On "knowing what you know"

The 95 percent figure for unconscious brain activity is bandied about on various Web pages. But the origin of this highly specific number is more of a story, and thus difficult to cite. As explained to me by Professor John Bargh, a social psychologist at Yale University, it starts with his article, "The Automaticity of Everyday Life" (*Advances in Social Cognition*, Vol X). This article is the lead article, which then includes commentary by other academics responding to Bargh's research; lastly, the book ends with a closing response by Bargh himself. It is in this closing response that the "95%" figure emerges. But it was intended, he clarifies for me, as a lighthearted reference to the "99.44% pure" slogan of the Dove soap ad, in a response to criticism by Dr. Roy Baumeister and Kristin Sommer—not as a serious measurement. Bargh states, "I think it is important not to take at least my and Baumeister's figures too seriously," as they were part of a friendly debate between social psychologists. Numbers aside, Bargh and other neuroscientists continue to maintain that the vast majority of brain activity is automatic or unconscious—numbers as high as 99 percent have been floated—but those exact numbers are for illustrative purposes only.

On the topic of writing as exploration and "unspeakable data," read the terrific writing of Peter Turchi in *Maps of the Imagination: The Writer as Cartographer* (Trinity University Press, 2004), and see page 90 for the first introduction of the term.

To gain insight as to the role of the body in cognition, look to the explosive new field of study called grounded cognition, and to the work of Emory University professor Lawrence Barsalou in particular. Video of Barsalou offers a simple, interesting overview of the field: youtube.com/watch?v=JZsckkdFyPM. For those seeking a fuller academic recounting, see Professor Barsalou's articles, such as "Grounded Cognition: Past, Present and Future," in *Topics in Cognitive Science* 2 (2010), pages 716–724, which provides an excellent overview of the state of the field.

On models, boundary objects, and prototypes

It is impossible to talk about models without pointing to the inspiring and insightful work by Hugh Dubberly on models and their role in creating The New. Hugh describes himself as a design planner and teacher, but his experiences at Apple and at Times-Mirror, and as co-author of the famed Knowledge Navigator video, add up to a vast experience base that informs a particularly refined point of view. His website holds all his articles and visualizations. For those addressing models, you can start here with the visualizations themselves: www.dubberly.com/models.

Why look to models as a means of aligning individuals? Star and Griesemer's work on information artifacts as boundary objects provides a new and useful frame for artifacts as a means of prompting exchange between individuals, not just delivering content. Boundary objects are so called because they are constructed in ways that satisfy the knowledge needs of very different user groups simultaneously, and so live at the boundary of various "communities of interest." Because the objects are recognizable by each user group, the objects can be used to bridge those user groups (prompting Hugh Dubberly's observation that they would be better named "bridging objects") through conversation and exchange. Star cites examples such as museum exhibits, libraries, forms, and templates. Each of these has enough structure to be of use within a given "social world"—the PhD student in biology or the casual specimen collector—but is also loosely structured enough to cross social worlds (for example, many individuals use the library). This notion that objects can mediate between different user groups has been taken up in interaction design (interfaces as "mediating objects") and in innovation management. Of particular interest to creators of The New, researchers are investigating the relevance of the boundary objects construct to create shared mental models and alignment across organizations. Star and Griesemer's 1989 original article, "Institutional Ecology, 'Translations' and Boundary Objects," is dense and likely out of context for readers of this book. However, Kenneth Fleischmann's "Boundary Objects with Agency: A method for studying the design-use interface" (*The Information Society* 22, 2006, pages 77–87) usefully places the topic within design. And Kaj Koskinen's "Metaphoric boundary objects as coordinating mechanisms in the knowledge sharing of innovation processes" (*European Journal of Innovation Management* 8, Issue 3, 2005, pages 323–335) applies the construct to organizational challenges of collaborating across disciplines or departments.

Stephen Few's terrific book on visualizing quantitative data, *Now You See It* (Analytic Press, 2009) offers a useful summation of how we do, indeed, think with our eyes. Colin Ware's *Visual*

Thinking: for Design (Morgan Kaufmann, 2008) also provides a detailed look at the eye-brain seeing apparatus for application in interactive systems, but it also has broader application for designing anything visual.

Martin Thaler and Anijo Mathew have not yet published their thinking on prototypes, but they should. They can be reached at the IIT Institute of Design in Chicago, if you'd like to prompt them to publish or invite them to speak.

On writing

Daniel Chandler, author and lecturer on media theory at the University of Wales, writes cogently about the theory of linguistic relativity and the Sapir-Whorf hypothesis at www.aber.ac.uk/media/Documents/short/whorf.html. He has a number of interesting online papers that summarize information theories of various kinds. For more on the language-thought debate, consider the interesting but not so easy to get through "A Review of the Language-Thought Debate: Multivariant Perspectives," by Parviz Birjandi and Somayyeh Sabah (2002) in *BRAIN: Broad Research in Artificial Intelligence and Neuroscience* 3, No. 2.

As mentioned, I found the work of Gail Fairhurst of great use in thinking about the role of language in making meaning. Her book, co-authored with Robert Sarr, *The Art of Framing: Managing the Language of Leadership* (Jossey-Bass, 1996) is particularly applicable to the challenge of encapsulating The New. George Lakoff's *Don't Think of an Elephant* (Chelsea Green Publishing, 2004) offers a short, reader-friendly tour of how framing through language, especially the metaphoric language used by Republicans in the 2004 election, controls the national agenda in the United States. Both are highly instructive about the power of language to shape not just what we think, but how we think.

On language

Hugh Musick's terrific essay "A Linguistic Model of Innovation (Use your Words)," can be found online at www.jenseiser.com/tag/hugh-musick/.

All throughout this chapter, my thinking and writing about language are heavily influenced by the theories of General Semantics and Alfred Korzybsky's *Science and Sanity* (the fifth edition was released in 1995 by the Institute for General Semantics). I appreciate both its rigor and its focus on the role of language as the cause of miscommunication and thereby much of human suffering. Observations about the false concreteness of language—that language is abstract, can offer only partial descriptions of reality, is static where reality is dynamic—are all from the rich analytic assessments of the General Semanticists. Other contributions include advocating that communication should

range up and down the "ladder of abstraction" (S. I. Hayakawa) to fully explain a given idea— we need abstractions to help us make sense of a pile of particulars; we need particulars to help illustrate the abstract. *Science and Sanity* is a 20-course meal; for a taster, Em Griffin offers a useful introductory summary in early editions of his textbook, *A First Look at Communication Theory* (McGraw-Hill), and that chapter is available online at www.afirstlook.com. Acolytes S. I. Hayakawa in *Language in Thought and Action* (1991 was the release of the fifth edition by Harvest Original) and Wendell Johnson, who applied the theories to psychology, are worth reading. Johnson is most readily available through back issues of *ETC: A Review of General Semantics*, on the Institute for General Semantics website, at www.generalsemantics.org/.

On metaphor

Any person curious about the power of metaphor, especially its formative role in thought, should reach for the reader-friendly and often cited *Metaphors We Live By* by George Lakoff and Mark Johnson (University of Chicago Press, 2003). It is authoritative and transformative.

Andrew Ortony's three communicative qualities of metaphor—compactness, vividness, and the ability to communicate obliquely—are first laid out in his article "Why Metaphors Are Necessary and Not Just Nice" (*Educational Theory* 25, Number 1, 1975, pages 45–53).

"Making the familiar strange" and "making the strange familiar" are the two organizing principles in the chapter on metaphor for new product development in the classic work by William J. J. Gordon, *Synectics: Development of the Creative Capacity* (Collier Books, 1961). Gordon, with others, believed creative problem solving could be studied, formalized, and taught; *Synectics* was his effort to do so. The book is out of print, but used copies can be found on Amazon, although not inexpensively.

On visual metaphor

Let me first address the obvious: The metaphor examples in chapter two are distinctive and impactful in no small part because they are visual, not just text-based. Pictorial metaphors are quite different from verbal metaphors in important ways, and to better understand this difference, I point readers to the important scholarship of Professor Charles Forceville, University of Amsterdam. His work on pictorial/visual and multimodal (any combination of text, pictures, sound, music, motion) metaphor has significantly influenced my teaching and is particularly relevant to this book because visual metaphors are powerful communicators of The New. Although Forceville would rather I point readers directly to his work—and I will do so in this section—in a recent e-mail to me, he offered a simple entry point into the complex world of nonverbal metaphor: "A metaphor, particularly a pictorial or multimodal one, is a very economic way to communicate something about a topic. In the 'A is B' format, where in advertising A is the product, using a well-chosen source domain in one (visual) stroke activates a whole range of connotations . . . and visuals communicate more easily than language inasmuch as we do not have

A metaphor is a comparison of two things

To create any metaphor, we create a comparison by mapping attributes of the *source* to the *target*. This creates new meaning: surgeons are rough and brutal, treating patients like carcasses to be carved up.

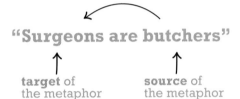

"Surgeons are butchers"

target of the metaphor   **source** of the metaphor

We might map:
rough
fast
brutal
slaughter
flesh
carcass

but not...
tradesmen
employee
crafts person

to learn visuals in the same way as we have to learn a language. But it is an error to think that we do not need a lot of knowledge to understand a picture, which means that infelicitous pictorial metaphors can baffle audiences, or even lead to misinterpretations."

Forceville is identifying an issue that may not be obvious to the casual reader—nonverbal metaphors operate by a different set of rules than verbal metaphors. Most scholarship around metaphor is derived from verbal metaphor and so misses issues that emerge when images are involved. For example, verbal metaphors use grammar that helps us distinguish the difference between "surgeons are butchers" and "butchers are surgeons," something pictorial metaphors do not have. Of great use to us, then, Forceville has developed a typology of pictorial metaphors that helps the viewer consider how the image works to distinguish the "source" of a metaphor from its "target."

A direct path to Forceville's work is his "Adventures in Multimodality" blog/website http://muldisc.wordpress.com/. It contains many of his papers—including some heading for publication—and a smattering of his students' work and presentations.

You can find his typology of visual metaphors here: "Metaphors in Pictures and Multimodal Representations," Chapter 26 of *The Cambridge Handbook of Metaphor and Thought*, edited by Raymond W. Gibbs, Jr. (Cambridge University Press, 2008). Another good survey of his ideas is the introduction and Chapter 2 in *Multimodal Metaphor*, co-edited with Eduardo Urios-Aparisi (Mouton de Gruyter, 2009), which contains chapters on advertising, cartoons, film, music, and gestures.

Forceville also looks explicitly at the use of metaphor in advertising, and, while I am not promoting an advertising mindset for the communication of The New, Forceville's investigation of nonverbal metaphors in advertising is instructive. See: "Creativity in Pictorial and Multimodal Advertising Metaphors," Chapter 7 of *Discourse and Creativity*, edited by Rodney H. Jones (Pearson, 2012) and Forceville's book, *Pictorial Metaphors in Advertising* (Routledge, 1996).

On mantras and catchphrases

Farhad Manjoo's *True Enough: Learning to Live in a Post-Fact Society* (John Wiley & Sons, 2008) is a fascinating exploration of using stories and language, including political catchphrases, to create persuasive experiences of "truthiness" that influence national dialogues and even elections.

See also Michael Pollan's groundbreaking article, "Unhappy Meals," which also ran under the headline "Nutritionism: How scientists have ruined the way we eat" on the cover of the *New York Times Magazine* on January 28, 2007. The book version, *In Defense of Food,* was released in 2008 by Penguin Press.

On wicked problems

Rittel's vintage but remarkably relevant article, "On the Planning Crisis: Systems Analysis of the 'First and Second Generations'" (*Bedriftskonomen* 8, 1972) introduces the concept of wicked problems—a vivid term that now has been adopted by mainstream business culture and is often used without informed connection to Rittel's meaning. Wicked problems, argues Rittel, pose a fundamentally different challenge than the "tame" problems that traditional systems-oriented processes, such as those found in operations management education (the "first generation") were designed to solve. In my discussion in the

"Artifacts and Images" section of this chapter, I have abridged Professor Horst Rittel's criteria for wicked problems; here is the full list:

1. A wicked problem has no definitive formulation—understanding the problem is part of the problem.

2. Any statement of a wicked problem includes its solution; unlike a tame problem, which can be stated separately from its solution.

3. Wicked problems have no stopping rule that tells you when you have finished.

4. Solutions to wicked problems are not true or false—it is the nature of the problem that this kind of thinking is not applicable.

5. Wicked problems do not have a finite list of possible solutions or permissible operations—it is not possible to identify and consider all solutions.

6. For a wicked problem, there are many possible explanations as to its cause, and the choice of explanation determines the nature of the resolution.

7. Every wicked problem can be considered a symptom of another problem, and therefore it's unwise to tackle the problem as stated—it might not be the right one.

8. For a wicked problem, there is no immediate or ultimate test of its solutions—each action can produce more consequences over time.

9. A wicked problem is unique—there are no prototypical solutions.

10. There is no opportunity for trial and error with wicked problems. Therefore, all solutions are a one-shot operation and count significantly.

CHAPTER 3:
Theories, writers, and references for "Targeting your constituents"

On mental models

As already mentioned, my thinking has been deeply influenced by Gail Fairhurst and Robert Sarr's *The Art of Framing: Managing the Language Of Leadership* (Jossey-Bass, 1966). The concept of mental models is integral to their explication of framing, but is first mentioned on page 10, and the content most relevant to this book continues through page 79.

On culture

The Interpretation of Cultures, by Clifford Geertz (Basic Books, 1976) is a collection of his articles and remains a classic text. But much of the core can also be found in standalone articles online, such as "Thick Description: Toward an Interpretive Theory of Culture." And, while academics may hate to hear it, the Wikipedia entry on his work offers a nice overview and a useful structure for anyone wishing to formulate a study plan of his work.

On the "Organization as Culture" framework

Michael Pacanowsky, with co-author Nick O'Donnell-Trujillo, wrote several articles advancing the study of organizations as cultures. For this book, I reference "Communication and Organizational Cultures" (*The Western Journal of Speech Communication* 46, Spring, 1982, pages 115–130), the authors' most explicit argument for Geertz's model as relevant to the study of organizations. A portion of the article contrasts traditional approaches and the cultural approach. This is also the article in which they first introduce the typology of vocabulary, stories, and rites and rituals as categories for study.

I also reference "Organizational Communication as Cultural Performance" (*Communication Monographs* 50, June 1983, pages 138–139) for more details about vocabulary, stories, and rites and rituals. In this article, Pacanowsky and O'Donnell-Trujillo pointedly challenge the cybernetic metaphor of communication as information processing ("transferring, processing, and storing," "feedback systems," etc.). They argue instead for an organizational culture metaphor in which human beings are more like tribes than computers, and communication is performative—a dynamic series of informal and formal rituals that human beings use to construct their "society"—rather than purely instrumental.

Harrison M. Trice and Janice M. Beyer's article "Studying Organizational Cultures through Rites and Ceremonies" (*The Academy of Management Review* 9, Number 4, 1984, pages 653–669) strives to define key terms, such as "culture," in the context of an organization, and to advocate for the study of rites and ceremonies as particularly compact expressions of an organization's culture. They propose a typology of six rituals, and suggest it be used as a way to organize the researcher's attention.

On Frederick Taylor and time/motion studies

Frederick W. Taylor put forth his comprehensive theory in *The Principles of Scientific Management* (Harper Bros., 1911, pp. 5–29). The key article in this book is also available online for free, and offers an interesting historical look at the rationale for standardizing production methods and for framing workers as a components of a system that can be optimized with proper study and codification: "Among the various methods and implements used in each element of each trade there is always one method and one implement which is quicker and better than any of the rest. And this one best method and best implement can only be discovered or developed through a scientific study and analysis of all of the methods and implements in use, together with accurate, minute, motion and time study. This involves the gradual substitution of science for rule of thumb throughout the mechanic arts."

On creating "pull"

In their book, *The Power of Pull* (Basic Books, 2010), John Hagel III, John Seeley Brown, and Lang Davison propose that businesses and individuals shift their mindset around information. When information has transformed from a precious commodity into an open river, they note, simply "pushing" information out into the stream is no longer sufficient. They propose we evolve our mental models and our business models toward creating "pull" for our content and ideas, so as to broadly attract the attention and interest of those who need them.

The opening quotation by John Seeley Brown is from *Seeing Differently: Insights on Innovation* (Harvard Business School Press, 1997, page 216).

On rejecting the "transfer" model and embracing the role of experience in learning

What I'm about to recount here is not news. Many have recounted this progression in more detailed and scholarly ways. If you are interested in learning more, the writing of Professor Robert T. Craig is quite brilliant: "Communication" (*Encyclopedia of Rhetoric*, ed. T. O. Sloane, Oxford University Press, 2001, pages 125–137), as is his award-winning article "Communication Theory as a Field" (*Communication Theory* 9, Issue 2 1999, pages 119–161).

Scholars classify communication theories into one of two categories: transmissive theories and constructivist theories. Transmissive theories conceive of communication as "transferring" or "delivering." We can draw a fairly straight line from these back to the famed Shannon-Weaver model of communication published in 1949. Claude Shannon, an engineer at Bell Labs, needed to increase the signal capacity of telephone lines and, being an engineer, drew a model to depict that technical process. Warren Weaver, a compatriot of Shannon's, took the model and proposed its relevance to human communication (something Shannon never really intended, although he is now tarred with the same brush as Weaver). This is important because, until then, a model of interpersonal communication did not exist. The Shannon-Weaver model was the first, and so arguably one of the most important theories of communication every proposed. It has been enormously influential in academic traditions of every kind, not just communications (which was not even a formal area of study at the time; this came later). As it turns out, it was also unhelpful and counterproductive in many ways.

Shannon-Weaver Mathematical Model, 1949

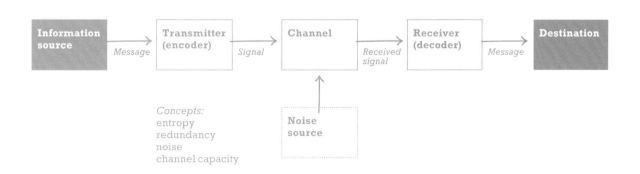

Nonetheless it fit the needs of mass media studies in the 1960s and early 1970s, and so persisted, although there were many attempts to update and improve on it.

It was in the late 1960s that constructivist theories, notably introduced by Piaget, Vygotsky, and others, emerged to explain more fully how individuals learn and integrate new information into their thinking. Constructivists posited that communication is not information transfer, but rather the active construction of knowledge by individuals, and that it takes place most effectively in a social context with dialogue. Information is not just received and stored; it is interpreted and integrated with one's preexisting knowledge. For constructivists, meaning emerges from interaction, especially interaction with other people through conversation. In sum, learning is constructing one's own knowledge, and learning is fundamentally experiential. An optimal learning environment, therefore, is one that creates social experiences and offers stimuli and structure with which participants can drive their own learning. It is these principles that are echoed in the five experience models outlined in the preceding pages.

The relatively new fields of embodied cognition and grounded cognition expand on constructivism to offer new dimensions, such as the role of the body and the physical environment in thinking and learning. We tend to conceive of learning as something that happens in the six inches between our ears, but new discoveries, such as that of mirror neurons in the body that connect to neurons in the brain, are convincing scientists that cognition is a whole-body experience.

Situated cognition studies, too, suggest that our understanding of information depends on more than just the "private mind" of an individual. Rather, it depends on the world of experience, almost always shared in social and cultural groups, as the core of human learning, thinking, problem-solving and literacy. Experiences, these studies suggest, provide a powerful platform for shared context that, in turn, directs the interpretation of information; such experiences also create the conditions for emotional connection to information, as emotion is a resource for understanding the content of an experience. To learn more about situated cognition, see J.P. Gee's article "Digital Media and Learning as an Emerging Field, Part I: How We Got Here" (*International Journal of Learning*, 2009, 1 (2):13–23.) For more on what's known of the role of the body and environment in cognition, look to the work of Emory University professor Lawrence Barsalou in particular. This is perhaps most simply accessed in an online video in which Barsalou offers a short, interesting overview of the field: youtube.com/watch?v=JZsckkdFyPM. For those seeking a fuller academic recounting, see his article "Grounded Cognition: Past, Present and Future" (*Topics in Cognitive Science* 2, 2010, pages 716–724) for an excellent overview of the state of the field.

On the role of emotion in attention and memory

It is widely accepted that emotions impact memory formation and recall—neuroscientists tell us we can thank our amygdala for that. A good overview of this can be found in Joseph LeDoux's *The Emotional Brain: The Mysterious Underpinnings of Emotional Life* (Simon & Schuster, 1998). More technical but equally interesting is Elisabeth Kensinger's "Remembering emotional experiences: The contribution of valence and arousal" (*Reviews in the Neurosciences* 15, Issue 4, 2004, pages 241–251). Among other gems in Kensinger's review of research on emotion and memory, is the finding that emotional content is prioritized over neutral content, so that in conditions of limited attention, individuals are more likely to process emotionally arousing items than neutral items. We are also more likely to remember emotional content than neutral content. Her work on the role of pictures and words in emotion is also pertinent to the use of artifacts and images in communicating The New. See also Kensinger's article, with co-author Daniel Schacter, "Processing emotional pictures and words: Effects of valence and arousal" (*Cognitive, Affective and Behavioral Neuroscience*, 6, Issue 2, 2006, pages 110–126).

CHAPTER 5:

Theories, writers, and references for "Expand the conversation"

John Medina's *Brain Rules* (Pear Press, 2008) offers an impressive synthesis of the research literature on 12 topics related to being a happy, productive human being in today's world. The quotation I excerpted is from page 74, in the section on attention.

The Power of Pull: How Small Moves, Smartly Made, Can Set Big Things in Motion, by John Hagel, John Seely Brown, and Lang Davison (Basic Books, 2010), positions the change in the information economy as moving from a twentieth-century "push" model, in which a few organizations control and push ideas to the masses, to a twenty-first-century "pull" model, in which consumers exert control, "pulling" what they need and value into their lives.

On the role of emotion in attention and memory

For a full accounting of the theories and references for this topic, please see the previous entry titled "On the role of emotion in attention and memory" in this chapter under the heading "Chapter 4."

On Consumer Insight Maps

See Kim Erwin's "Consumer Insight Maps: The map as story platform in the design process" (*Parsons Journal for Information Mapping*, Winter 2011) for how to structure and create visualizations of qualitative consumer data.

On the role of relevance and the need to garner attention to create "pull"

Back in the 1980s, researchers John Cacioppo from the University of Chicago and Richard Petty from Ohio State resolved a vexing problem in the area of attitude research. Attitude research is a branch of social psychology that looks to understand how individuals form their attitudes, and therefore might be influenced. For years, the field had failed to deliver consistent, reliable results. In fact, many studies produced contradictory results, and, after decades of work, the field of attitude formation was suffering a crisis of confidence and credibility. Cacioppo and Petty did something quite interesting. They took a step back and reviewed 20–30 years of studies, and concluded that the results were not contradictory, but were reflecting an unrecognized processing pattern in human beings. This pattern relied not on one, but rather on two routes to evaluate concepts and produce attitudes: a high-involvement route that involves careful reasoning, and a high-volume route that relies on surface impressions.

They summarized their findings in what they called the Elaboration Likelihood Model (ELM), a description of how and under what conditions individuals will engage with new messages to form new attitudes. This model has been vetted and expanded on by other researchers, and remains the dominant theory in explaining how individuals process messages designed to persuade. The model posits that we all have two modes of engaging with new messages, and therefore two routes to persuasion or decision making. We have two modes because individuals have limited cognitive resources to engage with all the information around us, and our brains have to make decisions about what deserves our careful attention. The central route is the high-

Elaboration Likelihood Model (ELM)

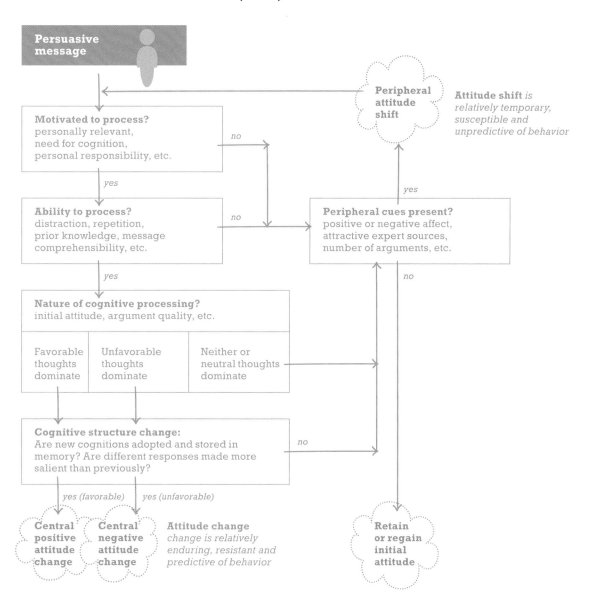

involvement route, and the one every creator of The New would prefer to have his or her concepts go through. In the central route, individuals look carefully at the content for its relevance, its clarity, its credibility and substance in an effort to form an attitude or conclusion about it.

But few concepts receive this kind of careful treatment, researchers concluded. Our high-volume evaluative mode kicks in when we don't care, or aren't prepared to consider deeply the content of a proposition. In this mode of engagement, we rely on surface cues about the presenter and the message to draw conclusions about the content: the attractiveness of the presenter or content, our ability to recognize expertise or authority in the source, the apparent thoroughness of the content. Advertisers rely on the peripheral route to engage potential buyers in their message, knowing that their audiences are unlikely to spend the time evaluating the factual content of their message.

What's notable about this model are two key findings. Finding number one: Attitudes formed through the central route are more stable, enduring, and predictive of behavior than attitudes formed through the peripheral route. Attitudes formed through the peripheral route are weaker, more unstable, and more likely to change when presented with new ideas or contradictory information. Clearly, we want The New to go through the central route. Finding number two: The gating factor for getting into the central route is the individual's motivation and ability to engage with the content. If an individual cannot see the relevance, or the relevance is weak, he or she will not be motivated to expend the brain power and focus required by the central processing route.

This research demonstrates what we intuitively already know, but often fail to act on, which is that in order to engage participants and earn time in their central processing route, we must establish the relevance of The New to them. Otherwise, participants will engage using their peripheral processing route, relying on superficial cues that we may not have in place yet, and making subconscious judgments that, even if in our favor, are tenuous, random, and disconnected. As Cacioppo put it to me, "Conditions that aren't meaningful can push people to the peripheral route. These can be a heuristic, a habit or a conditioned emotional response. Even when traveling the central route, though, one can show biased issue-relevant thinking. Just because one is thinking carefully doesn't mean one is thinking rationally."

To be informed enough to establish relevance, we must know something about our constituents—who they are, what they are engaged in, what they might need to know. But sometimes we don't. And here again the model comes in handy: "Both routes matter, and sometimes the peripheral route is where to start," offers Cacioppo. "This is something we actually argued in the '80s—sometimes you need to use cues in order to lure the person in enough so that they then start taking the information seriously . . . you know they're not going to engage in that kind of central route information processing if they see no reason." By way of example, John talks about seeding a small swell of activity on Twitter around a topic—using it as a means of drawing others in through the peripheral route—and then using that small swell as evidence of success that can be promoted more broadly. "If you have a localized focus initially it looks like it's going very fast. As information gets disseminated as a local success then others will pick up on it. The idea is like consensus information coming at them: it garners the attention you need to even start the central route operating. That's what I meant by this idea of using the peripheral route to gain access to do the central route processing. But you do it in gradations and you do it in ways that are specific to individuals, which is where you can see individualized material going to different users can be really quite valuable."

The ELM, with its insight that individuals manage their limited ability to attend to information using two modes of processing, might strike some readers as familiar. There is a notable similarity between the two routes of the ELM proposed in 1981 and Daniel Kahneman's "System 1, System 2" model, as presented in Kahneman's recent best seller, *Thinking, Fast and Slow*. Kahneman comes from a different academic discipline, a relatively new field called behavioral economics. In *Thinking, Fast and Slow*, System 1 thinking is characterized as the fast, intuitive, and emotional processing mode, while his System 2 thinking is slow, deliberate, and rational. System 1 is the high-volume processing mode we apply most often; System 2 is what we reserve for a much smaller number of evaluations.

There is also a notable difference between the two models—one that makes a difference to our mission in communicating The New: The ELM suggests that we can shift between the two processing modes. Petty and Cacioppo argue that individuals can be triggered to move from one processing path to another at multiple points. Kahneman's model does not suggest paths between the two processing systems, and moreover suggests that individuals engage in either one or the other, but not both, in any instance of thinking. The ELM way of looking at things offers us a bit of leverage: If we can engage constituents of The New in either path, the model suggests what we might do (and when), either to encourage central processing, or to keep individuals in that mode longer.

I find the lessons of the ELM useful when in "pull" mode. The highest and most productive use of our time is to understand our constituents deeply enough that we can identify and target the specific relevance of our work to them. If we can't do this (perhaps there are just too many distinct constituents, or we have inadequate access to information about their concerns and needs), then well-designed artifacts can generate the pull we need to draw in potentially interested constituents—and once we have their attention and commitment, we can engage them in a more substantive fashion.

See "Central and Peripheral Routes to Advertising Effectiveness: The Moderating Role of Involvement," by Richard E. Petty, John T. Cacioppo, and David Schumann (*Journal of Consumer Research* 10, September 1983, pages 135–146).

Index

#

5E framework 220, 254
    See also User experience model

A

Abrahamson, Lawrence 80
Allen, Jared 163, 179
An Inconvenient Truth 201
Arney, Mike 212
Arup 214, 215
Ask Jeeves 78

B

Bargh, Dr. John 237
Barsalou, Dr. Lawrence 237.
    See also Grounded cognition
Bernardo, Diego 164
Beyer, Janice M. 138, 140, 243
Bick Group 1, 72, 91, 107, 113, 119, 121, 132, 232
Bierut, Michael xi, 111
Biller, Gabriel A. 73
Birjandi, Parviz 238
Blue Mountain Labs 1
Böhm, Philipp 47, 52, 96, 99, 177, 190
boundary objects 237
Boundary objects 237, 238
Box, George P. 19

Brandenburg, Kathleen xi, 8, 10, 28, 209, 232
Braun, Lauren 216
Brown, John Seeley 143, 147, 186, 244, 245, 248
Burnett, Leo 108
Business concept visualization 224, 225, 226
Bussman, Paul 72, 91, 107, 112, 113
Buswell, John 47

C

Cacioppo, Dr. John xiii, 248, 250, 251
Cain, John xi, 28
Campbell, Dr. Ian 223
Cervantes, Miguel 110, 158, 159, 162, 166, 175
Chandler, Daniel 238
Chang, Mo 167
Cliver, Melissa 25
"Cloak" theory of language. *See also* Sapir-Whorf hypothesis
Cognition studies. *See also* Grounded cognition, Embodied cognition, Situated cognition
Communication conventions
    content 149, 150
    environment 151, 153
    interactions 151, 153
    materials 151, 153

Communication modes 231
    collaborative mode 141, 143, 231, 232
    experiential mode 143, 145, 185, 186, 231, 232
    "pull" mode 145, 185, 186, 209, 231, 232, 244, 248, 251
    "transfer" mode 149, 229, 231, 245
Concept maps 21
Conifer Research xi, 9, 22, 178, 181, 220, 221, 232
Constituents 3, 8, 25, 26, 112, 119, 120, 121, 122, 124, 125, 135, 136, 137, 141, 143, 144, 145, 185, 186, 187, 188, 233, 243
    continuous creators 141
    regular contributors 142
    voluntary accelerators 143
Constructivist theories of learning 245, 246
Consumer Insight Map 216, 218, 248
Continuum xi, 10, 25, 155, 157, 211, 212, 232
Cotton, Martha xi, 10, 165, 196
Craig, Dr. Robert T. 245

D

Davison, Lang 244, 248
"Design for experience" 14, 148
Design Research Conference 205
Doblin x, xi, 25, 93, 96, 99, 131,

190, 192, 221, 226

Drivers of Change cards 215

Dubberly, Hugh x, 20, 26, 180, 181, 229, 237, 238

E

Earle, Christina Payne 25

Edison, Thomas 106, 113

Elaboration Likelihood Model (ELM) 248, 251

Embodied cognition 246

Environments 123, 154, 155, 156, 157, 160, 181

Evans, Dr. Mark xiii, 223

Evenson, Shelley xi, 8, 25, 26, 27, 120

Experience model 151, 153, 154

   application experiences 146, 148, 172

   exploratory experiences 146, 148, 153, 155

   extension experiences 153, 176, 178, 179

   immersion experiences 146, 148, 160

   interaction experiences 146, 148, 165

F

fact list 52

Fairhurst, Gail xiii, 67, 92, 98, 116, 129, 133, 134, 239, 243

Fath, Megan xi, 22, 24, 220, 221

Few, Stephen 19, 238

Fisher, Jim 72, 91, 107, 112, 113

Fleischmann, Kenneth 238

Flench, Russell 45, 54, 161

Forceville, Dr. Charles xiii, 67, 240, 241

Frameworks.
   See Models and frameworks

G

Gabel, Katherine 169

Gee, J. P. 246

Geertz, Clifford 137, 243

General Semantics 115, 239

Gier, Gisela xii, 193, 196, 197

Goltz, Shlomo 179

Gordon, J. J. 70, 240

Gordon, William J. J. 240

Gore, Al 69, 80, 112, 201

Gravity Tank xi, 7, 10, 48, 165, 168, 193, 194, 196, 197, 207, 232

Griesemer, Dr. James 237

Griffin, Em 239

Grounded cognition 237, 246

H

Hagel, John 248

Harris, Dania 77

Hayakawa, S. I. 239

Hicks, Leslie Nichole 77

Holzworth, Chelsea 75

Horner, Jim 158

Hosmer, Chris 211

I

IA Collaborative xi, 8, 28, 232

iD cards 222

Illustrated narratives 100

Innovation processes

   closed processes 25, 121, 122

   open processes 122

intensity models 34

J

Jacobson, Ben xi, 9, 58, 131, 155, 172, 180

Johnson 67, 70, 77, 239

Johnson, Mark 70

Johnson, Wendell 239

Jump Associates 6

Just-in-place learning 86

K

Kahneman, Dr. Daniel 251

Keeley, Larry xi, 5, 11, 131, 134

Kensinger, Elisabeth 247

Kim, Eunkyung 179

King, Dr. Martin Luther 102

Kodinsky, David 78

Korel, Hanna 74

Korzybsky, Alfred 239

Koskinen, Kaj 238

Koziol, Ken 122

L

Lakoff, George 67, 70, 77, 239

Laundy, Peter x, 224, 226

Lavey, Jerad 167, 221

Leacock, Matt xii, 20

LeDoux, Joseph 247

Lee, Jennifer 163, 175

Leeke, Steve xii, 9, 192

Lim, Suk Jun 83

Lindholm, Amber 95

Lists

   fact lists 52

   hunch lists 52

   spark lists 52

   structured lists 51, 54

LL Bean 211, 212

Loughborough University 222

Luebkeman, Chris 215

M

MacTavish, Tom xii, 47, 131, 132, 180, 206, 208

Manjoo, Farhad 84, 241

Mathew, Anijo xiii, 42, 47, 86, 87, 148, 154, 163, 164, 167, 179, 238

Mathew, Nikhil 87

McDonald's xii, 6, 84, 116, 122, 123, 130, 139, 155

McDonald's Innovation Center 122, 123, 155

Medina, John 198, 248

Memorial Sloan-Kettering 164

Mental models 21, 54, 65, 66, 77, 98, 112, 125, 129, 130, 131, 133, 134, 136, 144, 165, 238, 243, 244

Miller, Tim 162, 166

Mind maps 29, 40, 41, 54

Mioduszewski, Scott 162, 166

Models and frameworks 19, 28. *See also* User experience models; *See also* Concept maps; *See also* Territory maps; *See also* Mind maps

impact models 36

priority models 34

sequence models 32

systems models 38

"Mold" theory of language. *See also* Sapir-Whorf hypothesis

Morgenstern, Judd xii, 5, 29, 208

Motorola xii, 9, 83, 132, 180, 192

Mulhern, Thomas xi, 128, 129, 130, 141, 145

Munger, Jamie 100

Murillo, Oscar 163

Musick, Hugh 66, 239

N

Narratives

analogous stories 106, 113

collegial stories 139

corporate stories 139

framing narratives 98

future stories 98, 102

illustrated narratives 100

parodies 99

personal stories 139

retrospective stories 104

unfinished stories 103

user stories 99

NCR xii, 47, 131, 132, 206

Netscape xii, 20, 21

Nierenberg, Danielle xii, 44, 45

Nourishing the Planet xii, 44, 45, 161

O

O'Donnell-Trujillo, Nick 138, 140, 243

O'Grady, Amanda 159

Oldenberg, Ray 116

Ortony, Dr. Andrew 67, 69, 239

P

Pacanowsky, Michael 138, 139, 140, 243

Panza, Adam 164

Parham, Andy xii, 1, 2, 3, 4, 72, 90, 91, 106, 107, 112, 113, 119, 120, 121, 132, 144, 232

Park, Jaesung 179

Passavant, Dave 25

Patel, Keta 164

Patnaik, Dev xi, 6, 165, 180

Patwardhan, Viraj 78

Pei, Dr. Eujin 223

Petty, Dr. Richard 248, 251

Pidgins 66

Pollan, Michael 85, 241

Portigal, Steve xi, 8, 129, 130, 133

Prototypes

build-to-decide prototypes 42

build-to-think prototypes 16, 42, 43, 47

business concept prototype 225, 226

frankenprototypes 42, 47

modular prototypes 48

paper prototypes 45

prototype "fidelity" 42, 47

prototype "resolution" 42, 43, 45, 157, 162, 163

writing as prototyping 51

R

Rao, Shilpa 88

Reavey, Heather xi, 10, 14, 43, 50, 58, 125, 155, 178, 209, 213, 232

Rittel, Horst 112, 241, 242

Roberts, Melody xii, 122, 123, 130, 131, 132, 145

Robinson, Rick x, 116, 205

Rockwell, Chris xi, 6, 176

Royer, Chris 204

S

Sabah, Somayyeh 238

Salvador, Tony xii, 8, 199, 202, 203, 228

SapientNitro x, xi, 28

Sapir-Whorf hypothesis 238

Sarr, Dr. Robert 239, 243

Sawant, Kshitij 167

Schumann, Dr. David 251

Scient 8, 25, 27

Shannon-Weaver model of
communication 245.
See also Communication
modes, "transfer" mode

Shaw, George Bernard 119

Shields, Joseph 83

Shin, John 109

Situated cognition 246

Skype xii, 168, 193, 194, 195,
196, 197

Sococo xii, 21

Star, Dr. Susan Leigh 237

Stories. *See* Narratives

Story platform 151, 152

Striebich, Jessica 173

Swift, Matthew 87

Sylver, Brianna xi, 188, 189

T

Taggart, Elizabeth 81

Taylor, Frederick 137, 243

Territory Map 8, 25, 26, 27

Thaler, Marty xiii, 42, 47, 83, 238

The New, three kinds of 3

the "complex new" 3, 231, 233

the "still-fuzzy new" 4, 231, 233

the "unfamiliar new" 4, 208,
231, 233

Transfer model 6, 11, 67, 149,
150, 152, 154, 181, 186,
245

Trice, Harrison 138, 140, 243

Turchi, Peter 17, 237

U

Unnikrishna, Aparna 87

"Unspeakable data" 17, 18, 237

User experience model 22, 29,
220

V

van der Doef, Thom 167, 218

Venema, Margaret 179

Vollmer, John 163

VSA Partners 1

W

Ware, Colin 238

Weil, Denis 122

Weinstein, Alisa 45, 161

Whitney, Patrick 161

Wicked problems 112, 241, 242

Wills, Helen 45, 56, 161

Winnick, Michael xi, 7, 9, 10, 48,
147, 148, 172, 207

Wolff, Michael and Michael Wolff
Design xi, 111

World Café 170, 171

Worldwatch Institute 44, 45

Wu, Yixiu 177

Y

Yang, Junyoung 179

Z

Zolna, Robert 232